This book analyzes the relation between the modern subject who emerges in seventeenth-century French literature, particularly in dramatic works, and the emergence of the first modern Absolutist state. It shows how in the works of the major writers of the Classical period (Corneille, Racine, Molière, Lafayette and others) a new subjectivity is formed in and through the representation of the family as the mediating locus of a patriarchal ideology of sexual and political containment. It examines why the theater became the privileged form of representation of this state, and why this theater concentrates almost exclusively on family conflict. Professor Greenberg argues that the narrative of Œdipal sexuality and subjugation central to this new literary canon reflected the conflicting social, political and economic forces that were shifting European society away from the universe of the Renaissance and guiding it towards the "transparency" of Classical representation.

Cambridge Studies in French 36

SUBJECTIVITY AND SUBJUGATION IN SEVENTEENTH-CENTURY DRAMA AND PROSE

Cambridge Studies in French

General editor: MALCOLM BOWIE

A complete list of books in the series is given at the end of the volume.

SUBJECTIVITY AND SUBJUGATION IN SEVENTEENTH-CENTURY DRAMA AND PROSE

THE FAMILY ROMANCE OF FRENCH CLASSICISM

MITCHELL GREENBERG

CAMBRIDGE
UNIVERSITY PRESS

Published by the Press Syndicate of the University of Cambridge
The Pitt Building, Trumpington Street, Cambridge CB2 1RP
40 West 20th Street, New York, NY 1001-4211, USA
10 Stamford Road, Oakleigh, Victoria 3166, Australia

First published 1992

Printed and bound in Great Britain by
Woolnough Bookbinding, Irthlingborough, Northants

A catalogue record for this book is available from the British Library

Library of Congress cataloguing in publication data

Greenberg, Mitchell, 1946–
Subjectivity and subjugation in seventeenth-century drama and
prose: the family romance of French Classicism / Mitchell Greenberg.
p.   cm. – (Cambridge studies in French)
ISBN 0 521 41293 5
1. French literature – 17th century – History and criticism.
2. Politics and literature – France – History – 17th century.   3. Power
(Social sciences) in literature.   4. Psychoanalysis and literature.
5. Subjectivity in literature.   6. Patriarchy in literature.   7. Sex
role in literature.   8. Family in literature.   9. Classicism –
France.   I. Title.   II. Series.
PQ245.G74   1992
840.9'358'09032 – dc20   91–33177   CIP

ISBN 0 521 41293 5 hardback

For Marie-Claire and Julia

"On ne sort de l'ambiguïté qu'à son détriment."
(de Retz)

CONTENTS

PREFACE

Our expectation is therefore directed towards two other possibilities: that the social instinct may not be a primitive one and insusceptible of dissection, and that it may be possible to discover the beginnings of its development in a narrower circle, such as that of the family.

(Freud, *Group Psychology*, p. 2)

In the general revolution of sensibility that occurred during the seventeenth century, the modern "subject," characterized most forcefully as a "psychological" interiorized being, as a privatized sense of the self, was given its first delineation. The central concern of this book will be to trace this delineation in the relation between French Classical literature (particularly, but not exclusively, dramaturgy) and the representation of the "family" as the mediating locus of a patriarchal ideology of sexual and political containment. Concurrently this study attempts to adumbrate the relation between sexual/ political constraints, the ideology of the subject (the subjugation and the subjectivization of the individual) and the creation of a literary "canon" that represents and naturalizes this subjugation. Here, in defense of my privileging of literary texts in the analysis of the workings of seventeenth-century (French) ideology, even if I do not necessarily share his particular definition, I must appeal to Terry Eagleton, who has so vigorously argued for viewing literature as the prime object of such analysis. "Literature," he writes, "is the most revealing mode of experiential access to ideology that we possess. It is in literature, above all, that we observe in a peculiarly complex, coherent, intensive and immediate fashion the workings of ideology in the texture of lived experience ..."[1]

The scope of this book is necessarily limited. It is not intended as a totalizing study either of the seventeenth century or even of "Classicism" in its most varied forms: very little reference is made to those paragons of French Classical thought and aesthetics, La Rochefoucauld, Bossuet, Pascal or Mme de Sévigné. On the other hand, the texts I have chosen, in the majority selected from the tragic and comic repertory, respond to what seems to me to be the essential question we must ask ourselves about the peculiarly inter-woven patterns of politics, representation and sexuality in the devel-opment of the Classical subject: "What is the relation between the emergence in the seventeenth-century of the first "modern," Absolutist, State and theatricality? The central focus of this book will be, therefore, the theater and rather than a panorama of the entire scope of Classical dramaturgy, it will focus on only a few chosen examples of the enormous corpus of works produced for the stage in seventeenth-century France. I have chosen these works because they strike me as symptomatic texts, texts that help us respond to the next important question we address to the Classical canon: why did the theater become the privileged form of represen-tation of the emerging Absolutist state and why is it that this theater, whose splendor existed for a relatively brief moment, was exclusively the theater of familial conflict, of family? For it is, I would argue, on the late sixteenth and seventeenth-century stage (that is, in and as a "vision," a vision that is always an illusion) that the modern family, as a subject of representation, was born. We would have to look far afield, even return to that other great period of the theater, to fifth-century Athens, before finding a similar insistence on representing the human subject within the sexual/political con-fines of the family. Medieval and Renaissance literature is particularly lacking in great familial narratives: heroes exist, lineages abound; we find passionate lovers and, in the tradition of the fabliaux, feuding married couples, but no clearly articulated familial scenarios. It is, I suggest, upon the seventeenth-century stage that both the family and the subject formed in a closed familiar scenario were brought forth. The great theatrical productions of the seventeenth-century, in France but also in England and Spain, introduced into modern western literature the "family" as the privileged site of individual subjugation; in its plots and peripeteia we are called upon to witness the submission (and resistances) of every human child to those societal codes that pre-exist his or her entry on to the stage of social existence and which s/he must internalize in order to participate in communal life. The dramatic scenarios of the Classical stage become the site where the sexual and political demands of society are most acutely represented in conflict with a "personal" desire that those demands paradoxically inform.

Without wishing to jump too far ahead, we might speculate that the dialectics of theater produced, at a precise historico-political juncture, an originary narrative of Oedipal sexuality as the "imaginary" scenario of the conflicting social, political and economic forces that were, at the same moment, shifting European society away from the universe of the Renaissance and guiding it towards the "transparency" of Classical representation.[2] It will come as no surprise, therefore, that the discipline most invoked to analyze this emergent subjectivity will be the discourse of freudian and post-freudian psychoanalysis. Surely no other modern theory of the subject is more at home on the stage, weaves so intimate a relation with the theater, in both its external and internal strictures, and the individual whose subjectivity is lived as a perpetual intermeshing of public and private scenarios. Rather than appearing as a discipline foreign to Classical culture, psychoanalytic discourse will be regarded as continuing, in another register, the dialogue between individual desire and societal law that was first articulated with seductive elegance by the passionate protagonists of the seventeenth-century stage.

INTRODUCTION

Narcissus

Enfin la gloire et la grandeur des Spectacles ne pouvoient mieux
venir que de celuy qui s'estoit rendu luy-mesme le plus glorieux
et le plus grand Spectacle du Monde.

(d'Aubignac, *La Practique du Théâtre*, p. 15)

Although a final verdict may never be forthcoming on the political
acumen with which Louis XIV directed the affairs of France during
his long and often turbulent reign, few can doubt that he had a particular genius for making a spectacle of himself. Louis was, in his
self-representation, the most "theoretical" of monarchs: his persona
was both a theory and a theater of kingship. Having perceived that
the essence of political power resided in the images and imaginary
of majesty, he proceeded to project these images into the world in
a way that had never been seen before. Whereas his reign is most
often associated, in the works of literary historians, with a turning
away from the excesses of the Baroque, certainly his insistence on
living his persona as a royal "role" squarely situates him at the
pinnacle of an entire Weltanschauung, where, if all the world was a
stage, Louis knew that his was the leading part. In this he seems to
have understood the enormous power inherent in the manipulation
of representations, to have grasped what every great political actor
has perceived: his force comes from his ability to orchestrate reality
around spectacular scenarios.[3] The evidence of his *Mémoires* suggests that Louis XIV intuitively apprehended the political potential
of the *theatrum mundi* metaphor and used it to glorify his being:

il fallait conserver et cultiver avec soin tout ce qui, sans diminuer mon autorité
et le respect qui m'était dû, liait d'affection avec moi mes peuples ... Cette
société de plaisirs qui donne aux personnes de la cour une honnête familiarité
avec nous, les touche et les charme plus qu'on peut dire. Les peuples, d'un
autre côté, se plaisent au spectacle, où au fond on a toujours pour but de
leur plaire; et tous nos sujets, en général, sont ravis de voir que nous aimons

1

ce qu'lls aiment, ou à quoi ils réussissent le mieux. Par là nous tenons leur esprit et leur cœur.

(*Mémoires*[4])

Certainly an entire tradition inherited from the Renaissance equated princely largesse with its manifestation in/as spectacle, and, at least since Machiavelli, the political necessity of spectacle was recognized as an essential component of power. The ties binding subject to sovereign are not rational but emotional.[5]

Freud, following the work of Le Bon, was perhaps the first modern theorist to comment suggestively on the workings of "mass psychology." In *Group Psychology and the Analysis of the Ego*, Freud argues that "groups have never thirsted after truth. They demand illusions," he says, "and cannot do without them. They constantly give what is unreal precedence over what is real."[6] The dialectic of "truth" and "illusion" masks, as we shall see, a still more profound "passional" tie, the coupling of mastery and submission, of sadism and masochism elevated to the level of political theory. The group, Freud intimates, "wishes to be governed by unrestricted force; it has an extreme passion for authority ... it has a thirst for obedience."[7] This thirst is quenched, he claims, by the charismatic leader who assumes, in his own person, the desires and fears of his group. In Freud's terminology, this leader locates himself in the (dangerous) place of the "primal father," and reflects back to his subjects their own desires and ideals.

This, I would suggest, is very obviously the role that Louis played for himself and for the nation, presenting himself as a "representation," that is the "desired illusion," of what a king is; at the same time this illusion is inseparable, historically and politically, from a highly charged social investment in the patriarchal family, where kingship and paternity go hand in hand: the monarch is, first and foremost, the "father" of the nation.[8] It was the importance of representation − the illusion of paternal power that is projected by the king, and that is desired by his subjects − that Louis mastered.

The Renaissance prince was, as I've said, obliged to please his court and subjects. Among the most pleasurable of courtly occupations were the various "spectacles," ballets, masques, tournaments, parades, and, of course, the royal "entrées," the elaborate courtly processions from town to town which celebrated the significant dates of the reign: births, baptisms, marriages, ascensions to the throne, victories in battle.[9] There is, nevertheless, a remarkable difference in degree and in kind between the courtly spectacles of the Renaissance and the spectacular court life which Louis XIV orchestrated around his own person. While we could speak of the extravagant "Plaisirs de l'Ile Enchantée", of royal ballets and the patronage of the theater, of painting, of music, of architecture and of science, this list would in no way be exhaustive. Louis's entire reign, in its political, literary, architectural and military dimensions, was, as Louis Marin has exhaustively shown, a representation of the Princely body: the reign become but so many blinding rays emanating from the central body of the Prince, a body quickly lost, disseminated in the very representations that mirrored its glory, and by so mirroring, constructed it.[10]

When we look at the works that represent the king — Versailles, the medals struck to reflect the momentous occasions of the reign, the histories and poems written to celebrate the sublime monarch — and when we read Louis's own words, where we hear an authoritative "I" that, with incessant repetition, constructs the world around itself, sees itself as the center of a world, we cannot but be struck by the fact that these self-representations manifest a paradoxical desire, a desire for an apotheosis, for the transcendence of a merely earthly existence that, in the terms of that existence, would entail the disappearance of the self in its image: Louis, making a spectacle of himself, finally eclipses that "self", scatters it in its own representation, disperses it in its own disappearance. For this reason, his choice of the "Sun" as his personal emblem strikes me as heavy with meaning, and more resonant than just the apparent analogies to his own resplendent majesty would at first suggest:

Ce fut là que je commençais à prendre [cette devise] que j'ai toujours gardée depuis, et que vous voyez en tant de lieux. Je crus que, sans s'arrêter à quelque chose de particulier et de moindre, elle devait représenter en quelque sorte les devoirs d'un prince, et m'exciter éternellement moi-même à les remplir. On choisit pour corps le soleil, qui, dans les règles de cet art, est le plus noble de tous, et qui, par la qualité d'unique, par l'éclat qui l'environne, par la lumière qu'il communique aux autres astres qui lui composent comme une espèce de cour, par le partage égal et juste qu'il fait de cette même lumière en tous lieux, produisant sans cesse de tous côtés la vie, la joie et l'action, par son mouvement sans relâche, où il paraît néanmoins toujours tranquille, par cette course constante et invariable, dont il ne s'écarte et ne se détourne jamais, est assurément la plus vive et la plus belle image d'un grand monarque.   (*Mémoires*, 135–136)

We may speculate that inextricably attached to the image of the sun, as that which is everywhere and yet cannot be seen or gazed upon, is the equally analogous but hidden association with death. Such an insistent self-representation leads us to the rather obvious conclusion that this Monarch, that this monarchy, that aims to be Absolute — that is non-contingent — was infused not only with the myth of the sun god Apollo, but also with that other, melancholic figure of self-absorption and death — Narcissus.

Narcissus, too, contemplates himself only as a spectacle. He, like Louis, or rather Louis like him, can see himself only as his own reflection. The circle, the sun, turns in on itself blinded by its own self-enclosure in which the subject of representation and the object of representation are one. Absolutism, as a state system, is perhaps the first modern avatar of totalitarian government. Georges Balandier offers us a definition of totalitarianism that I find particularly telling for my purpose. It is, he says, a government that desires "la soumission de tous et de tout à l'Etat" where "la fonction unifiante du pouvoir est portée à son plus haut degré. Le mythe de l'unité ... devient le scénario régissant la théâtralisation politique."[11] In this definition we understand that if the underlying drive of Absolutism is "le désir de l'Un,"[12] it must constantly interweave politics and passion, the individual and the collective. Narcissism, like Absolutism, appears as a totalizing drive, the desire for a unity of being that necessarily must ignore, repress, what precisely would sunder that being, its own desire. André Green offers the following definition of Narcissus, of the narcissistic personality:

Portrait du Narcisse: être unique, tout-puissant par le corps et par l'esprit incarné dans son verbe, indépendent et autonome dès qu'il le veut, mais dont les autres dépendent sans qu'il se sente porteur à leur égard du moindre désir. Cependant séjournant parmi les siens, ceux de sa famille, de son clan et de sa race, élu par les signes évidents de la divinité, fait à son image. Il est à leur tête, maître de l'Univers, du Temps et de la Mort, tout rempli de son dialogue sans témoins avec le Dieu unique qui le comble de ses faveurs — jusqu'à la chute par laquelle il est l'objet élu de son sacrifice — intercesseur entre Dieu et les hommes vivants dans l'isolement rayonnant de sa lumière. Cette ombre du Dieu est une figure du même, de l'immuable, de l'intangible, de l'immortel et de l'intemporel.[13]

Green's description of Narcissus is eerily consonant with Louis's own self-presentation. What I find particularly appealing in this description is the way it inserts Narcissus into a "social" context. Green portrays Narcissus as a political leader; he exists in society as its charismatic chief, among the people but above them, and radically non-desirous. It is this "indifference" that makes others desire him, attaches them to him. His own lack of contingency is the sign of his divine election. The idol of his people, he is also their victim. Narcissus in his self-sufficient totality is the perfect representation of a desire for closure, for unity, that Michel de Certeau, among others, has hypothesized as being one of the undercurrents of seventeenth-century French society:

Telle est la situation au XVIIe siècle. Les conflits mettent en cause des formations hétéronomes. Cet éclatement fatal de l'ancienne religion de l'unité reporte progressivement sur l'Etat la capacité d'être pour nous l'unité référentielle. Une unité qui se développe sur le mode de l'inclusion, par un jeu subtil de hiérarchisations et d'arbitrages ...[14]

But, as we can see from the history of seventeenth-century France, this unity is apparently obtained only through the erection of a difference, an "other." This other takes many forms, be it the religious other — the Huguenots, the colonialist other (the natives of the colonies of "la Nouvelle France"), or the other that inheres in society, the feminine that must be encircled, contained, repressed. Narcissus remains deaf to Echo, to her and to his desire.

Both Richelieu and Louis XIV, in very different ways, warned of the troublesome, chaotic consequences of allowing women any influence in the politics of the realm. Richelieu, for instance, establishes a contrast between the "vertu mâle"[15] that is necessary for the good ordering of the state and the intrigues of Marie de Médicis, whom he accuses of causing the state's fragmentation.[16] There is a slippage in his rhetoric between "femininity," "maternity" and disorder that is always in conflict with "male virtue" and order. This is a slippage that will often be repeated in the tragic and comic scenarios of the Classical stage. Louis XIV, in another tone, is equally concerned to warn the Dauphin not to let sexual passions get in the way of reason:

Dès lors que vous donnez la liberté à une femme de vous parler des choses importantes, il est impossible qu'elles ne nous fassent faillir. La tendresse que nous avons pour elles, nous faisant goûter leurs plus mauvaises raisons, nous fait tomber insensiblement du côté où elles penchent; et la faiblesse qu'elles ont naturellement, leur faisant souvent préférer des intérêts de bagatelles aux plus solides considérations, leur fait presque toujours prendre le mauvais parti. Elles sont éloquentes dans leurs expressions, pressantes dans leurs prières, opiniâtres dans leurs sentiments ... (*Mémoires*, p. 259)

This desire for unity, this narcissistic desire for the Absolute, must, in order to protect itself from itself and the other that inheres in that self, be seen as existing in a dialectical relation in which a highly charged dose of masochistic self-denial is coupled to an aggressively sadistic desire for subjugation. This dialectics comes to rest on and in the person of the King, his "moi," which is, as we know, "l'Etat".

This desire for closure, for an ego that must constitute itself in as closed a system as possible, may be said symptomatically to represent narcissism's intimate connection with death.[17] Either as an "individual" personality or as a collective societal impulse, narcissism attempts to effect a closure of the world, a sideration of the body that can best be thought of as the body's elimination. The body's radical otherness is closed, objectified.[18] Louis' exhaustive dissemination of his presence into all corners of his realm can be seen precisely as this desire, so typical of narcissism, to recreate the world in one's image by having that image become the world.[19]

Architecturally speaking, Louis did, with the construction of Versailles, turn himself into a monument: we know how the entire massive edifice was constructed and reconstructed around the symbolic (absent) center of the place of the King, reduced to his most "vital" symbolic function, to his bedchamber. The architectonics of Versailles is a celebration of royal copulative power, of Louis as phallus, extinguishing himself in his own pleasure, only to rise anew as a self-sufficient phoenix. Louis is fetishized as an invisible reproductive force; he becomes that function that ensures the permanency of the dynasty, its eternal propagation into the future.[20]

Nevertheless, when we look at Versailles as the commingling of a solar topology with an elaborate symbolism of sexual potency ("le soleil ... produisant sans cesse de tous côtés la vie"), we are also in danger of overlooking the nether side of that force, the inextricable involution of eroticism and death. While Versailles may be an architectural materialization of the solar topos, it can also be seen to represent an imperious death drive: its obsessive reconstruction monumentalizes Louis, turns Louis into a monument to his own desire, to his own death. It becomes a narcissistic monument to Louis as death: the great Pyramid of the Classical age.

In her study of Absolutism, Nannerl Keohane underlines the almost visceral and seemingly paradoxical connection that existed between the King and his subjects:

It would be hard to exaggerate the importance of the concept of the French King as the representative of the common interest, the source and embodiment of the good of all ... There was a sense of security when the monarch was personally in charge of things, a trust in the benevolence of his will, which can only be explained by the belief that he apprehended and spoke for the good of the entire society in a way no other human being could approach.[21]

Introduction

Although E. Kantorowicz has taught us to look at the long theological tradition that traduced the "eucharistic" body of Christ and the Church into the sacred relation that bound the King to his people, and although this fusion of the "holy" dimension of monarchy with the body of the king was reinforced by all the apologists of divine-right rule, an intriguing question still remains.[22] How are we to understand this extraordinary bond between a king who existed only by representing himself as the Sun, that is, as a narcissistic self-enclosure, as Death, and his "subjects?" This bond does not admit of "logical" explanation. Rather, it seems to me, if we are to understand the attraction of Narcissus we must risk an exploration across apparently separate disciplines – history, literature, psychoanalysis. I will be borrowing and comparing different concepts from domains that have traditionally been kept separate in a preliminary attempt to explore those areas where politics and desire interweave in a set of overlapping dynamics. As I have suggested, a certain freudian sado-masochism seems to be inextricably connected to both a certain group psychology and a dynamics of spectacle where spectacle implies a mediation between and an inherent reversibility of both collective and individual desire, between the personal and the private. In a monarchical state, this dialectic between the personal and the private may be seen to come together in the "passionate" tic uniting the king/father and his subjects.

Opening the 1694 *Dictionnaire de l'Académie Française* at the entry "sujet," the first definitions read as follows:

Sujet, adj. – soumis, astreint, obligé à quelque dépendance, à quelque charge. Nous sommes tous sujets aux lois et aux coustumes des pays où nous naissons. Il est d'ordre qu'une femme soit sujette à son mari, qu'un fils soit sujet à son père, qu'une fille soit sujette à sa mère ...

Sujet/ette – Qui est sous la domination d'un prince, ou d'un Estat souverain.

Two things are immediately striking in these definitions. First, for the seventeenth century only one of the definitions of "subject" that we have come to recognize (since Kant) existed: a subject is one who is subjected, that is who is obliged, dependent on the will of another. The seventeenth-century sense appears closer to its Latin origin "sub-iectum" than the later variations found in modern usage. Secondly, this subjection is hierarchically established. It follows a sexual and a familial pattern that is presented as "natural," while at the same time the family pattern becomes confused with a "political" one: a subject is one who is subjugated to a prince. The gap separating politics from family is bridged by the ambiguous "naissons." We are "born" into a family and into a state. The relation between family and state is implied, slipped in, and thereby an entire hierarchy of sexual and political imperatives returns us both to the Sovereign and to the family as an inseparable continuum in which and by which all who are born, are born subject(ed). Contrary to Rousseau, and much more in keeping with a certain strain in Althusser's thinking, man (not to mention woman) is born subjected, in chains that tie him to his Prince, his father, in a perfectly enclosed world of masculinist devolution and duty.

Although Narcissus is not a God, he does mediate the passage between God and man, partaking more of the former than the latter:

Il en est sans doute de certaines ["fonctions"] où tenant, pour ainsi dire, la place de Dieu, nous semblons être participants de sa connaissance, aussi bien de son autorité ... *(Mémoires,* p. 232)

In the history of patriarchal monarchy the interchangeability of the metaphors subtending the sacred and terrestrial realms are papered over, "naturalized," precisely by the slippage the word "father" precipitates, a slippage from "God the father" to the Monarch, father of his people, to, finally, the father, head of each individual household. (This metaphoric chain of course works simultaneously in ascending and descending order.) This is not an invention of French monarchy: Bossuet, perhaps the most eloquent apologist for that monarchy, reminds us that "from the beginning," monarchy, patriarchy and state religion were intertwined, and that the heavenly city of God was reproduced on earth in the well-run patriarchal state:

Les hommes qui avoient vu, ainsi qu'il a été dit, une image de royaume dans l'union de plusieurs familles, sous la conduite d'un père commun, et qui avoient trouvé de la douceur dans cette vie, se portèrent aisément à faire des sociétés de familles sous des rois qui leur tinssent lieu de père.[23]

Recent historians such as Georges Duby underline Christianity's specific contribution to the tightening and naturalizing of this system:

Cependant, par suite d'abord de la christianisation de la royauté, le roi, tenu pour le représentant de Dieu, mais de Dieu le Père, apparut peu à peu lui-même comme un père, investi d'un pouvoir analogue à celui de ces pères qui gouvernaient dans chaque maison.[24]

At the beginning of the seventeenth century, following the societal anarchy of the wars of religion and the traumatic assassination of two kings, this politically vital metaphor was given new rigor, as the gradual re-patriarchalization of French society was strengthened by the increased emphasis accorded to "Roman" law. Louis constantly comes back to this imaging of himself as "père du peuple":

C'est pourquoi, bien loin de mépriser aucune de ces conditions, ou d'en favoriser l'une aux dépens de l'autre, nous devons être le père commun de tous, prendre soin de les porter toutes, s'il se peut, à la perfection qui leur est convenable ... (*Mémoires*, p. 221)

Je parus enfin à tous mes sujets comme un véritable père de famille qui fait la provision de sa maison, et partage avec équité les aliments à ses enfants et à ses domestiques. (*Ibid.*, p. 111)

Ce n'est que pour leurs propres avantages que nous devons leur donner des lois; et ce pouvoir que nous avons sur eux ne nous doit servir qu'à travailler plus efficacement à leur bonheur. Il est beau de mériter d'eux le nom de père avec celui de maître, et si l'un nous appartient par le droit de notre naissance, l'autre doit être le plus doux object de notre ambition.

(*Ibid.*, p. 90)

At the same time the ubiquitous power of the perfect father-monarch is represented precisely by his ability to be not only the most sublime spectacle of his realm, but the most perceptive spectator as well. He is, in his new incarnation, reduced to being — as Louis tells the dauphin — like the sun, an all-seeing, unseeable eye:

Tout ce qui est le plus nécessaire à ce travail est en même temps agréable; car c'est en un mot, mon fils, avoir les yeux ouverts sur toute la terre; apprendre à toute heure les nouvelles de toutes les provinces et de toutes les nations, le secret de toutes les cours, l'humeur et le faible de tous les princes et de tous les ministres étrangers; être informé d'un nombre infini de choses qu'on croit que nous ignorons; pénétrer parmi nos sujets ce qu'ils nous cachent avec le plus de soin; découvrir les vues les plus éloignées de nos propres courtisans, leurs intérêts les plus obscurs qui viennent à nous par des intérêts contraires ... (*Mémoires*, p. 42)

Narcissus and Echo: the tain of ideology

"le lien social est un lien tragique"
(E. Enriquez, *De la Horde*, p. 389)

All these allusions to omnipotence, to Paternity, to kingship as spectacular self-representation, bring us back to the question of political and sexual subjectivity as a product of ideology. "Ideology" is an extraordinarily elusive concept not only when we try to define it and its modes of operation but also when we become aware of the often contradictory political charges it carries in modern discourse. In this study I shall use ideology first in Althusser's celebrated although much-debated definition as "une représentation du rapport imaginaire des individus à leurs conditions réelles d'existence."[25] Furthermore, ideology is not conceived of here as something "outside" the experience of social existence, or the products of that existence, but as inhering in that experience.[26] Following this definition, ideology would be those practices that "constitute individuals as subjects." The production of seventeenth-century subjectivity will then be read, in what will certainly be seen as a deviation from Althusser's definition, as both the "origin" and the object of current psychoanalytic discourse where "the unconscious ... must be seen as the site where social meanings and practices are negotiated prior to and simultaneously with any activity of the conscious agent."[27]

I would like to quote here, at some length, that part of Althusser's discussion of ideology where he introduces the concept of interpellation. For Althusser, it is the individual's response to interpellation that constitutes him/her as subject. Furthermore, for Althusser, the "hailing" by which individuals are constituted as subjects is essentially a specular relation. The subject is "called" into his/her place by the "transcendent" Subject who in turn is ratified by the response of the object to this interpellation. This definition, despite its very modern vocabulary, does not strike me as essentially foreign to Louis XIV's own conception of the power of monarchal self-imaging:

Il apparaît alors que l'interpellation des individus en sujets suppose l'existence d'un Autre Sujet, unique et central, au nom duquel l'idéologie ... interpelle tous les individus en sujets. ... La structure de toute idéologie interpellant les individus en sujets au nom d'un Sujet Unique et Absolu est spéculaire, c'est à dire en miroir et doublement spéculaire: ce redoublement spéculaire est constitutif de l'idéologie et assure son fonctionnement. Ce qui signifie que toute idéologie est centrée, que le Sujet Absolu occupe la place unique du Centre et interpelle autour de lui l'infinité des individus en sujets, dans une double relation spéculaire telle qu'elle assujettit les sujets au Sujet tout en leur donnant, dans le Sujet où tout sujet peut contempler sa propre image (présente ou future) la garantie que c'est bien d'eux et bien de lui qu'il s'agit.[28]

Now, although this functioning of ideological interpellation has been severely criticized, particularly because it seems too dourly deterministic, and because it does not allow for the concept of "human agency,"[29] I wonder if that criticism is not more pertinent to our modern bourgeois societies with their purportedly more "open" subject positions than to the Absolutist society of seventeenth-century France?[30]

Althusser's "Sovereign Subject" seems remarkably close to the "primal Father" that Freud mythologized in *Totem and Taboo* and elsewhere as that ruthless, all-powerful, self-contained leader who was the object of desire and fear for the lesser males that revolved around him.[31] It was the collective murder of this "father" and the subsequent shared guilt among the brothers that, according to Freud's myth, was at the origin of all civilization. With the murder of this first "father," guilt (that is, the beginnings of an individual and social conscience) comes into existence. At the same time this reorganization of society around the "dead father" transports the individual out of the contingency of biology and into the realm of culture and politics. The important lesson of this fiction is that the Father, as Green says, is always already dead, sacrificed.[32]

All great leaders, all those capable of fixing on themselves the inchoate and often contradictory desires of a population, do so by placing themselves, for their people, in the non-contingent place of the dead father. They all capture and hold their subjects in their thrall by an ambiguous promise, the promise of love and the promise of their own immolation, their own narcissistic self-immolation to the people or nation they represent.[33]

What is important in this "imaginary" description of the death and resurrection of the primal father is precisely the necessity for the myth. The actual father is never more than a surrogate for the laws that structure society, underpinning all political formations:

It is the place of the father, not the actual father that is thus here significant.... The symbolic father, for whose prehistoric death the boy pays the debt due, is the law that institutes and constitutes human society, culture in the fullest sense of the term, the law of order which is to be confounded with language and which structures all societies, which makes them in fact, human.[34]

In the above quotation Juliet Mitchell, one of the most influential feminist interpreters of psychoanalysis, re-scripts Freud's initial scenario, inflecting it with Lacanian echoes. For with Lacan, and with Lacan's influence on Althusser,[35] we can begin to understand the coming together in the image of the primal father of those structural laws that interpellate all individuals as they move from the state of "infans" to the position of subject − subject of law, subject of language and subject of desire − in the dialectics that inscribes them in any given (human) society.

It is in the metaphoric weaving of political and familial power that we will attempt to establish the mediation between individual and collective subjugation in Absolutist France. During the last thirty years the work of historians of various and often contradictory theoretical persuasions has attempted to define the exact nature of this mediation. Although they generally agree that something portentously revolutionary occurred during the period 1580–1680, corroborating the premonitions of the privileged witnesses of the time,[36] the exact nature of the "crisis of the seventeenth century" and its particular characteristics, causes and effects, has not, of course, met with any form of consensus.[37] To some, the major transformation was economic: seventeenth-century mercantilism is seen to negotiate the passage from an essentially agrarian to a market economy, thus serving as the intermediary in the economic evolution from a pre-capitalist to a capitalist society. To others, of whom Foucault is the leading figure, the change represented a fundamental break in epistemology, shifting Europe out of the sphere of analogical reason and into the realm of (Classical) representation. To others still, the fundamental innovation was essentially political: Europe moves from an outmoded feudal system, with its Aristotelian concept of a "shared" monarchy (shared between nobles and king), to a non-contractual "Absolutist" state: the centralization of legal, judicial and financial power in the hands of a newly created corps of functionaries at the service of the king.[38] The king, in turn becomes, in the words of Keohane, "the ordering principle of all social life, the ultimate source of authority and energy within the state."[39] Finally (although this list is not exhaustive), yet others, demographic historians and historians of society such as Ariès and Flandrin in France or Laslett and Shorter in Great Britain and the United States, would view the seventeenth century as the period which sees a general reorganization of affective familial and sexual ties. This reorganization radically altered the way human beings reflect their own lived experience and relate it to the socio-political structures in which they are born and evolve.[40]

Nevertheless, one thing does seem certain. The seventeenth century, in its flight away from heterogeneity towards the order of the "One," in what Foucault has called the "grand renfermement," reinforced the image of the Father at the same time as (again following Foucault's stimulating hypothesis) it began, through its religious and economic practices, to encircle a sexuality that in its excessive drive would have proved too threatening to this unitary order. Sexuality, newly scrutinized, was gradually enclosed in a tightened family circle.[41] As Foucault suggests, it was at this time that the family became "l'échangeur de la sexualité et de l'alliance: elle transporte la loi et la dimension du juridique dans le dispositif de sexualité: et elle transporte l'économie du plaisir et l'intensité des sensations dans le régime de l'alliance."[42]

This view is consonant with the findings of those social historians who see the seventeenth century as precisely the period that witnessed the "actual" transformation of the family. "En effet il paraît clair qu'entre le xvie siècle et la fin du xviiie la famille a changé de nature et qu'une nouvelle morale familiale s'est ébauchée," writes J. L. Flandrin.[43] According to these historians the family gradually shifted away from that large, inchoate unit for which the term "household" ("maison," "maisonnée" in French) would be more appropriate and towards the "family" as that smaller, affective bourgeois unit the eighteenth century was to cherish. This family comprised, and was usually limited to, the biological unit of mother, father and their offspring.[44] It is during the seventeenth century that the more archaic "economic" definition of family gradually gave way to the newer "affective" one.[45]

No ideology is ever completely total(izing): zones of resistance exist, are allowed to exist, by the dialectical nature of all social change. The radical imposition of a new socio-economic structuring of sexuality and polity does not occur without opposition. Robert Mandrou reminds us that French society was not necessarily ready for this restructuring. As we know, the nurturing of the Absolutist ideal in the reigns of both Louis XIII and Louis XIV met with nobiliary hostility, corporate resistance, religious tensions and peasant uprisings. Nevertheless, as Mandrou also informs us, the elaboration of the new political archetype, the creation of "Classical" French society, was ceaselessly impelled by a new ideal of government that inextricably tied its success to the manipulation of the passions, by and through the arts. From Richelieu's premiership on, the arts were strategically enlisted into the political program.[46]

That the theater should be the most dynamically volatile of the arts, that it should be the art form privileged by both Richelieu and Louis XIV, should not surprise us. Let us recall that both for Louis XIV and for Althusser, in the two quotations cited above, the importance of spectacle, of specularity, appears as essential in any political program. Each places an extraordinary emphasis on that most ineffable of all interpellations, the "look," the spec(tac)ularity of the hailing. Not only is this consonant with the intense interest the seventeenth century brought to bear on the study of optics,[47] but it is particularly apparent in the theater, whose seduction is based, according to that critical paragon of seventeenth-century theater, the abbé d'Aubignac, on an intense visual appeal:

Ce poème est nommé Drama, c'est à dire, Action, et non pas Récit; ceux qui le représentent se nomment Acteurs, et non pas Orateurs; ceux-là même qui s'y trouvent presens s'appellent Spectateurs ou Regardans, et non pas Auditeurs; Enfin le lieu qui sert à ses Représentations, est dit Théâtre, et non pas Auditoire, c'est à dire, un lieu où on regarde ce qui s'y fait, et non pas où l'on Ecoute ce qui s'y dit.[48]

It is this emphasis on the active visual dimension rather than on the other aspects of dramatic art that strikes me as particularly revelatory of the theater's importance in the elaboration of a classical ideology. As the century unfolded this ideology was reinforced, gradually becoming hegemonic.[49] The dynamics of theatrical vision can of course be approached from two different directions: either from the point of view of theatrical architecture, the changes in the very structure of the theatrical edifice; or from a discussion of the psychical function of the *Schautrieb* or "scopic drive."

Timothy Murray, in his recent *Theatrical Legitimization*, offers an illuminating discussion of the ideological construction of Richelieu's "théâtre cardinal," the first private theater in France to be built according to the new "Italian" scheme. Murray insists on the political importance of this construction, an "ordered and hierarchical setting," a construction that divides the parterre from the "scene" of the play by means of the proscenium arch, that uses perspectival backdrops, and that seats the spectators so that they too view the scene in "imperfect" perspective. Imperfect because perfect perspective was available only from one seat, the Cardinal's.[50]

But another aspect of the perspectival theater is also highly significant. The introduction of perspective in Renaissance painting (and the perspective of the seventeenth-century court theater was essentially Renaissance − that is, it had a single vanishing point; multiple vanishing points were not incorporated until the eighteenth-century stage backdrops)[51] forcefully subjugates the viewer of that painting to its geometrical optics, one that reduces the viewing body to an "all-perceiving eye."[52] This reduction effectively eliminates the body from the dynamics of viewing and constitutes the subject as a point trapped in the specular construction of the painting's perspective. In other words, the painting interpellates its subject as an "eye," an eye that gazes at the painting in its subjugation to it.[53] I find it compelling that the theater − and here I am speaking of the official court theater, whose emphasis on the perspective of the Renaissance vanishing point must be distinguished from the more "primitive" perspectival apparatus available at either the "Théâtre du Marais" or the "Hôtel de Bourgogne" – was attempting to reconstruct this visual capture of its audience, at the very moment when the "body," the heterogeneous unruly "other" of Classical decorum, is coming under greater scrutiny. The gradual triumph of the Classical doctrine also implies that the theatrical text is itself being dis-embodied.

The years that witness the emergence and implementation of Richelieu's Absolutist project of "raison d'Etat" also see the imposition of the "Classical" ideal in literature, the triumph of the Malherbian revolution in the "mise-en-place" of the three unities, of the bienséances, of the purification of prosody and language. Is it merely a coincidence that Classical dramaturgy, an art of ellipses, of abstraction and of ideality, becomes the privileged form of representation in the seventeenth century by tracing in its internal strictures the very effacement of the body as textuality at the same time as it places this body on the stage, offers it to the "eyes" of the spectators? What are we to make of a form of representation in which textuality is "embodied" on the stage at the very moment that the body becomes off-limits to "textuality" – when, that is, those talking "bodies" are not bodies at all but the sign of the body's repression? This repression is incorporated as guilt, as sacrifice, and reappears as sublimation, as the conflict of allegiances, represented as the split between (say) "love and honor," "duty and pleasure," "man and woman." How are we to interpret this body that has become merely a "talking head" speaking with a disembodied voice its subjugation, its subjection in a political/sexual economy whose effacement of the body, its internalization as difference, forces it to forever mourn, in fantasies of utopian plenitude, its sacrificed other?[54]

To answer these questions we must return once more to the theater as the site/sight, the zone, of interference between social and individual desire. In the confusion of changes taking place in the period 1630–1680, the theater, by its very mediating function, its situation "at the crossroads of the individual and the collective,"[55] seems to double and relay, in an uncanny fashion, the role that Foucault attributes to the family. Just as the latter becomes the internalized interchange between the political and the personal, the theater, functioning at the junction of the public and private spheres, can be seen to relay, in a spectacularly seductive fashion, the dynamics of the law and desire as incorporated in plots of family strife. The theater mirrors back to the spectators, who are already structured in a reciprocal perspectival function, the role of the law, the law of the Father, and through its pleasure elaborates this law as subjugation and subjection.

The theater functions in the seventeenth century as a heavily charged apparatus combining state and family politics in scenarios of guilt and retribution which I call the "family romance of French Classicism." I am, of course, borrowing this broad and mobile term from Freud, who uses it, in general, to describe the narratives children invent to compensate for their own disappointments or fears about their real parents and their relation to them. These narratives can either be of an exalting kind, e.g. the child narrates that s/he is really the secret child of a noble house, or of the debasing kind, e.g. s/he was abandoned/or taken in by poor peasants. In either case the narration is the way the child's imagination deals with a real or fantasized conflict in the relation with the parents.[56] Here, however, I wish to expand the term and use it as a heuristic device to describe the plots and scenarios of seventeenth-century theater as a social "family romance," those stories a society told itself, represented to itself, as the "imaginary" projection of the real (that is, irreconcilable) differences, contradictions and social struggles that were occurring in that society and which radically altered the way individuals were interpellated as subjects.

In essence, the seventeenth century mediated the change from an essentially outmoded feudal system of kinship to a (pre-)capitalist family network. The psycho-sexual consequences of this shift from kinship to non-kinship social formations have been the subject of much theoretical speculation by Claude Lévi-Strauss (*Structures élémentaires de la parenté*), the social theorist Serge Moscovici (*Société contre nature*) and by theoreticians of the unconscious, beginning with Freud (*Totem and Taboo, Civilization and Its Discontents, Moses and Monotheism*). In *Psychoanalysis and Feminism* Juliet Mitchell, attempting to elucidate what some have seen as the apparent anachronistic universalization of the freudian Oedipal scenario, returns to Lévi-Strauss's discussion of the structural importance of the kinship system in the development of human society. For Lévi-Strauss, kinship is primarily a system of exchange, the exchange of women among men, and it would be this activity of exchange that distinguishes human from non-human societies. Lévi-Strauss underlines the importance of the exchange as such, rather than the object of that exchange. It is the exchange that institutes kinship.[57]

16

The exogamous network that this exchange establishes is coterminous with the imposition of the incest taboo, not because the taboo is "biologically" impelled, but because it is socially necessary.[58] As kinship societies evolve into large, more complex networks, and particularly as western society moves into the capitalist era, the structures of kinship – that is, those laws that determine which men might exchange which women – tend, with the disappearance of kinship communities in favor of smaller family groupings, to be internalized. What in kinship societies was an external structure of prohibition becomes, so the theory goes, through its internalization in the (pre-)capitalist family, the crux of the modern, i.e. Oedipal, scenario:

It is as though the Oedipus complex of Western man were heir to the kinship structure whereby man became human, but the further mankind gets from overtly employing kinship relationships for social organization, the deeper repressed and hence more clamorous these become, for they are expressed within a context that tantalizes them. The mother and sister or father and brother you sensually cannot have are also the only people you are supposed to love ... It would seem that it is against a background of the remoteness of a kinship system that the ideology of the biological family comes into its own. In other words, that the relationship between two parents and their children assumes a dominant role when the complexity of a class society forces the kinship system to recede.[59]

Continuing along the same line of thought, this time with the use of similar psychoanalytic theories applied to the realm of anthropology, Eli Sagan, in his provocative study of "primitive" societies, *At the Dawn of Tyranny*, advances the hypothesis that "central to any society is the definition and locus of 'political authority.' Authority has its origins in the family; political authority results from the transformation of family hierarchical relationships."[60] He further suggests that the most radical change in political structure occurs, that the State emerges, precisely when "nonkinship forms of social cohesion are as important as, or more important than, kinship forms."[61] In his discussion of how archaic societies – by which he means societies that have not evolved past the limits of the kinship system – develop into more complex societies, he theorizes the need for a passage, mediated by the figure of the King, whereby kinship ceases to be the dominant political structure in that society and where power is now displaced among those whose position in the social structure depends solely on their relation to the leader. This leader's position, in turn, must be fixed, made to seem independent of a grounding in merely contingent social relations: it must be

17

supported rather by the "sacredness" of his own lineage, a sacredness inherited by his family's supposed "descent from the God(s)."[62]

Without wishing to establish an false analogy — France on the cusp of the seventeenth century was by no means a "primitive" society: rather it was a highly complex, political network — I nevertheless find both Mitchell's and Sagan's hypotheses intriguing because they allow us to theorize several of the key aspects of those changes that we see emerge in French society and on the French stage in the seventeenth century. It was a society where precisely those transformations Sagan theorizes were taking place: the old feudal class of nobles, historically a kinship society, saw its economic and political power decline. In the 1620s and 1630s it was effectively brought to heel by Richelieu and Louis XIII. Its rights and privileges were steadily eroded. At the same time, the royal government, in order to bolster its new-found economic and political desires, allied itself to the third estate, the world of emergent pre-capitalist families, choosing the sons of merchants, doctors and magistrates to man its bureaucracies. Power was effectively disseminated, strengthening the monarchy by making this class dependent on the royal government for its social and political advancement. Could we, then, see the emergence of these familial scenarios of conflict and change, these "family romances," as the impossible attempt at mediation between the fantasies of a declining feudal class and the proleptic utopian projection of a rising bourgeoisie, in their commingling of mutually inclusive desires with a mutually exclusive political antagonism?[63] To understand this ambivalence we must see this theater as functioning both as a structural pivot, in the way all theater is seen to do, mediating the conflicts and desires of its audience and offering as a solution to them the aesthetic pleasure of the spectacle. In that pleasure great amounts of libidinal energy are released by the spectators' identification with characters, plots and peripeteia; but also, due to the formal constraints of Classical theater, this energy is reharnessed just as quickly as it is released.[64]

Both Richelieu and Louis XIV were ardent admirers of the theater and no less ardent patrons. Both realized that in some ambiguous way the theater represents the state, that it can stand in for the Prince who is its privileged spectator and for whom it is the privileged spectacle. There is a mirroring in which the point of view of the Prince — that point that excludes, totalizes, subjugates and pleasures — is returned from the stage to the parterre, becomes internalized in the individual spectator as the Law, without, of course, the necessity of the Prince's actual presence, without his actual gaze. The presence is disseminated as spectacle, as that which is offered to view, as the drama. The play, tragic or comic, reproduces the law in familial scenarios of social dilemmas with potentially tragic (or comic) outcomes. It is this imbrication of the presence of the Sovereign Subject in the visual mirroring of family romances, represented by the theater/parterre dichotomy, that is essential for explaining the elaboration of subjectivity.[65] In the instances of both tragedy and comedy, the Classical theater may be seen as a particularly overinvested site of Absolutist desire, where an imperious "sadistic" drive towards "Integrity" comes up against the inchoate, anarchic drive of individual passion, and where, "masochistically," this passion is brought to conform to, or be eliminated from, the Law.

I should like to go even further and suggest, but only suggest (the details will be seen in the following chapters) that this effacement of the textual body, that I have adumbrated above as being integral to the elaboration of French seventeenth-century dramaturgy, reflects the textual/sexual ideology of Classical patriarchy. For the body that is repressed is coded as "feminine," in so far as "femininity" in the vocabulary of the political leaders is what is dangerous to the social order. To claim that this attitude towards women, but even more pointedly towards their own desire, should be integrated into the ethics and aesthetics of Classical doctrine as a manifestation of patriarchal monarchy, is not particularly novel.[66] The way in which the aesthetics of Classicism work to eliminate the discordant female presence from its structures of harmony and symmetry is directly connected with the politics of vision that we have already described as essential to the ideology of subjection that functions in Absolutist aesthetics.

The theater functions, we have said, like a mirror. It holds up to view both the individual desires of the spectators and the societal Law that informs these desires and prohibits their fulfillment. The spectators in front of this spectacle – a spectacle that is, in its symbolic dimension, a representation of the Prince, of the Law – are rather like Lacan's famous infant in front of the "mirror" that presents him with an image of himself as "total," One, unified, in which he jubilates. Classical theater reflects back to the spectator an image, social and individual, that is totalizing: the play, tragic or comic, plays out a scenario subtended by an aesthetics of wholeness and closure, a "theological" scene of the One that points, as Jacques Derrida has argued, to God, to the King, to Narcissus.[67] That this theological scene is also a mirroring of the one, that it functions primarily as an instance of, and appeal to, the scopic drive, is part of its illuding pleasure. For precisely this image of totality, the illusion of vision, is that image that most successfully avoids the confrontation of castration, that acts as its apotropaic talisman, eluding it, playing with it, holding it off.[68] The "pleasure" of the spectator is informed by this vision of a totality that is necessarily a lure, a seduction, a jubilation. That this image is also essentially alienating is never allowed into discourse: rather the "pleasure" in the spectacle papers over the rift of alienation, the rift of castration and death, that the plays thus both confirm and deny. Rather it is the illusion of totality, an illusion that is the "hailing" of a necessarily split, divided subject sutured in the reflection of his own narcissism. It is a narcissism that is offered to him by the supreme Narcissist in whose image the play is validated, and that holds out to each individual spectator the illusory totality as the fulfillment of his own desire to be One.

This pleasuring of the spectator is done more in the sense of French "plaisir" than in the sense of "jouissance." The latter term, as P. Smith suggests, is much more radically upsetting of social law, while the former is complicitous with it, upholding the illusion of the stability of the subject.[69] At the same time, I would tend to define this pleasure as masochistic because that in which the spectator is made to pleasure is his own alienation, that is, his/her own castration, separation from an ideal that is held out to him/her, and yet that is forever unattainable. The only "person" who really has such perfection, who really is complete, non-desirous, is the Prince/Narcissus, who is, as we've seen, always already dead. In fact, what the theater promises is the jubilation in the scenario that re-enacts over and over again the spectator's alienation in the law that marks him as a split, that is desirous, being, while allowing him and us the illusion of a "unitary" self.

Narcissus refuses to respond to Echo's desire. He can look only at himself, at his own image. Echo is reduced to pure ephemerality, a non-presence, a disembodied voice – the sensuality of Classicism's verses – in this world of vision. And yet this voice is part of the dialectic that both joins Narcissus to the world and forever keeps him from it. It is the haunting return of difference, in the seductive image of the one, of the Absolute absence of alterity, of the refusal to exist in the world of contingency. Perhaps, rather than the triumph of the idea of a unitary subject/state, Echo whispers its already inevitable exhaustion. Just as the seventeenth century mediated the enormous change between a feudal past and a capitalist future, the theater, mirroring the family, became the "imaginary" site of this change; for it was, I would suggest, on that new stage of Absolutism that the "modern" conflicted subject was born, torn between a desired image of integrity that is constantly rent, rendered problematic by the murmur of difference. It is this conflicted subjectivity that the tragedies and comedies of the Classical age first performed and that we, to our horror and pleasure, never tire of rehearsing.

As I've attempted to make clear in the above paragraphs, this study is not a work of "literary *history*" but a work of speculative ideological criticism that uses as its symptomatic texts some of the most highly invested works in the French canon. This study suggests large and difficult changes in sexuality and subjectivity, changes that cannot be proved (by recourse to traditional historical categories) but can, I believe, be theorized. I continue to use those tools of theoretical speculation, especially psychoanalysis and feminism, that do not allow for any univocal grounding, but rather insist on the inevitability of ambiguity. It is this ambiguity that best corresponds to the extraordinarily complex notion of epistemic change, to the complex notion of "episteme." It would be a mistake to see these changes as univocal, one set of structural, symbolic, discursive practices replacing another. These changes are never absolute. Rather what we see, as we attempt to decipher them, render them into an intelligible, discursive form, is a fascinating pattern of survivals, anticipations, throwbacks and concurrencies that are all contained, at the same time, in the epistemic fabric of any particular epoch. What is particularly important is the emergence of certain dominant patterns, certain nexes of meaning that come to impose themselves on and over other less vital clusters of meanings or possibilities, over long periods of time.

The readings that comprise this study all examine the role, explicit or implicit, of the family as it is created, denied, impinges on, or is in other ways essential to, the power and seduction of the texts under discussion. Each in its own way relates to one or several of the theoretical concerns discussed above. They all refer to the constitution of the subject as a product of a family scenario, of the family lived as "spectacle" under the gaze of an omnipotent, panoptic Sovereign.

Although the individual essays are meant to stand on their own, it does strike me, with hindsight, that when read in sequence the chapters of this book can be seen to trace, as a parabola, the "mise-en-scène" of patriarchal heterosexuality. At the same time the chapters offer glimpses of a "counter-discourse" that although often heard only in echoes is nevertheless persistently present. From what we can call the amorphous, pre-Oedipal sexual textuality of the *Astrée* (chapter 1), with its very floating familial and subject positions, we move to the imposition of the Law of the Father in Corneille (chapter 2). This imposition implies the dichotomization of the sexes. In Corneille, as we shall see, sexuality is presented as an already essentialized opposition, the heterosexual splitting of the world into male and female difference. In a certain sense we might say that Corneille introduces "sexuality" itself on to the seventeenth-century stage as an inextricable part of each of his protagonist's history. This splitting that is shown to be "natural" is nevertheless presented as antagonistic: the paternal and maternal poles of this sexual opposition are opposed in hierarchical ordering that implies and enforces the repression of a certain excess coded as "feminine". Chapters 3, dedicated to a reading of the "autobiography" of Jeanne des Anges the possessed nun of Loudun, and 4, which discusses Corneille's *Rodogune*, investigate the resistances to this patriarchal imposition. In each, the role of a non-reducible femininity is shown to represent a nevralgic point of both resistance and repression in the active sexing of the seventeenth-century subject. Once more firmly established, however, the consequences of the imposition of a rigidly defined sexuality return to haunt the very structures of patriarchy as its own indeterminacy, its own desires for an other who dangerously eludes the totalizing drive towards the order of the One. Chapter 5 on Molière's *Tartuffe*, deals with this elusive other by concentrating on scenarios of homosexual desire that, while never allowed into consciousness, nevertheless appear as an ever-present threat to the integrity of the seventeenth-century masculine subject. Chapter 6 continues this discussion of the dangerous other by focusing on a different threat to patriarchal hegemony, the vexed relation between parents and children in Racine. This most primordial of family scenarios is given a compellingly tragic dimension in Racine's theater. Although Racine's placing of children on the stage marks an innovation in seventeenth-century dramaturgy, their presence situates Racinian theater in a frightening network of monstrosity and sacrifice. Racine brings children on to the Classical stage to immolate them. Finally, in Chapter 8, on Lafayette's *La Princesse de Clèves*, we leave the theater and return to the scene of narrative fiction. It is in this most "theatrical" of novels, however, that the exhaustion of the normative and prescriptive system of patriarchal sexuality is given its most subtly scathing denunciation. *La Princesse de Clèves* traces the impossibility of "sexual relations" within the world of Absolute monarchy.

Introduction

By subtly playing with the injunctions of patriarchal law, Lafayette offers the greatest resistance to the totalizing drive of a sexual and political Absolutist world order that the Classical theater had, with great effort, succeeded in imposing both on the seventeenth-century stage and on that "other scene" of our own cultural memory.

1

L'ASTRÉE AND ANDROGYNY

O Dieu! comme quelquefois ceux qui font plus de semblant de vouloir mettre l'ordre, sont ceux qui désirent plus de désordre.
(*L'Astrée*, IV, vii, 376)

Ici les choses ont depuis longtemps perdu leur ombre (leur substance). Autre chose que le soleil les éclaire, un astre plus irradiant, sans atmosphère, un éther sans réfraction − peut-être la mort les illumine-t-elle directement, et leur ombre n'a que ce sens?
(J. Baudrillard, *De La Séduction*, p. 87)

Let us begin at the end, with a scene that to my mind represents, in its precarious equipoise, the apogee of a certain Classical ideal. In the first book of *La Princesse de Clèves* Mme de Lafayette includes a detailed description of the engagement ball of Claude de France and the Duc de Lorraine. The staging of this spectacular royal "fête" allows Lafayette to bring Mme de Clèves and the Duc de Nemours together for the first time. It is here that they initially see each other and are first seen by the court. I take this originary scene to be emblematic of what I will call the scenario of Classical desire:

Elle passa tout le jour des fiançailles chez elle à se parer pour se trouver le soir au bal et au festin royal qui se faisait au Louvre. Lorsqu'elle arriva, l'on admira sa beauté et sa parure; le bal commença et, comme elle dansait avec M. de Guise, il se fit un assez grand bruit vers la porte de la salle, comme de quelqu'un qui entrait et à qui on faisait place. Mme de Clèves acheva de danser et, pendant qu'elle cherchait des yeux quelqu'un qu'elle avait dessein de prendre, le roi lui cria de prendre celui qui arrivait. Elle se tourna et vit un homme qu'elle crut d'abord ne pouvoir être que M. de Nemours, qui passait par-dessus quelques sièges pour arriver où l'on dansait. Ce prince était fait d'une sorte qu'il était difficile de n'être pas surprise de le voir quand on ne l'avait jamais vu, surtout ce soir-là où le soin qu'il avait pris de se parer augmentait l'air brillant qui était dans sa personne; mais il était difficile aussi de voir Mme de Clèves pour la première fois sans avoir un grand étonnement.

L'Astrée *and androgyny*

M. de Nemours fut tellement surpris de sa beauté que, lorsqu'il fut proche d'elle, et qu'elle lui fit la révérence, il ne put s'empêcher de donner des marques de son admiration. Quand ils commencèrent à danser, il s'éleva dans la salle un murmure de louanges. Le roi et les reines se souvinrent qu'ils ne s'étaient jamais vus, et trouvèrent quelque chose de singulier de les voir danser ensemble sans se connaître.

(*La Princesse de Clèves*, ed. E. Magne, in *Romans et nouvelles* (Paris: Garnier Frères, 1961), pp. 261–262)

Although this scene is remarkable in many ways, I would like to comment on only a few of them here. What first strikes us is its almost perfect rhetorical symmetry ("se parer" – "se parer", "surprise" – "surpris"), which reflects and reinforces the sexual symmetry of the protagonists. Each is offered to our gaze as a perfect example of his/her sex. At the center of this scene we are first presented with the division of the sexes, and then with their perfection:

Ce prince était fait d'une sorte qu'il était difficile de n'être surprise de le voir quand on ne l'avait jamais vu ... mais il était difficile aussi de voir Mme de Clèves pour la première fois sans avoir un grand étonnement.

It is the apposition of their difference, their exclusive and mutual "perfection," and then the harmony of the ensemble that surprises. It surprises them and it surprises the court. Their appearance is an epiphanous moment that transcending the narrative level carries us back to the rapturous world of myth. It is as if two demi-gods, each realizing in his/her person the aesthetic and metaphysical desires of an entire society, suddenly appeared in its midst: grace descends upon the world confirming its metaphysical desires as a physical reality.

Next, the surprise ("étonnement") of the court, of the two protagonists, is a "visual" surprise, a delight for the eyes. This divine vision is immediate, total and penetrating. It is a self-perpetuating and self-enclosing vision that passes from outside to inside, from Mme de Clèves to Nemours, from him to the King and queens and then to the court at large. An encompassing vision, the enchanting gaze is at once totalizing and exclusive. In *La Princesse de Clèves* the vision of the loved object is both political (that is, exterior, in the "world") and passional (interior, individualized). Circumscribed within the frame of this vision both its signifier and signified, Mme de Clèves and the Duc de Nemours are one with it. To satisfy the desire of the court, a desire to see itself reflected in the perfection of its two most perfect members, they must desire each other. Their love is predetermined for them, for in it it is not so much they who love but an entire world that loves them, and through them loves (that is, affirms) its own being.

Finally, and most important, this desire, an aesthetic become a blinding, troubling vision, is mediated and thus authorized by the King: 'Le roi lui cria de prendre celui qui arriva ...' The King — center of the world, point of reference and vanishing point of his subjects' gaze — orders Mme de Clèves to "take" the young man who has just made such a forceful entry, "climbing over chairs to fray a path to her," as her partner. What the King's order does is at once to institute this circle of surprise and to dictate a Law that, cutting through the circularity of desire, establishes a clearly Œdipal linearity of sexual/social relation. The dictate of the King descends on the assembly, describing the line of sexual difference — the placing of the two in opposition in the gaze of the world. This opposition is affirmed as a "re-union"; the surprise—ecstasy of the vision; a recuperation of difference in a harmony that subtends the entire ideology of Classical Absolutism.

What I would like to insist upon in this already too long preamble is how Classical desire is structured by this passage so that it works for us as a "verisimilous" narration of sexual recognition, and pleasure. Nevertheless the narrowness of this world, its all-encompassing suffocating gaze, proves, as we know, to be too threatening for the Princess. She will leave it and the desire it has formed for an "outside." It is to this outside that all of Classicism's misfits — Alceste, Bérénice, Mme de Clèves — must journey, to be free. Their freedom, however, is the freedom of loss, the loss of the world and of one's self in that world: it is tantamount to death.

The apogee of the Classical moment would be, then, a symmetrical patterning that, closing in upon itself, creates a world of total difference and total (but failed) reciprocity. It is a world whose desire is mediated between the public and the private where each reflects the other in a ritual mirroring. This reflection, however, ends up in its own exhaustion — in the withering of love, in its exile to "l'orient désert." There, and only there, released from the internalized gaze of the Father, Classicism's exiles are free of his Law; but that freedom is, as I have suggested, their end.

This metaphoric desert to which Classicism condemns its recalcitrant heroes is, of course, only its own internal emptiness, the structuring loss that is at its very center. The fear of its own closure haunts Classicism at the heart of its being. Being or nothingness: that is the unresolvable dilemma that is both hidden and revealed in the blinding vision of perfection that Classicism imposes on itself for its own pleasure and for ours.[1]

What, then, is the relation between the withering brilliance of the Classical gaze – as it institutes and yet forecloses passionate love – and the sylvan glades of the Forez? Can the verdant lushness of the *Astrée* prefigure, as origin, the passion of the Classical subject? Is it enough for us to have incorporated the lessons of J. Ehrmann and G. Genette, who have looked through the smiling veils of the pastoral to see the dark eroticism and profound disillusion that are at its center, to allow us to establish an unambiguous link between this "Baroque, pre-Classical" text and the Classical universe that was so enamored of its characters and its world as to make them over as its own?[2] Is the *Astrée*, as generations of scholars have claimed, already Classical in "style" and can we already see in it the beginnings of all Classical psychology – the "first modern novel"?[3] Does a rhetoric of love, such as we find in the *Astrée*, allow us to presume a Classical psychology of love? What do such sexually fluid characters as Astrée and Céladon, ready at the drop of a (shepherd's) hat or a Druid's veil to change clothes, to change sex, to change social stations, have in common with Mme de Clèves and the Duc de Nemours? While we all seem willing and able to accept the inverisimilous verisimilitude of seeing Céladon dress in women's clothes and be described as "she" for almost two thousand pages of text, to believe the textual travesty, how many of us would not be disconcerted were the Duc de Nemours to appear at the engagement ball dressed in drag?

Something very radical has changed in the fifty or so years that separate the *Astrée* from *La Princesse de Clèves*. In that separation we see, literally, and literarily, a new world. If we are to understand the long road Classical subjectivity (by which I also mean, in great part, our subjectivity) traveled from the "love" experienced by Céladon for Astrée and the "love" felt by Nemours for Mme de Clèves, we must turn our gaze to that difference, a difference in textual subjectivity, as we attempt to describe both the *Astrée*'s prefiguration of the Classical world and its radical otherness.[4]

Situated precisely at that moment of transition between the world of the Renaissance and the Classical universe, at that moment Foucault so eloquently describes in *Les Mots et les choses* as the moment of transition between two epistemological systems through which and by which the human subject defines the world and his own place in that world, at the interstice of that never possible differentiation, the *Astrée* stands as their partition, their parturition, separating and connecting, differentiating and eliding all difference, in that impossible moment that is at once a beginning and an end, the birth of one world order and the death of another.[5] It is precisely this impossibility of division, this "partage" that is both other and same, that makes the reading/analysis of the *Astrée* both fruitful and frustrating.

Containing the past and the present within the confines of its world, the *Astrée* figures its own paradox within the metaphorical trajectory it traces as it attempts to suture its own ambivalence in a resolution that eludes it. One way we might figure this transformation from a pre-Classical to a Classical subjectivity would be in spatial terms: dispersion as opposed to concentration, surface as opposed to depth. Surely, the mark of the "modern" subject, at least since Descartes, is a certain self-reflexivity that is spatialized as an interiority. The move to modernity is metaphorized as an endless journey inward.

The two poles of this trajectory, and the trajectory itself, exist, I would suggest, as metaphors structuring the general form and quest of the *Astrée*. The goal of the quest, the ultimate desire of all the characters of the novel and of the narration itself, is "self" knowledge, the discovery of the grounding truth of their own passional existence, the truth of love revealed by the "Fontaine de la vérité d'Amour". The entire novel moves towards this end that constantly retreats before it, that eludes it and that, by eluding it, eggs it on. The end that is promised and desired, the end that is not possible, would be the fountain, the inner well of love.

The novel's beginning, the origin of the quest, is, like all origins, difficult to situate, infinitely elusive. It is not, of course, the circumstantial beginning of the plot − Céladon's attempted suicide − although the means of his attempt, his throwing himself into the Lignon, certainly is of interest to us. The plot, however, does not really begin at a beginning, but "in medias res." The "origin" of the novel is coterminous with the origin of the Forez itself, that is, with the "creation" of this never-never land of love, with the creation of the stage − and its reality − upon which the lives and loves of the characters of the *Astrée* find their authorizing principles. And, in the beginning, the Forez was significantly not a "land" but a sea:

Sçachez donc, gentil berger, que de toute ancienneté ceste contrée que l'on nomme à ceste heure Forests, fut couverte de grands abysmes d'eau, et qu'il n'y avoit que les hautes montaignes que vous voyez à l'entour, qui fussent découvertes ... Mais il peut y avoir quatorze ou quinze siècles, qu'un estranger Romain, qui en dix ans conquit toutes les Gaules, fit rompre quelques montaignes, par lesquelles ces eaux s'escoulèrent, et peu après se découvrit le sein de nos plaines, qui luy semblèrent si agreables et fertiles, qu'il délibéra de les faire habiter. (I, ii, 44–45)

On the one hand, then, the origin of the universe of the *Astrée* mimics and inscribes in itself its cultural model, the Old Testament: it emerges from the sea. Its "origin" is the ocean, "de grands abysmes d'eaux." On the other, this origin is constantly re-inscribed in, is represented by, the text itself. The "ocean of words" that is the *Astrée*, that attempts to recreate a world that never was, a utopian other, loses itself in the shining surface of its enormous verbal expanse.

It is precisely the text's involution of itself on itself, its recreation of itself as oceanic, that, I believe, signals its belonging to the mimetic order of the pre-Classical. The *Astrée*, in form at least, is part of the mimetic tradition of the sixteenth century, the tradition that sees the world as the great book of nature, and the book as the reflection of the "natural" world. At the same time, in its quest, in its desire to find the "well of truth," it also signals, even as an impossibility, another grounding, another, new origin in the depths of self-knowledge.

The move from sea to well, from limitless expanse to concentrated interiority, follows the flow of the Lignon. Nevertheless, precisely because of the river's central and complex status both in the geography of the Forez and as the metaphoric representation of the inconstancy of Love, as both the threat of death and the source of rebirth, we intuit that the novel can never reach its goal, can never arrive at the "modernity" towards which it moves, precisely because it can never escape from the limits, or rather from the lack of limits, its own metaphoric structure imposes on it. The essential fluidity of the narrative, a fluidity that is both real and metaphoric, refuses to be contained. The "Fontaine de la vérité d'amour" is off limits, is "hors texte." It exists beyond the representational imperatives of the *Astrée*. Yet by this same foreclosure it impels the text on. It is in this tension, perhaps the tension of a "sea change," that the entire ambivalence, and the ultimate undecidability, of the text reside, its pleasure and its ennui, its past and its present.

M. Foucault has theorized the encyclopaedic enterprise of the sixteenth century as an attempt to "reconstituer par l'enchaînement des mots et par leur disposition dans l'espace l'ordre même du monde" (*Les Mots et les choses*, p. 53). Surely, it would appear that the monumental "novelistic" enterprise of d'Urfé participates in this particular form of encyclopaedia as it attempts both to transcribe and to circumscribe, in the representation of this "other world" of "perfect" love, the "real" socio-historical context which serves as the *Astrée*'s negative, authorizing other.

Let us briefly recall that in its general outline the *Astrée* recounts the vexed love of Céladon and Astrée: their separation caused by Astrée's mistaken belief that Céladon has been unfaithful; her admonition to him never to present himself to her unless she orders him to do so; and the adventures, disguises and misprisions necessary for this love to finally reach its happy end (it never does). Secondly, to this master narrative are added all the subsidiary narratives of other loves, other lovers, all of whom journey to the Forez seeking amorous advice. The "Fontaine de la vérité d'amour" acts as a vacuum, aspirating all the secondary narratives into its center until all the characters, and their stories, are integrated into the main plot. They all end up (in Book IV) either besieged in Marcilly or captives of the besieging army. At this point d'Urfé's death cuts (short) his narrative.

We might see, in the very narrative structure of the *Astrée* − a series of "exemplary" intradiegetic micro-narratives,[6] caught within the overriding general sweep of the main diegesis, of which they are at once subsidiary and integral − the general "world view" of the late Renaissance, a division between (in Foucault's terms) a sublunary sphere of mutability and mortality, of change and difference, and an overriding cosmic form, a perfect, immutable, unchanging (static) circle. What, of course, this would represent "formally" (and what would be constantly repeated, in all the dyadic oppositions of the book) is a desire for stasis − for a world fixed, in an unwavering constellation − in which change, if it is allowed (that is, if it is not to produce too great an anxiety in the social corpus), must be seen to be not really change at all, but rather just one more twist in the eternal return of the same.

The textual world of the *Astrée*, despite its enormous expanse, strikes me as forming a seamless whole which ignores any radical alterity in geography, in history or in politics. The 5000 pages of d'Urfé's text may wander far afield: we are taken on journeys to Africa, Italy, Paris, London, Byzantium; we travel back in time to (more) ancient Rome, to the narration of the "history" of the diverse families, their ties and associations; nevertheless, we never really leave the imaginary present nor the fantasized "here and now" of the Forez. No matter what adventure, no matter what intercalated story, we are involved in, no matter to what country or to what distant time these stories transport us, we are always within the same essential structure, within the same love story, that never varies. Love is presented as a monolithic invariable, the "yes/no" of passion that transcends time and space. Only Love *is*, and it is like it is here, in the Forez.

As we know, "Love" is the "politics" of the *Astrée*. For a book written in a period of enormous political, religious and economic upheaval by an author whose vital interests were so intimately threatened by these revolutions, the *Astrée* strikes us first and foremost as a "fantasy" (a "romance") whose essential predicate is the exclusion, repression, of that reality (the world of political struggle).[7] It might seem redundant to point out the obvious: as a fantasy, a utopian idyll, the *Astrée*'s contract with its readers requires their acquiescence in the generic "given," that this is a "perfect" world which (as everyone knows) excludes, purposefully and forcefully, the intrusion into its sylvan glades of ugly, quotidian reality.

One of the first consequences of the apparent absence or refusal of the political in the *Astrée*, a consequence resonant with meaning for any analysis of the "novel" as a whole, a consequence that is both shockingly simple and perversely complex, is that this amorous world that refuses politics also denies sexuality. Or, put in simpler terms, where there is no politics (and here I am using politics in its broadest, originary meaning as the distribution and organization of power through the differentiations of economic, gender and legal distinctions, both real and imaginary, that legislate the possibilities for individual and collective activity in a given human community) there is no sexuality (if by sexuality we mean the way that biological bodies are inserted into signifying systems, as masculine or feminine, within whatever parameters the political assigns to them).[8] Is this to say that we cannot read the *Astrée* politically and sexually? We know that it is not possible to be presented with a human artifact, and especially one that presents a model for human subjectivity, no matter how idealized it may be, and not to see that as a political/sexual enterprise. Normally, however, it is only through a reading that is situated in the margins of the text rather than at its center that we can begin to detect those symptomatic areas where the work of textual repression may yield up its own unspoken drives, where the return of both the political and sexual repressed can be glimpsed. In the *Astrée*, however, I suggest that we take another tack and that we look not so much to the margins of the work but to its very center, to the discourse/depiction of love, to the "master plot" which both hides and reveals the political and sexual investments of the fantasy that is this text.[9]

31

In the *Astrée*, love, as the *primum mobile* of the world of the novel, is essentialized, and this essentialization effaces any difference, figuring the haunting fear of change. This essentialization refuses any notion of evolution (of progress) in the exquisite stasis of a rhetorical standoff that competes with the "real" in a monolithic drive to engulf it, reflect it, control it. Everything in the world, reduced to "love" (although that term is not univocal), is reduced to a rhetoric, to a verbal jousting, to a game whose parameters circumscribe the entire fictional universe, stretching its borders out to infinity; and yet, at the same time, within those borders, we float eternally in the same space, in the space separating "yes" from "no," in the space of desire, in the space of love, on a shining and shallow sea of words. This textual sea rejects any distinguishing marks that would allow for the possibility of differentiation. In its refusal of difference, in its inability to fix sexual or textual distinction, the fantasized world of the Forez comes very close to undermining the very structures it elaborates as it attempts to protect itself against the reality it fears.

This helps to explain the most salient feature of the *Astrée* which we have already noticed: its sheer bulk, the "physical" weight and density of its investment in its own textuality. This investment in words, the obvious pleasure in the accretion of narrativity, traduces, it seems to me, the anxiety of the "signifié" on the level of the "signifiant". The "oceanic" reality, the weight of the words, the never-ending compilation of language, indicates the attempt of the written medium of language to triumph over the spoken, even as the spoken is given (in the interior universe of representation) as the means to both knowledge and power in the world of the shepherds and shepherdesses. At the same time this seeming contradiction helps, I believe, to explain the mutual imbrication of the narrative "invraisemblance" of characterization, the almost total lack of narrative individuation and the philosophical subtext of Neoplatonic love that these characters espouse.

It will come as no surprise if I suggest that, for modern taste, d'Urfé's characters lack any semblance of "real" psychology just as they lack any distinguishing physical characteristics. There is never any individuating trait (as we find, for example, in the fiction of d'Urfé's contemporary Cervantes) that would particularize, and therefore "fix," a character as unique and inimitable. In the *Astrée* there is no "physical" individuation, there is only "rhetorical" difference. The endlessly repeated arguments about "love" create a fictive world in which all the characters are potentially interchangeable.

Everyone can become, or can be made to represent, everyone else.

This lack of physicality, the refusal of the body, is symptomatic of the metaphysical parti-pris of the novel.[10] In the Neoplatonic conception of "love" (desire) that underpins d'Urfé's text, true passion is defined principally as a metamorphosis, a transmigration. When one truly loves, one dies to oneself in order to be reborn in the loved object, to be changed into the loved object:

Sçavez-vous bien que c'est qu'aimer? C'est mourir en soy, pour revivre en autruy, c'est ne se point aimer que d'autant que l'on est agréable à la chose aimée, et bref, c'est une volonté de se transformer, s'il se peut, entièrement en elle. (I, viii, 290)

Or,

Car, il faut ... que vous sçachiez, que tout ainsi que les autres eaux représentent les corps qui luy sont devant, celle-ci représente les esprits. Or l'esprit qui n'est que la volonté, la mémoire et le jugement, lorsqu'il aime, se transforme en la chose aimée, et c'est pourquoy lorsque vous vous présentez icy, elle reçoit la figure de vostre esprit, et non pas de votre corps, et vostre esprit, estant changé en Silvie, il représente Silvie et non pas vous. Que si Silvie vous aimoit elle seroit changée aussi bien en vous que vous en elle. (I, iii, 93)

On the narrative level this metamorphic capacity is mirrored precisely in the non-physicality of bodies, by their essential fluidity (non-differentiation) which permits them to pass, by a simple change of clothes, into another sex, or into another social rank (thus all the "misprisions," all the stories authorized by disguise, and all the totally improbable doublings). Just as the narrative is in constant evolution – the intercalated narratives becoming part and parcel of the main narrative sweep of the story and the main narrative fragmenting into subsidiary stories, all oscillating around an absent center (the ideal of love) – so it would seem that despite its enormous scope, its interminable digressions and apparent inability to end, the *Astrée* is motivated by a very basic binary desire: the desire for the same, for a unity, an integrity that is constantly deferred while constantly sought: and the desire for stasis, for the abolition of a difference which is perceived and denied at the same time, for repetition which is death, and a death that is perhaps desired as much as it is feared.

In the *Astrée*, therefore, sexual difference is purely a verbal distinction (a difference of rhetoric). In the final analysis it is a difference between the "Yes" ("more") of the shepherds, and the "No" of the shepherdesses. From this simple and irreconcilable opposition wells forth the never-ending debate, the unquenchable thirst of the narrative for ever more examples of how and why this simple dichotomy spawns limitless variations.

We could schematize this underlying structuring principle of the *Astrée* as an attempt to resolve, through the constant repetition of the same, the unresolvable social and sexual contradictions that are repressed in its representational universe. The compulsion to repeat, of which the *Astrée* offers one of the most glaring examples in literature, is, as we know from Freud's theorization, an attempt to establish control over forces – impulses, traumatic memories – that prove too threatening to the integrity of the organism (i.e., the textual corpus). In *Beyond the Pleasure Principle*, Freud speculates that the compulsion to repeat both reveals the desire for mastery, (repetition inverts what was first a traumatic passive experience into an active dominion), and at the same time, reveals at the very heart of this desire for mastery a more radical competition between forces of regression – a drive to return to a state of non-existence, to death – and forces of conservation, sexual forces; the two are emblematized as Thanatos and Eros.[11] If, therefore, we are to understand the interrelations of the repetitive structuring of the narrative of the *Astrée* not just as an unmotivated vestige of literary history, but as a motivated attempt to express in literature a situation of social and sexual conflict, we must turn to the very heart of the *Astrée*'s investment in repeated ambivalence in an attempt to reveal what that repetition signifies.

The *Astrée* figures, disguised as an allegory of perfect love, the negative correlative to an imperfect historical reality, the reality of those feudal vassals whose own place in the world was slipping, both economically and politically.[12] The ideological underpinning of this political reverie is a patriarchal genealogy in which possession and power devolves from male on to male. It becomes evident, therefore, why in such a system the importance of family, of the history of the "family," should bear so heavily on social interrelations. Paradoxically, for a world so preoccupied with and conscious of social hierarchy, a hierarchy that is determined by genealogy, by the importance and "place" of one's family in the general distribution of wealth, influence and power, the *Astrée* strikes us as contradictory because on the level of narrative development it is glaringly family-less.

Although there is the constant presence of a "symbolic" interdiction that is associated with the absent father, there is the no less striking absence in the represented universe of parental figures.

In general parents, if they exist, exist only as a narrative ploy. They are mentioned as an initial obstacle to desire, and then disappear from the representational universe.[13] In the 5000 or so pages of the *Astrée*, the actual presence of parents (especially of the father) is restricted to two or three narratives. In the rest they conveniently die or rather are the victims of their offspring's incipient love (cf. story of Mélandre, I, xi, 459: "Je ne sçay que devindrent mes parents me trouvans partie ... bien m'asseuré-je que la vieillesse de mon pauvre père n'aura pas resisté à ce desplaisir"). In this world desire kills, but it kills strategically. Its victims are characters unnecessary to the narrative, unnecessary, that is, as presences. They are, in fact, much more intriguing absent. Dead, their power is all the greater: it is the imperious power of an interdiction tinged with the taboo of guilt that is as pervasive as it is invisible.

The essential model for this disappearance of the parental presence and its re-inscription as interdiction is, of course, the story of Astrée and Célandon whose love is marked, from the start, as a contravention of a parental taboo. Their passion is inscribed under the sign of transgression. The ancient rivalry of their fathers has placed them forever out of each other's reach. Nevertheless, once the narration begins (and except for a flashback to recount Alcippe's amorous adventures) they are eliminated from the storyline almost at once. No sooner has Célandon thrown himself into the Lignon and drowned (*sic*) than − "comble de misère" − Astrée learns of both her parents' death.

In a strange sense the (fantasy) world of the *Astrée*, in its political and sexual density, is wholly enmeshed in a universe of familial-patriarchal law while at the same time totally insouciant of the narrative representatives of that law. Parents exist as the invisible imperative to renunciation that informs the entire narrative network of the novel. They are the invisible authority which structures the desiring machine of the *Astrée*; the authority that informs sexuality as a deferral, as the "no" of the female characters, as well as the "castration," the chivalric proofs of fidelity − the servitude, the hope, the constant renunciation of the male characters.

While there is, therefore, no "real" family structure that would individuate characters by inserting them in the "real" of sexual difference, while all the shepherds and shepherdesses seem to exist in a parentless world (another aspect of the "utopic" vision), there is a dissemination of family on the level of a more generalized, structural imperative in the text. Could we, in fact, see the entire world of the *Astrée* (and in this we would only be pointing once again to the

35

obvious ideology of a certain feudal class self-consciousness of the book) as one extended family? The heads of this family are obviously the nymph Amasis and the druid Adamas, who combine, in not insignificant ways, the temporal and spiritual seats of power of the Forez within a figuration that both affirms and effaces maternal and paternal authority.[14] Because they are indistinguishable, because they all exist as "young lovers," all the shepherds and shepherdesses, all the knights and ladies, are essentially an unruly but basically stable group of siblings, all the offspring of this "Ur-couple." In relation to the two representatives of the older generation, representatives who are both, interestingly, "sex-less," the young people are constantly in a position of subservience. Their dutifully respectful, filial role prefigures not only the ideal bonding of child to parent, but that of vassal to liege lord. Under the guise of a diffused, indistinct familial discourse lurks an entire power structure which, through repetition and displacement, inscribes a static configuration of authoritarian control.

Finally and perhaps most perversely, let us not forget that politically the world of the Forez is described as a matriarchal society; women rule (i.e. power devolves through the female line, from Amasis to Galathée, etc.). The Forez is presented as a "terre-mère" rather than as a "patrie." In one more twist to the confusion of politics and love, women are represented both as the arbitrators of sexual passion (their "No") and as the actual holders of legal authority.

It would seem, therefore, that on the level of the represented universe (that is, the world of the book presented not in its materiality as words but in its "immateriality" as a textual "reality" – a "verisimilous" experience of the text as true), the Neoplatonic deification of the woman serves as one more instance of the "utopic" nonreality disguising the actual functioning of power in the extra-textual world.[15] For in that world, again following Foucault's hypothesis, real power would reside in the "written," in "l'écriture" which he defines sexually as the "intellect agent, le 'principe mâle' du langage," which alone contains and manifests "truth." The spoken word is reduced to the subsidiary role of being the passive, female part of language: it is untrustworthy, inherently unreliable (*Les Mots et les choses*, p. 54). The sheer presence of the monumental weight of the text would function, therefore, as a counterbalance to the power that is supposedly affirmed within the narrated universe. The real power that the text masks would be the framing, structuring power, which is invisible, being the "matter" of the book itself, those neverending words which create the text and yet (paradoxically) remain exterior to it. But this "exteriority," this "masculine" presence of language, finally, has the role of arbitrator, of, in Derridean terms, the always-already-there, the invisible presence from which and through which all the rest exists and to which it must necessarily remain obedient.

These distinctions, while apparently too general to be at first glance convincing, gather weight when we see them informing the general ideological parameters of d'Urfé's text, which bear down upon it from the outside (its negative other, the real) and which appear inside of the represented universe as the constant oscillation and repetition, the very problematization of the role and function of language between the masculine and the feminine, between the seen and the spoken.

Readers of the *Astrée* have not failed to be struck by the total interdependence in the novel of vision and speech. On the most elementary level, the level of narrative motivation, this interdependence figures simply a primitive discursive technique that, in its constant repetition, signals the lack of what will come to be known as "an authorizing, or motivating psychology" (or at least an interior psychological impetus to narrative evolution). Quite simply, in the *Astrée* narrative evolution depends on an ocular witness; vision is constantly and instantly transcoded into discourse.[16]

As a general rule of narration, characters are constantly happening upon couples, plotters, isolated shepherds, shepherdesses, knights and ladies, who in their supposed solitude give voice to their most intimate feelings, secrets, plans. They are speaking to no one, to themselves, to the rocks, trees, streams that surround them, and, of course most importantly, to those "eavesdroppers," those "voyeurs-raconteurs," whom fate, chance, but most especially, narrative necessity have placed exactly in the position to "see" and *a fortiori* to hear and then to repeat. There is, in other words, operative in the *Astrée* a strange "slippage" between the visual and the vocal.

In a recent book, *Vision and Painting*, the art critic and historian N. Bryson, in an invigorating attempt to redefine the production and reception of painterly representation, appeals to Lacan's theorization of the "gaze of the Other" to articulate how one general form of painting ("Byzantine") interpellates and produces its viewing subject in a radically different way from that which the Renaissance canvas will introduce:

So far from being a spatial or temporal point, the viewer [of a pre-Renaissance painting] of the ecclesiastical image is an embodied presence in motion through a circular temporality of text and a choreographie (in the full sense) space of vision; the substance and mobility of his physique are fully involved in the work of receiving the images, as he receives the Eucharist, the Doxology, the Word. *The body does not see itself*; the gaze under which it moves is not yet the introjected gaze of the Other, but of God.[17]

One can, I believe, make a similar analogy for the function of "vision" in the *Astrée*.

The vision that plays so large a part in the narrative functioning of the *Astrée* is always glancing, that is, fragmenting, superficial and exterior. It remains on the surface because in a sense it is always subservient to a more imperious necessity, the necessity to tell, to narrate. In other words, the importance of the visual in this text is both enormous, and yet indicative of an entirely other perception of the world. Its glance never pierces the surface, perhaps because there is nothing *but* surface: no depth as yet exists. In the *Astrée* characters are continually under the eyes of other characters, yet this gaze is never internalized. This explains why in this book, where so much depends on the look for the transmission of knowledge, for the discovery of secrets, for, in fact, the fate of "nations," this look is at once pervasive as a narrative ploy, and utterly shallow. It is both the agent of knowledge (and thus power) and also powerless, participating as it does in the mere play of surface illusion that is the text, and explaining the seemingly total "invraisemblance" of psychological motivation: it authorizes the text's constant "travesty" — the reliance on misprision, on transvestitism, on the fluidity of sexual identity, and, with this travesty, the possibility of a never-ending repetition of the text itself.

It is therefore hasty, it seems to me, to make the leap that Ehrmann makes when he announces that the "theatricality" of the *Astrée* (the fact that everyone sees everyone else, that everyone therefore is in some sense a performer on the great stage of the world) is a sign of the text's modernity.[18] What we have is perhaps a pre-stage, that is a world that "appears" theatrical, but which lacks, or does not need, the depth of the theatrical gaze that will appear and radically reinterpret the subject body and that body's inscription in the world, in the middle years of the seventeenth century.

The slippage of the visual and the textual in the *Astrée* is indicative not of an incipient "modern" subjectivity, but rather of the old. It would seem to correspond to a certain network of power in which there is an essential non-distinction between what one sees and what one reads, "entre l'observé et le rapporté" (Foucault, *Les Mots et les choses*, p. 54), a non-distinction that would correspond to the not-yet-split, sexed modern subject, the subject of a division of the world into public and private domains, into an interiority and an exteriority. In the *Astrée*, as N. Elias claims, we are in the presence of a world of "configurations" (constellations) where "subjectivity" depends on a generalized identity within a group and within the mobility that that group authorizes; it is a general dance, but one in which all of the participants move when each one moves.[19] In this world the subject floats at the interstices of exterior and interior, at the criss-crossings of seeing and speaking (writing, of course, encompasses them both, for the seeing and speaking is also always writing – seeing and reading) in a network that, precisely like the *Astrée*, constitutes "une nappe unique et lisse où le regard et le langage s'entrecroisent à l'infini," (Foucault, *ibid.*) and where distanciation, difference and interiority do not exist as possible modes of self-definition. What we have in the *Astrée* is, therefore, a text that precludes differentiation, that pre-exists the sundering that institutes the modern subject and his interiority.

This formal reality is intimately connected to the philosophy of love that the text continually repeats in its narrative of desire, in its representation of the plight of all the lovers in the universe of the Forez. It both grounds their love and determines its ultimate but impossible goal.

Although much has been written about the Neoplatonic infrastructure of the *Astrée*, curiously an essential Platonic myth has been glossed over. This myth proves to be relevant not only to the understanding of the formal construction of the text, but also for the intimate mirroring of form and both the internal dynamics of plot and the psycho-sexual representation of power in the world of the novel.

In the *Symposium*, the grounding text for all discussion of western love, Plato introduces the Androgyn myth to explain the origin of desire as an innate sense of lack, of a feeling of "incompletion" that impels the desiring subject to seek union with the object it perceives will complete itself:

for the original human nature was not like the present but different. The sexes were not two as they are now, but originally three in number; there was man, woman, and the union of the two, having a name corresponding to this double nature, which had once a real existence, but is now lost, and the word 'Androgynous' is only preserved as a term of reproach. In the second place, the primeval man was round, his back and sides forming a circle; and he had four hands and four feet, one head with two faces, looking opposite ways, set on a round neck and precisely alike; also four ears, two privy members, and the remainder to correspond.[20]

In the beginning, Plato makes Aristophanes say, there were three, not two, sexes and each of these three sexes existed in a self-enclosed state of union, a state that made them formidable opponents to the Gods. It was, in fact, the threat that this self-sufficiency represented that caused the Gods, in an act of self-protection, to sunder them and in effect, to create desire – sexuality:

At last, after a good deal of reflection, Zeus discovered a way. He said: 'Methinks I have a plan which will humble their pride and improve their manners; men shall continue to exist, but I will cut them in two and then they will be diminished in strength and increased in numbers ... After the division the two parts of man, each desiring his other half, came together, and throwing their arms about one another, entwined in mutual embraces, longing to grow into one; they were on the point of dying from hunger and self-neglect, because they did not like to do anything apart. And when one of the halves died and the other survived, the survivor sought another mate, man or woman – as we call them – being sections of entire men or women – and clung to that.[21]

What the myth of the Androgyn does, as I have said, is to explain the origin of desire as the impulse towards suturing an elementary wound – a wound that is an enforced splitting of a primary integrity into difference. What it also posits, however, is that initial indifference, that original harmony – which is described as a self-contained circularity:

Now the sexes were three, and such as I have described them; because the sun, moon, and earth are three; and the man was originally the child of the sun, the woman of the earth, and the man-woman of the moon, which is made up of sun and earth, and they were all round and moved round and round like their parents.[22]

The Androgyn myth can be seen then as a structuring metaphor uniting the narration, as plot (the stories of the lovers), and the narration as form, that particular structure that is constantly fragmenting itself into opposing stories, only to re-suture itself in the on-going swell of its own elaboration. In Plato's explanation of passion there is a significant place left to homosexual desire. Those sexes that were originally male or female continue to seek each other out – men, men and women, women. It is only the products of the Androgyn who seek the opposite sex. At the same time this "opposite" is reversible, can always revolve around itself to become its other. Sexuality, grounded in the Platonic myth of the Androgyn, is indeed indeterminate-reversible.

The *Astrée*, as "androgynous" text, would therefore be a text that refuses the differentiating gesture, that establishes itself as existing before scission, before the division of the world into subject and object, into fixed, sexed, gendering. It is a text that formally and thematically posits the impossibility of subjectivity founded on the internalization of difference as a sublimation of Œdipal sexuality, refuses to choose a fixed individuation (in the role of father, mother, child), but assumes the innate fluidity of these roles, their interconnectedness rather than their difference. It is a text that inscribes itself as another representational mimesis in which dominates a certain circularity, a certain turning in of the text on itself, a turning in which both posits and escapes its own demise, its own ending.

It is precisely this configuration of the text, both in its formal and narrative features, as that smooth, shining, indistinct surface, that authorizes what appears to modern readers as its greatest "invraisemblance": those narrative sequences in which characters appear garbed in the clothes of the opposite sex, and where they are taken for members of that sex, where no one can "see" any anomaly. In turn, it is also precisely because of these sequences that what appears "invraisemblable" in "reality" (that is, a certain transcoding of "physicality") is "naturalized" ("vraisemblabilisé") in the representational universe of the *Astrée*.

What strikes me as being profoundly at stake in these central episodes of cross-dressing, in which all the codes of the text, ethical, amorous, political and lexical, are invested, is the play of forces, of power – even, I might add, of the pleasure of repression and its sublimation. Céladon's transvestism is, of course, also a travesty, confusing all these codes, revealing their own "naturalness" to be not givens but productions, productions of the invisible ideology that informs the possibilities of representation and subjection of the text.[23]

What happens in the *Astrée* when Céladon appears in drag is that the text, in a way that is perhaps unknown to itself, is seduced into a spiraling play of signifiers, where its own explicit codes are decentered by the constant oscillation of a (hetero-)sexuality that is situated in contradiction with itself. As the text disguises itself in drag, seduces itself in its fascinating play of mirrors, the text as Androgyn reveals itself to be a production of (social) paranoia. Turning in on itself, doubling its own impossible imperative of renunciation and castration, the sameness of the Androgyn reveals its other face: death, in a narrativity of repetition and repression.

When Alexis first appears in the world of the shepherds and shepherdesses of the Forez, she seduces men and women alike. Not only is Astrée smitten by her beauty, her grace, and a certain "je ne sais quoi" that reminds her of Céladon, but Hylas, the greatest amateur of feminine beauty, is also enthralled. Having seduced the most potent example of male heterosexuality in the Forez, Alexis proves to be equally seductive to Astrée. It is, of course, the exquisite teasing of this situation that proves so titillating for the reader who participates, voyeuristically, in the innocent games of the two "girls." Much has been written on the sensuality of these scenes of intimacy: the dressing and undressing of Astrée by Alexis, Alexis' night-time vigils at the foot of Astrée's bed, the coy caresses, sighs, ecstasy of the two young women, and their mutual vows of eternal friendship and fidelity. I will not, therefore, reiterate the obvious. What I would like to stress, however, is the general malaise that these scenes of "erotic" encounters produce, a malaise that is caused precisely by the lexical/textual indeterminability, the confusion of sexual identity. What is sexy, stimulating, in these scenes is the constant oscillation between innocence and taboo, the flirting with limits and the interdiction they impose, and with the ambivalence of both transgressing and recuperating those limits.

Carried to its extreme, however, the cohabitation of Astrée and Alexis, their constant intercourse, has consequences that take the sexual translation a step further: not only are the bounds of sexuality transgressed, but as a natural consequence of this first transgression the initial tenuous idea of Alexis or Astrée as individual, desiring entities is also fragmented, undone. In one further twist of the spiral of cross-dressing (and ignoring a discussion of "fetishism"), Alexis, enthralled by Astrée's clothes, cannot resist putting them on and becoming, therefore, Astrée:

Amour qui fait trouver des contentemens extremes à ceux qui le suivent en des choses que d'autres mespriseroient, représenta à cette feinte Alexis un si grand plaisir d'être dans la robbe qui souloit toucher le corps de sa belle bergère, que ne pouvant la despouiller si tost, elle commença à la baiser et à la presser cherement contre son estomach, et regardant sur la table, elle vit sa coiffure, et le reste de son habit. Transportée alors d'affection, elle les prend et les baise, se les met dessus, et peu à peu s'en accommode, de sort qu'il n'y eust personne qui ne l'eust prise pour une bergère. Et encore que la robbe d'Astrée luy fust trop estroite, si est-ce que se laçant un peu plus lasche que ne souloit faire la bergère, il y eust eu peu de personnes qui s'en fussent pris garde, mesme que sa beauté et sa blancheur ne dédisant point l'habit qu'elle prenoit, estoient de grandes trompeuses pour la faire croire telle. (III, xi, 593)

L'Astrée *and androgyny*

When Astrée wakes up to find Alexis dressed in her clothes she has no other choice but to put on her companion's garments:

Alexis mouroit d'envie de posseder tout le jour cet habit, luy semblant que le bon-heur de toucher cette robbe qui souloit estre sur le corps de sa belle maistresse, ne se pouvoit égaler. Astrée qui aymoit passionnément cette feinte druide, et qui desiroit de laisser tout à fait l'habit de bergère pour prendre celuy de druide, afin de pouvoir demeurer le reste de sa vie aupres d'elle, avoit un desir extreme de porter les habits d'Alexis.

(*Ibid.*, 596)

Thus dressed, each in the clothes of the other, they sally forth, and as we now expect, no one sees any difference, recognizes the change:

Et parce qu'Astrée et Diane luy firent signe de feindre d'estre estrangère, pour voir si Hylas et Laonice la recognoistroient, car elles avoient dit à Phillis le change qu'elle avoit fait de ses habits, elle contrefit de sorte son personnage, qu'Hylas la mecogneut, et Laonice aussi.

(III, xi, 608–609)

What the cross-dressing permits, of course, is the elimination not only of the sexual and social barriers but of all difference, so that in the end Alexis and Astrée become one — the Androgyn:

J'ordonne donc qu'Astrée sera Alexis, et qu'Alexis sera Astrée, et que nous bannirions de nous, non seulement toutes les paroles mais toutes les moindres actions qui peuvent mettre quelque différence entre nous.

(IV, i, 44)

Although this union is, on one level, true to the expressed (rhetorical) desire of Neoplatonism, the elimination of all difference is too threatening not to go unchecked. It throws out of all kilter the possibility for any subjectivity, even of the most fluid kind. Caught up in the dizzying spiral of his own desire, a desire that is set free and becomes an uncontrollable game of signifiers, a game in which "he" is lost, Céladon comes up against his own androgyny, his own dual desire, where there is no "he," no "she," just a play of signifiers, refusing any signified:

Mais quand je veux rentrer en moy-mesme, qui suis-je, qui redoute et qui desire? Suis-je Alexis? Non, car que peut davantage desirer Alexis? Suis-je Céladon? Non, car que peut craindre celuy qui est parvenu au comble de tous les mal-heures? Qui suis-je donc qui desire et qui crains? Car il est certain que je ressens ces deux passions. Je suis sans doute *un meslange*, et d'Alexis et de Céladon ... Je suis donc et Alexis et Céladon meslez ensemble ...

(IV, v, 252)

A mere twenty years before Descartes's similar reasoning, Céladon/Alexis' questioning, instead of producing certitude, instead of grounding the subject in its own interrogation, disperses it. The inquiring subject is a mixture, an amalgam, finally a no-thing. This unstable "one," the reunion of the Androgyn, the coming together of the "two halves" each seeking the other in the elimination of all difference, passes first through the codes of "natural" (rhetorical) sexual desire, then through the register of the repressed (homosexual) desire, to arrive at the elimination of all desire in reunion, the figure of non-difference.

Androgyny thus both blurs and reveals forces of sexuality that the text's entire philosophy and rhetoric must obfuscate. It is a sexuality that is more definable by its drive than by its object. When this sexuality surfaces in the text, it is always condemned as an impossibility, as the ultimate limit of representation. The text of the *Astrée* is (and this comes as no surprise) a text of deferment, a text that refuses the sexuality that is at its very center, and displaces it. Pushing sexuality beyond its own borders, the text creates its "jouissance" as shining in an impossible distance. Thus, the text can always claim to be heading towards it, while in reality avoiding it. (Re)-union is precisely what the entire thrust of the novel in its rhetoric strives for, all the while refusing it. This reunion, the end of desire, would be at the same time the end of narration itself, the end of the text, death.

In order to escape this end, in order to circumvent the law of reality, the text must constantly invent new obstacles in its own routeing, must constantly re-route itself, away from an ending. To do this the text falls back on its own narrative "vraisemblance," that is, on those narrative traditions it issues from and changes: the pastoral, the romance, the tales of chivalrous adventures. The text delves into these, its own authorizing fictions, to produce constantly new obstacles to its own narration, producing ever-renewed fictions for its self-perpetuation.

Nothing ever ends in the *Astrée*. Impelled by the mechanisms we have been discussing, and others we have been forced to leave aside, the novel can and does go on forever. Nothing except death, which as the ultimate destruction of difference may be metaphorically synonymous with the indistinction of androgyny, can stop it. Yet even death, in this text, is never "real": people die and resuscitate to meet the needs of narration (Céladon is once again the best but not the only example). Finally death, too (at least the death of any of the main characters), is banished from the world of the

Astrée. Death must be imposed from the outside in order for this narration to reach its limits.

In 1624 d'Urfé died, suddenly, unexpectedly. Strangely, with this death his text both stops and goes on. It stops in an eternal moment of openness with Astrée and Alexis/Céladon bound and exposed, suspended between the hostile army of Polémas and the menacing arms of their friends besieged in Marcilly. They are left hanging in mid-air between life and death, between "plaisir" and "jouissance," clinging to their past and ignorant of their future. It goes on in the continuations of Gomberville and of Baro, and in the interminable fights over which of their endings is the "true" one. Yet there is no "true" end. Death came to d'Urfé, but left his characters exactly as we found them, *in medias res.* They are about to be, at some future moment, in some time and place even more perfect than the ideal world of the Forez.

Curiously, the very fact that the *Astrée* has no ending, cannot be "finished," refuses narrative closure, is itself indicative both of the novel's place in the evolution of seventeenth-century subjectivity and of its own part in that evolution. Closing our own circle, the moment of eternal suspense, of eternal "suspension" of Astrée and Céladon in that unfigurable point of passage between past and future, returns us to our own point of departure, the *Astrée* as partition, separating and joining through the enigma of representation the pre-modern and the modern.

Finally, we too are left hanging in our attempts to articulate this difference, suspended between the various critical idioms available to us to explain and circumvent this ambivalence. We could, for instance, attempt to define the ineffable in post-freudian terms where the *Astrée*'s textual dynamics could be described as more closely allied to a "pre-Oedipal" economy rather than to an Oedipal schema of desire. It structures the human subject formed in its meanderings as fluctuation, fluidity, fragmentation. It traces the parameters of a subject subjugated to a primitive relation to an indeterminate "maternal" corpus. Thus, it would be opposed to the more rigidly ordered Oedipal text – the *Princesse de Clèves*, for instance, a text of sacrifice subjected by and to the law of the Father, a text of completion, of closure, of death.

On the other hand, we could look to the *Astrée* more in terms of "myth" (which obviously does not exclude but rather subsumes the post-freudian discourse) both in the "classical" definition given to myth by Lévi-Strauss as the representational compromise of irreconcilable differences, and in the more recent, more "philosophical" vocabulary J. L. Nancy employs to describe the ideological functioning of literary myth in the constitution of a community.[24]

If we, with Nancy, understand myth to be the undefinable bond uniting and separating individuals in a "community" – that it is, therefore, a form of "ideology" – and literature as an instance in which that ideology is made manifest and deflected (if only to become itself, mythologized), then we might see how the *Astrée* functions as an "originary" myth of/for Classicism while remaining itself at a distance from what it helps define.

What I believe attracts Classicism to the *Astrée* is an apparent essential structuring of the world through a sexual iconography whose limits repeat and trace a congenial "naturalization" of social parameters. These parameters will be incorporated in a Classical aesthetic that is itself informed by the possibilities of an evolving sexual and political ethos. Although the entire thrust of the novel in its narrative, aesthetic and symbolic dimensions undermines the possibilities of the essentialization of sexuality – any grounding of sexuality in a "nature" that is given rather than produced – what will seduce, or be eminently congenial to, an emergent Classical order of the One will be the figure of natural sexual symmetry, the figure traced by the coupling of the characters, the male–female coupling that divides and joins the world of the novelistic universe into a "natural," therefore a-political, realm of the harmonization of opposites into a total, unified structure.

The literary thrust of the *Astrée* is its reworking of, and re-insertion in, an Edenic myth. This mythic return to some pre-lapsarian Eden, in turn, helps echo and shore up the entire Christian tradition upon which the social, monarchical system of seventeenth-century Europe was grounded. The Forez, like all pastoral, rejoins the foreclosed garden of Eden as the figure of a pre-lapsarian universe, a world before sexuality, before politics, instituted from above, from God. It functions as a perfectly self-adequate social structuring of the human in a male/female economy, the order of an Adam and an Eve – guardians and principal victims/beneficiaries of that structure. It also, by the remythologization of that order in the context of the seventeenth century's turmoil, sustains its effort to situate itself, to order itself. What this reinscription of myth implies, however, what it also carries along, surreptitiously, in its mythic seduction, is its impossibility. As myth the *Astrée* also transports the weight and burden of what is repressed in myth, of what, occulted, also informs the parameters of self-representation, condemning the Classical universe and the subject it spawns to its own exhaustion, its "épuisement" in the quest for the promised completion that eludes it, that it can never attain within the symmetrical sexuality that is offered it as its goal.

And this, too, the *Astrée* told us in its telling, in its endless repetitions and constant deferrals of what it could not "see" either because its own "focus" was directed elsewhere, at a different subjective configuration, or because a certain alignment of sexual and political forces existed beyond its horizon. It is this alignment and focusing that, I believe, Classicism does finely tune; and in so doing it is able to offer to our gaze a new sighting of perfect love that is as tantalizing as it is impossible. It is this difference of visions, the difference between an impossible blindness and an equally impossible insight, between the lack of interiority and its too painful apotheosis, that explains, in large part, the abyss that both separates and joins the shining, depthless subject of pastoral romance and the passionate tragic subject of seventeenth-century Classicism.

2

THE GRATEFUL DEAD: CORNEILLE'S TRAGEDY AND THE SUBJECT OF HISTORY

> Le passé est le lieu d'intérêt et de plaisir qui situe hors des
> problèmes présents du prince, du côté de l'"opinion" et de la
> curiosité du public, la scène où l'historien joue son rôle de
> technicien-substitut du prince.
>
> (M. de Certeau, *L'Ecriture de l'histoire*, p. 17)

Although Corneille entered the tragic universe through the door of myth (*Médée*), his great tragedies, those plays that in his own time set him apart from his contemporaries as the creator of a new, powerful dramaturgy, are firmly rooted in history. *Le Cid*, *Horace*, *Cinna* and *Polyeucte*, despite the obvious differences in their plots and dramatic peripeteia, are all subtended by a historical imperative, a recourse to history as the impetus and motivation of tragic mimesis. In Corneille's plays the imbrication of history and tragedy forms a locus of overlapping, and at times contradictory, forces that circumscribe the emergence of the Classical subject. This subject, in turn, is implicated in the forms pleasure and power take in Cornelian dramaturgy as it reflects and traces the parameters of the nascent Absolutism of seventeenth-century France.

The Cornelian gesture of tragic "translation" from the universe of myth to the world of history is significant in its own right. Could we not see in this shift that initial move separating what J.M. Apostolidès has, following contemporary sociological discourse, described as the distinguishing feature of two types of societies, "those without history and those with access to historical understanding"?[1] On one level at least, Corneille's abandonment of the mythic could be seen to parallel a contemporary shift in early seventeenth-century society. This society, still reeling from the chaos of civil war, still tottering on the brink of religious, social and political divisions, emerged during the 1620s garbed in the vestiges of a feudality that was waning, but far from dead. The "history" of feudal societies is tautologically cyclical. Clannic rivalries are repeated in systems of legality, economy and thought that trap time in the circularity of an eternal return of the same. Myth freezes institutions and entire societies in a compulsive need to repeat.[2]

Concurrently, however, the early years of the seventeenth century witnessed, in the works of Bodin, La Popelinière, Sorel, and others, the emergence of a "modern" form of historiography.[3] These writers, influenced by the work of Machiavelli and Guicciardini, eschewed a providential view of history and elaborated a theory of action in the world around the figure of the Prince. In the first decades of the century history began to collaborate with the dominant ideology of "raison d'Etat." It and its practitioners were corralled into the service of the monarchy.

As the prince becomes the center of History, the main agent of human affairs, so too does he become the symbol of subjectivity as the focal point of legal, grammatical, and sexual authority. At the same time and paradoxically, as the object of desire of his subjects, the prince becomes also the vanishing point of individuality. Any conception of individual difference, that is, the possibility of the individual's representing himself as existing outside of the forms of sociality that define him — those hierarchical values that situate them both synchronically and diachronically as pertaining to a transhistorical "national" essence — are foreclosed as this sociality becomes itself inextricably bound to the subjugation of the citizenry to the Prince's history. Citizens and monarch are bound together, "incorporated," in the emerging national state. Together they form a "corpus," whose integrity is reflected in the princely body.

The emergence of the modern form of Absolute monarchy around the image of the Prince was based, in part at least, on the historian's ability to articulate a difference within a continuity. Society was made to look at its own past, at its own dead, as Other.[4] From this demarcation of past and present, from this (arbitrary) investment of the past by the present needs of the Monarchy, history becomes both the sign corroborating the present, and the proof that the present is part of a progression. In other words, history is presented as a form of genealogy, a linear progression in which death is both affirmed and denied, in which a present is created that is inextricably bound to a past with which it becomes confused, separable only in and through the "person" of the Monarch. In its immediacy the present, and the present Monarch, is always an apogee, the proof of its own transcendence.[5] When seen in these terms, the relation between history and tragedy, as it was brought to the stage by

Corneille in his revolutionary dramaturgy, becomes for French society of the seventeenth century particularly charged with significance. For our own world as well, where we continue to stage for our pleasure these icons of the Classical stage, they continue to represent the scene of inchoate, yet radical social change (a change in historical consciousness) that reflects an ideological shift in how one defines oneself in relation to both the past and the present. The theater becomes the locus where the conflicting demands of individual pleasure and societal renunciation meet. By tracing in its internal strictures the social revolution that informs its parameters, the stage becomes the mirror of a new "subjectivity." This subjectivity is directly connected to the ideological imperatives that Cornelian tragedy in its historical illusion is elaborating for and through the pleasure of the spectator.

What exactly is at stake in Corneille's shifting of his tragic locus from the universe of myth to the world of history, what does Corneille abandon when he moves from *Médée to Le Cid*? C. Lévi-Strauss has taught us that one of the essential attributes of myth is its "eternal" quality, a quality which negates "time" and ignores "progress."[6] Situated at an eternal moment of conflict before the imposition of the Law, before the radical separation of the universe into the domains of nature and culture, and coterminous with the scission of the sexes, myth traces the shifting parameters of these undefined borders. At its most extreme the mythic universe defies all order and seeks refuge in the illogical mode of the magical and the sacred.[7] Was it, therefore, just a coincidence that Corneille chose as the subject of his first tragedy the destruction by a woman of that social unit, the family, that would continue to play so important a role in his great plays?

The origins of family, its constitution and disintegration as recounted in myth, provide the most compelling of tragic scenarios because it is here, in this vortex of conflictual passions, that the desiring subject is most radically affected in those sexual, political, and economic structures in which s/he is most invested. It is here that the subject becomes the object of the most violent threat to his/her own dispersion.[8] In *Médée* we witness the inability of the family, as a Patriarchal unit, to be. We witness its destruction by Medea, the barbarous other, the sorceress, come from the far reaches of the world, from savage Scythia, who in her excess refuses the symbolic Law of the Father. Medea refuses containment and triumphs over any semblance of (masculine) order, over any ideal of genealogy by and through the Father — over, that is, what was coming to be thought of as "history."

50

Corneille's tragedy and the subject of history

As the author most associated with the elaboration of the Classical edifice, an edifice which reflects while representing the Law, Corneille poses as the first stone of this edifice a tragedy that refuses this Law. By placing at the entrance of his own tragic universe a myth that portrays the reign and victory of excess as woman, Corneille institutes that excess as the desire/fear his great tragedies must mask. It is with the troubling conundrum of *Médée* (not just an excessive myth, but an excessive "representation," a "Baroque," irregular tragedy) that the subsequent tragedies must struggle as they elaborate the strictures of symmetry and order that are attained only through repression, the repressions of *Médée*, of Medea.

The move from myth to history is a complicated transference for Corneille, for it is a move that is fraught with ideological consequences. This "translation" both implies an investment in a metaphysics of sexuality (the imposition of a Patriarchal essentialization of sexual difference and the hierarchy of power that essentialization implies) and betrays a concern for the representational imperatives – for the arduous development of "tragédie régulière" – that was to affect the course of French and European drama for more than two hundred years.

The distinctions between myth and history that I have been elaborating are not as simple as it would at first seem, especially when we are caught up in the Cornelian world, in the universe of theatrical mimesis. I would like, for the moment, to leave aside the very real and pressing contradictions that are apparent to us all (the theater is not history, and history, or rather historiography, is not dramatic representation), in order to delve into first the ideological implications of writing history and writing tragedy, and then the explorations of the differences and overlapping premises of these two rhetorical exercises.

In a quite paradoxical fashion, could we not speculate that for those societies that have passed over into the "historical," that have abandoned the explanations of myths, "history" as a form of narration, a narration that explains origins, conflicts and resolutions – that explains, that is, the present – becomes its own form of myth? "L'histoire est sans doute notre mythe," writes M. de Certeau. "Elle combine le 'pensable' et l'origine, conformément au mode sur lequel une société se comprend."[9]

In *L'Ecriture de l'histoire*, de Certeau argues powerfully for seeing historiography as an exercise of ideological control. He points out the difference between actual historical action ("faire l'histoire") and its narration ("faire *de* l'histoire") and the political and ideological implications of the latter. In its attempt to resurrect and yet contain the past, to make the dead speak, think or act ("Les chers disparus entrent dans le texte parce qu'ils ne peuvent plus nuire ni parler," p. 8), history as a form of rhetoric constantly invests the past with its own present:

Le discours sur le passé a pour statut d'être le discours du mort. L'objet qui y circule n'est que l'absent, alors que son sens est d'être un langage entre le narrateur et ses lecteurs, c'est à dire entre des présents. La chose communiquée opère la communication d'un groupe avec lui-même par ce "renvoi" au tiers absent qu'est son passé.   (p. 60)

In this sense, history would be a dialogue with the dead where the present asks questions about itself and listens to its own answers, to its own ways of explaining itself as invested with the powerful, mystical pronouncements of its other. As a rhetoric, history is always a desire, a desire to capture, repossess the dead other, to speak from the place of that other. This desire would situate itself beyond death, in the empyrean transcendence of the Law, which it articulates as coming from the hereafter, but which echoes the here and now.[10] This rhetoric would confer upon "history" as discourse what all desire desires, to be consubstantial to itself, to be both its own subject and object, to be, therefore, out of the realm of contingency, to be the "truth," the "one," divine and transcendent, the origin and echo of the Law of the Father. History, in these terms, would always seem to be the ideological explanation of the present by the past, because it represents the imperialistic colonization of the past by the present.

Tragedy, on the other hand — that particular form of historical tragedy Corneille perfected in the 1630s and 1640s — presents itself, disguises its present, as past. It is clear that for Corneille, as for Aristotle, "(past) action" (*muthos* = "history") was the heart of all tragic representation:

La tragédie est représentation non d'hommes mais d'action, de vie et de bonheur (le malheur aussi réside dans l'action) ... De sorte que les faits et l'histoire sont bien le but visé par la tragédie ...
(Aristotle, *Poétique*, p. 55)[11]

l'âme de la tragédie c'est l'histoire, les caractères viennent en second.
(*Ibid.*, p. 57)

Corneille is always careful to refer his readers to the histories he has used to authorize his tragedies:

Au reste, comme les tragédies de cette seconde partie sont prises de l'histoire, j'ai cru qu'il ne serait pas hors de propos de vous donner au devant de chacune le texte ou l'abrégé des auteurs dont je les ai tirées afin qu'on puisse voir par là ce que j'y ai ajouté du mien et jusques où je me suis persuadé que peut aller la license poétique en traitant des sujets véritables.

("Au lecteur," 1657, p. 5)[12]

History is always used to authorize tragedy, but it never quite contains it, never quite limits it to its own laws. In a strange "chassé-croisé" history and tragedy contaminate each other, history being the origin of tragedy, tragedy the end of history.

This crossing simply repeats the initial chiasmus we have already alluded too, and to which we must return. History colonizes the past with the present, while historical tragedy represents the present as past. The point of their intersection, the meeting of the two unassimilable terms of this opposition, is in the immediacy, the always-now of the moment of spectacle. Here the opposition between the past and the present vanishes in the eternal moment, always displaceable, always renewable, of the tragic catharsis. It is to this eternal moment of immediacy, the focal vanishing point where history and tragedy meet and are inverted, that we must turn our gaze if we are to understand their imbrication as a form of desire for the Other, a desire that, materialized as spectacle, contributes to the elaboration of Absolutist ideology as a form of hegemony.

When Corneille moved from myth to history, when he wrote *Le Cid* and had it produced, he was immediately embroiled in scandal. The reaction to the *Cid* was unique in the annals of the French stage. No other theatrical début was to have such a momentous impact on its contemporaries and on successive generations as Corneille's new tragi-comedy. Once the storm of protest, the accusations and counter-accusations, had subsided, once the Académie had made public its own thoughts on the play, the crux of the scandal remained as troubling as ever. Implicated in this crux were two distinct but interrelated areas of theatrical and "historical" tension. On the one hand, what most scandalized the play's audience, what sent a shiver of pleasure throughout the parterre, was Chimène's reaction to her predicament, a reaction that marked her as "unnatural":

Amante trop sensible et fille trop *dénaturée*. Quelque violence que luy peust faire sa passion, il est certain qu'elle ne devait point se relâcher dans la vengeance de la mort de son père et moins encore se ressoudre à épouser celuy qui l'avoit fait mourir. En cecy il faut avouer que ses mœurs sont du moins scandaleuses, si en effet elles ne sont pas dépravées.[13]

On the other hand, Corneille censors himself for his awkward handling of the unity of time. The temporal dimension of the play is described by him as being "invraisemblable." It, too, is un-"natural": "Je ne puis dénier que la règle des vingt et quatre heures presse trop les incidents de cette pièce ..." (*Examen*, p. 703).

When Corneille moves from *Médée* to *Le Cid* he leaves the realm of myth for the domain of history. Yet the two essential components of scandal — women and time — are the same we meet in *Médée*, and they set this new play off from the "Classical" perfection towards which it tends. The move from myth to history does, however, imply certain differences within the apparent similarities. The move displaces the scene of the drama from a universe existing before time to a world already structured within the limits of a very definite chronology. What was not possible in *Médée* — the triumph of the Law of the Father and the concomitant organization of society in sublimation — is present as an "already-there" by *Le Cid*. While the world of *Médée* represented a stance outside of time, the world of *Le Cid* is anchored in the curious interstice of diachrony and synchrony that meet in the embrace of Castilian history. This history is the narration of a "race" whose roots reach into the past and whose ambitions send it forth into the future. In this, Corneille's first venture into history, temporality will take the form of genealogy.

And yet the historical moment Corneille chooses for his tragedies is always a "dramatic," fraught, moment, a moment of "history" becoming, a moment of passage, a threshold where what has been vanishes into what must be. Corneille's historical tragedies, from *Le Cid* to *Polyeucte*, are always situated at the point where ideologies collide. Corneille's history always appears threatened with a return to chaos, to social and cultural disintegration. Curiously, all of these plays reflect this moment of passage in the twists of their plots and in the inscription of this "threshold" at the very center of their "dramatic" dilemmas. In a large sense the moment of representation, the moment we are called upon to witness, is the threshold (the "hymen") of History.[14] In *Le Cid* we are present at the unsteady beginnings of Castilian monarchy. Fernand is the first king of Castile. He is the first great lord to separate himself from his fellow nobles and to impose his rule on them. Nothing could be less sure than this rule. The old feudalism, represented by Don Gomès, is very much alive as the play begins. It is only in his duel with the count, in his killing of Chimène's father, that Rodrigue will mark the end of that threat to Fernand's rule and the emergence of the new order of Castilian hegemony.[15]

This same structure pertains, I believe, to all the great tragedies. All of the major dramas figure moments of passage; history as tragedy is always a threshold, always an indeterminacy. In them all the moments of historical passage from one order to another are mirrored as a psycho-sexual passage, a ritual sacrifice, the coming together of the masculine and feminine lines in the promised and yet infinitely displaced moment of marriage ("l'hymen-ée").

It is in this conflated space where history is mirrored in tragedy, where the context (the "real") is analogous to the "private", personal dilemma of the protagonists, that history is represented as "desire." The desire for the Other that is history, the desire for the past/dead, is conflated with the desire that is internal to the drama. Finally, in the moment of representation both appeared fused with the desire of the spectators.[16] It is in these interweavings that we can discern the reciprocal investments of Tragedy and History where the one informs and constitutes the other as its Other.

Although Cornelian tragedy always evolves within the confines of the family, always turns around the conundrum of marriage, we must remember that tragedy for Corneille is primarily political. The imbrication of the family and the polis is never questioned in this world which ignores any separation of private and public spaces. In Corneille the family doubles the State.[17] All existence is political existence and it is here, at the very heart of the tragic dilemma, that we see the inseparability in Corneille of desire and "action," of tragedy and history. The tragedy that is played out for us, that engages us in its structures of desire, informs our sense of history and creates for us history that is as ideologically seductive as it is pernicious.

As we know, ideology is both elusive and illuding. Although reproduced materially – in the everyday gestures and rituals of a populace – ideology remains always beyond representation, informing those invisible limits that make representation possible.[18] Yet the forms of representation remain at an asymptotic distance from "ideology," always supplementary and insufficient. According to L. Althusser's definition that we have discussed in the introduction to this book, "L'idéologie représente le rapport imaginaire des individus à leurs conditions réelles d'existence."[19] I would like to insist, here, that it is this "imaginary" (in the sense of unconscious) that we glimpse in the theater, and I would like to add that we glimpse it only as "symptoms." Ideology becomes apparent to us only in those strategic moments when the characters who are offered to our gaze as "subject" (both subjugated and subjected) become dramatic ("dramatis personae"). This happens at that moment when their particular form of subjectivity is put into question. In Corneille this discord always appears at its most intense where sexuality and history are joined as tragedy.

In order to approach the ideological imperative that is at work in the Cornelian spectacle, we must for the moment try to see beyond the individual predicaments that each of the great plays proposes to our gaze, and attempt to find a more general *archè*, a structure that the "history"/plot both masks and reveals. It is only when we see through the trappings of plot, that always situate Cornelian drama in far-removed cultures and historical situations, and perceive the underpinnings of its archaeological structures that we can attempt to analyse its role in the elaboration of an aesthetics of Absolutism, and to understand, through this elaboration, its hold on us.

It is my contention that the central structure of the great tragedies repeats the gesture Corneille traced by leaving the world of myth for the universe of history. By this I mean that Corneille's great plays all represent, in the structures of symmetry (sexual as well as formal) which they elaborate, the (shaky) triumph of order (the Law of the Father) over chaos, of ideality over materiality, of metaphor over metonymy and of masculinity over femininity. What this means, in the first instance, is that Corneille sexualizes history: he makes history play out, through his characters' actions, a metaphysics of Patriarchy, constructed around a "naturalization" of biological sexual difference essentialized into a political and ethical difference. The battle that is constantly waged in all of the great tragedies, the epicenter where the real ("history") is invaginated in the tragic, always replays the never-ending triumph of the Father over Medea.

The world of the *Cid*, for instance, is firmly rooted in history. Yet it remains on the near side of the margins separating the universe of ordered, progressive chronology from the indifference of disorder. We are in history, but, as I have suggested, in history that trembles on the brink. The society of the *Cid* is young and it is still prey to uncertainties that transcend the political and are confused with the anxieties of the metaphysical. It is these anxieties that Chimène more than any other of the play's characters embodies.

While *Médée* showed us the victory of matter, of the chaotic forces of nature metaphorized as both woman and mother (Medea as *mater*), over form (Jason as representative of the *polis*, of the Law of the Father) *Le Cid* is clearly a mise-en-scène of a patriarchal society where we have moved from the frightening world of an all-powerful Phallic mother to a smaller, but ever so much more rigidly organized, stage of the Law. From a world of vengeance, hostility and aggression played out as natural forces exterior to the person of the heroine (but metonymically representative of her) we are now in a world where these same passions are interiorized. The conflicts that in the former play could still be resolved in the world with which they were one are in this play (and this is not the least of its major innovations) all internalized. Paradoxically, when we move from the realm of myth to the domain of history that sphere of the human psyche that ignores chronology, the unconscious, comes to the fore.[20] It is perhaps for this very reason, for the radical new stakes that were at issue, that chronology is what gave Corneille the most difficulty in composing his play, and is what, throughout the play, Chimène refuses.

The first scenes of the play clearly establish the locus of dramatic tension within the space of desire and chronology, at the juncture of "clannic" history and individuality that defines all of the play's characters. In this schema we see the conflict between an emerging centralized Monarchy that predicates its existence on a concept of linear history (time as genealogy) and the remnants of a feudal horde which exist in an inchoate, inordered synchrony. Don Gomès, Chimène's father, is the representative of this feudal threat. He refuses the sublimation to the King that is required in the newly emerging monarchy:

> Monsieur, pour conserver tout ce que j'ai d'estime,
> Desobéir un peu n'est pas un si grand crime ...
>
> (II, i, 365–366)

But, of course, his disobedience is a crime, a crime of "lèse-majesté," and for this reason Gomès, and what he represents, must be eliminated.

Genealogy in *Le Cid* spatializes temporality. It imposes a metaphorical essence (masculinity) on a metonymical (biological) displacement. It is this shift that allows Patriarchy to exist in history and yet to transcend the particular historical moment. History as genealogy creates a transhistorical "essence" that can be transmitted from man to man.[21] It is for this reason that the marriage of Rodrigue and Chimène remains the central troubling conundrum of the play. On its acceptance or rejection hangs the entire system of genealogy-history that is emerging and that subtends the ideology of Monarchy that the drama plays out. For whatever the "psychological" reasons the plot brings to the fore forming the tragic dilemma of the play, "structurally" the marriage ("l'hymenée qui à tous ... importe") must be resolved, in order for history to triumph over dispersion. Chimène is "unnatural" in this play because she refuses history; she can no more accept the past than the future:

> Le passé me tourmente et je crains l'avenir.
> (II, iii, 480)

Chimène lives in an eternal present. She is trapped in a self-negating narcissism that mirrors her father's feudal backsliding, and remains the stumbling block to the triumph of the newly centralized monarchy. Chimène remains the troubling refusal of the evolution of the society of the *Cid* because she refuses, or is incapable of, the right "historical" choice. This choice would break her off from the old regressive order of her father and ally her to the new order towards which the whole of her world tends. She remains as divided, "indifferent," at the end of the play as at the beginning, caught up in a battle for the past, the death that cannot endure:

> Et toi, puissant moteur du destin qui m'outrage,
> Termine ce combat sans aucun avantage,
> Sans faire aucun des deux ni vaincu ni vainqueur.
> (V, iv, 1665–1667)

Chimène is most scandalous not because she accepts the marriage to Rodrigue, but because she postpones it.

By the end of the play much has been changed politically. Time has been skewed out of all verisimilitude (cf. the entire battle with the Moors) in order to demonstrate the uncomfortable moments of the passage of history, of a new order being born and imposed in a society that still lives very much on the tremulous borders separating sublimation in chronology and the celebration of death in the evanescent present. Yet some things remain unresolved: Chimène's protest, although silenced, remains real. The last words of the king:

> Le temps assez souvent a rendu legitime
> Ce qui semblait d'abord ne se pouvoir sans crime.
> (V, vii, 1814–1815)

are a deferral of the paradox that neither he nor the play can resolve. It manifests, nevertheless, a new desire, a desire that time, a new chronology finally put in place by the Cid, should triumph over Chimène.

The *Cid* that begins the construction of Corneille's Classical edifice does so by imposing certain constraints as imperative for that edifice's success. First, when Corneille moves from myth to history he eliminates the threatening (m)Other: in the great plays, all of which turn around the conundrum of family and State, individual and society, there is no mother: all the female roles are reduced to wife, sister or daughter. Then – and this is probably a direct consequence – genealogy, the descent of male to male, is elevated to the essential role in the distribution of societal power: genealogy implies hierarchy. The great anxiety that this investment in genealogy awakens in the Cornelian universe is precisely the need for the female as vessel, as the unavoidable container through which males must pass, and yet this vessel proves to be recalcitrant to its own effacement, unreliable, and usually untrustworthy. It is in order to circumvent the above that the female characters are usually split, first internally (the sign of the feminine in Corneille is precisely this "split," both an excess and a lack), then into two camps: those women who mime the Father and his Law (the Infanta, Julie, Livie) and those who remain ambivalently engaged by/with this Law (Chimène, Camille, Emilie, Pauline). At the same time, it is precisely these same women, the erotic objects of the heroes' and the audience's gaze, who, as females, are made to represent a form of narcissism that in its self-enclosure, in its obsessive negative drives, is pinpointed as the stumbling block to all cultural evolution (that is evolution in and through the Law of the Father).

Nowhere is this recalcitrance made more apparent than in *Cinna*. The entire drama plays out, along the axes of sexuality and politics, conflicting perceptions of history. All the characters of *Cinna* are the products of a fiercely traumatic past. They have been radically sundered from this past which in their fantasies and rhetoric is reconstituted as a moment of utopian plenitude: then they were linked to a genealogy that defined them socially, politically and economically. In their articulation this past is metaphorized as "Republican" Rome. Although forever inaccessible to them, this metaphor survives in the form of fragmented memories, fantasies and desires which, constantly intruding in their present articulations of their predicaments, continually contaminates the present with the past, making any separation of the two impossible. Each of the main characters of the play is given a monologue where s/he attempts to explain his/her present by the past. Perhaps nowhere in Cornelian theater does the weight of history lie so heavy upon the actions, ambitions and desires of his characters. History, as it is described in *Cinna*, is a fatal cycle which unfolds in the narratives of each of the characters and which seems to entrap them in a constant impasse. The present is immediately engulfed as a simulacrum of the past. No differentiation is possible. The present can only repeat, in an endless cycle, the "same" thing as the past:

> Salvidien à bas a soulevé Lépide;
> Murène a succedé, Cepion l'a suivi:
> Le jour à tous les deux dans les tourments ravi
> N'a point mêlé de crainte à la fureur d'Egnace,
> Dont Cinna maintenant ose prendre la place.
>
> (IV, iii, 1199–1203)

One cannot get out of history. Origin and end continually reflect one another and in this reflection no idea of progress, no ideal of individuation is possible.

The essential drama that is played out in *Cinna* works out of this outmoded form of history, works out of the endless cycle of repetition of the same, and into a new "linear" model of progressive, evolutionary history. Obviously this working out is done through the subjugation of the most recalcitrant character, Emilie, who is also the most subversive, combining politics and eroticism to control the hero. Space does not permit me to go into the details of this subjugation. Suffice it to say that Emilie's (and the conspirators') epiphany occurs precisely at that moment when Auguste eliminates the feminine that inheres in his own character (the "split", the essential division, that is metaphorized as his double being "Octave–Auguste") and effaces the fault that condemns him to repeat his past. By this gesture he becomes, in his splendid, isolated integrity, the impossible reflection of all self-containment – the model and reflection of all desire for his subjects. By placing himself above the demand of the plotters (the demand to punish them) he has established a new system of power: instead of a system of circular exchange that has united all of them along a horizontal axis (Auguste = Cinna = Emilie = Maxime = Auguste) we now have a vertical structure where all meaning flows downward from Auguste, become godlike.

Auguste breaks out of the system of repetition that had condemned Rome to constantly replay her internal strife in dissension and fragmentation. He has constituted a new order of history where all is sacrificed to the Monarch, and where the supreme pleasure of the subject is to die so that the Law may live:

> Puisse le grand moteur des belles destinées,
> Pour prolonger vos jours, retrancher nos années.
>
> (V, iii, 1779–1780)

Contrary to other initial acts of foundation, which have traditionally been a transgression of the body — a murder/sacrifice — the
action that establishes this new political order is a (re)birth. By his
gift of life Auguste successfully replaces the (dead) Fathers of past
history and becomes their substitute. Each plotter owes his existence
anew, to Auguste. Their allegiance from now on is not to the past
but to Auguste, who has created himself as both their past and their
future. This debt, paradoxically, is articulated by them as what
makes them entire:

> Souffrez que ma vertu dans mon cœur rappelée
> Vous consacre une foi lâchement violée,
> Mais si ferme à présent, si loin de chanceler
> Que la chute du ciel ne pourrait l'ébranler.
>
> (V, iii, 1745–1748)

The end of the play sees, then, a complete reversal that affirms a
political system that was only shakily in place at the tragedy's start.
For a tragedy, the play ends quite joyously. We witness the institution
of official well-being, the happiness of a monarch who has achieved
the voluntary sacrifice of Republican values (values that have been
constantly identified with Emilie). From his place among the im-
mortals Auguste contemplates all of his former enemies, now vying
to outdo one another in sacrificing to their new history. Is it not the
ultimate ruse of a tyrant to make his subjects happy, to give them
a sense of their self as inseparable from the repressions of his Law,
and to have them articulate this repression as their supreme pleasure?

Both S. Doubrovsky and B. Dort have discussed the evolution of
the Cornelian hero in ways similar to those I have been sketching
here.[22] I could continue my description of this *archè* in *Horace* and
in *Polyeucte*, where we find the final apotheosis of the masculine
imperative in its transcendence into both a universal and eternal
principle. The new Leader — Christ/God — at the end of *Polyeucte*
installs an order that is both temporal and divine, that transcends
pagan history in itself, and leads the way forward in the ever greater
unfolding of providential history. However, having identified this
structure at work in the great plays I would like to dwell a moment
on the initial conundrum I started with, the use of history (instead
of myth) for tragedy, as part and parcel of the development of
Absolutism's hegemony.

As Corneille moves from *Le Cid* to *Polyeucte* he firmly imposes
the Classical edifice on the French stage. This edifice is marked by
many things, but perhaps foremost among the structural, aesthetic,

and philosophical tropes that underlie it is a drive towards a harmonious integrity based upon the metaphysics of symmetry. Aesthetic symmetry – the union of two halves forming a whole – is predicated on a sexual symmetry, the supposed "natural" pairing of heroes and heroines (masculinity and femininity), whose dilemmas and sufferings form the tragic knot of the dramatic plots. This sexual symmetry is presented as a given at the same time as it is naturalized in/by the plays.[23] There is a constant struggle to repress elements that are seen as heterogeneous, dangerous and threatening. These elements, aesthetic – the Baroque aspects of the theater before the *Cid* – and sexual – the presence of a too powerful, too destructive maternal/female presence – are eliminated in the great tragedies. Their elimination accounts for both the beauty and the tension of these plays, but also for the malaise that grows more and more unbearable as we move towards the epiphany of *Polyeucte*.

It is, however, from this symmetry, and from the hidden hierarchy this symmetry both implies and renders explicit, that the figure of the Integral Monarch Emperor-God can be seen to emerge. In another way, we can turn this around and say that the emergence of the One authorizes the structuring of the symmetrical separation of the world into complementary halves whose desire it is to join together in mimetic adoration of the Monarch. This Unitary imperative reinforces itself by imposing difference, investing in concepts of divisions, of dyadic oppositions as the tautological proof of its own prominence.

In the seventeenth century, the theater seems to have been the privileged locus where this Absolutist imperative received its most definitive and seductive form.[24] As we noticed at the beginning of this chapter, the stage is precisely the central point in the chiasmus that history and tragedy form, the point where the colonization of the past by the present (the desire for the Other of historiography) meets the disguising of the present by the past of tragedy. The eternal now of the spectacle both accentuates and obfuscates still another, perhaps primordial, symmetrical investment. What this "now" projects is the collapse of the desire for the past with the desire of the spectacle – that is, the mutual pleasure demanded by an audience and provided by a (successful) play in the image of the King that appears at their join.

That image, the idea of the Monarch as integral, is confirmed in history's disappearance into tragedy. Past and present are eternally available in the immediacy of representation. At the same time, history validates and authorizes tragedy, making it both more and less available. It represents both the immediacy of the contemporary political situation and its effacement as other. In their chiasmus, where the past and the present are fused, there emerges, as their unique point of reference, the image of the Monarch, the only object that transcends time: he becomes the Absolute referent for time, for history, and for desire.

As I have suggested in the introduction, Absolute monarchy would be impossible without a metaphoric substructure of patriarchy, without the structuring of sexual and familial organization, of genealogy/history, around the center/sun of the father. Politics becomes a family affair where the State doubles the family, where each is inseparable from the mirror image of the other. In the confines of this double enclosure the King is, as we have said, first and foremost "le père du peuple."

The unity of the Father is the unity of exclusion. All that contravenes, or is opposed to, his mimesis is exiled to the frontiers of representation, to its outside. An obsessive drive against dispersion, a constant dread that chaos/disruption is always ready to break loose in the world, a horror of the loss of control, is the constant negative other of Paternal order. Integrity is achieved only with the greatest vigilance, the greatest sacrifice. This sacrifice is part of the desire, part of the pleasure of the ambivalent dialectics between Law and chaos, between mastery and submission, between ideological subjugation and subjectivization that is at work in the aesthetics of tragedy. The juncture of these apparent antitheses, the focal point of the tragic — the icon of the Monarch's integrity — is also a vanishing point. It is the point where the pleasure of the spectator, perhaps a masochistic pleasure like the pleasure of the Roman conspirators, finds its grounding in the pleasure of the Monarch, in his adoration.[25]

It is perhaps not a mere coincidence that the plays of Corneille that have been signalled out by the centuries and the canon as the most "perfect," the greatest examples of Classical aesthetics and ethics, are precisely the plays where the imbrication of history and tragedy works the most seductively, where the repressions that are built into the edifice are most compellingly contained. After *Polyeucte* something changes in the Cornelian œuvre. But that is, of course, another story. I will only suggest that the plays that follow see the return of the monsters that have been so strategically banished from the great tragedies. In these plays, the Mother returns, precisely as "uterus", that is as mad, as the hysteric (Cléopâtre, Arsinoé, etc.), and this return signals the contamination of history by myth, the return of Medea. This return of the repressed in Corneille's theater decenters it, sending the structures it elaborates into disarray.

Nevertheless, what seems important for the Absolutist adventure is not the exceptions to the rule, but the rule itself, the Law as it is elaborated in the canonical plays. For is not their very existence as "canon" still the best proof that the desire they elicit and satisfy is very much with us? The tragic world of the great plays represents, not unambiguously, the interrelation of the sexual and political roles of the individual in the patriarchal family/state. It is only when we see the workings of this Absolute quest for totality that we can, I believe, also try to demonstrate what is at stake in the pleasure we take in these tragedies. The violence that is inherent in them is the same violence at the origin of modern Law and thus of the modern subject. It was Corneille who, in the great plays, first elaborated this violence with such seductive elegance as to command our pleasure and our obedience. The great tragedies serve as a troubling reflection of our continued investments in systems of representation − history and tragedy − as a repression that we, perhaps as much as the Frenchmen of 1640, both desire and fear.

3

PASSION PLAY: JEANNE DES ANGES, DEVILS, HYSTERIA AND THE INCORPORATION OF THE CLASSICAL SUBJECT

> For centuries, hysteria has named an incapacity to ... be the difference, "the woman." To explain hysteria by the problem of sexual identity is to miss the struggle in female hysteria against *that* assumption of difference, against *that* identity, is to refind hysteria as a nature of women and not the site of a resistance − nothing to do with an essence − in culture.
> S. Heath, "Difference," p. 57

The Renaissance, as we know, was obsessed with the body. It has even been said that the period that turned its back on the "Dark Ages" did so by discovering, and more importantly displaying, in painting, in sculpture and in literature, the body that, freed from its vestimentary fetters, took its place (as Ronsard put it) "net, libre et nu" as the privileged symbol of human perfectibility. This vision, an exultation, is the utopian promise of a body that exists only for the eye to embrace, to encompass, to penetrate and to possess. At the same time, it must be said that this vision of the body, that the body exposed, caressed by the eye of the beholder, responds to a new, or at least, a newly invested desire, the desire to see. Seeing, that is, the subjective incorporation of the world, becomes a metaphor for knowing that world, the privileged mode for seizing exterior reality and making it a part of the self. The Renaissance's visioning of the body, the body as visibility, was coupled with, inseparable from, the appetite of the eye. This *Schaulust* so amply and so continually teased by the explosion of visual signs, informs not only the being of the other I gaze upon, but my own as well. In this play of showing and seeing, the "I" of the modern subject constitutes itself as surely as it constitutes and is constituted by the object of its gaze.

In the poetry of the Renaissance the body that is offered to our readerly gaze is almost exclusively the female body. It is proffered to the mind's inner gaze in those thousands of petrarchan sonnets, in the myriad "blasons," as fragmented, fetishized, disjointed −

65

le beau téton, la belle lèvre, les belles dents, les jambes, les cuisses, les fesses – and of course, les yeux. In a strange reversal these fragmented bodies can only remind us of the other side, the sadistic side of this visionary drive, this visioning of the female body venerated and vilified by those same men who need its visible otherness as a proof of their difference, as a proof of "the" difference, the political/sexual difference that structures their place in the world.[1] Was it only a coincidence that this period of the poetical display of the female body was also the moment that saw the publication of the first "modern text of anatomy," Vesalius' *De humani corporis fabrica* (Basle, 1543), whose cover shows, as M.A. Descamps reminds us, the savant "dans son amphithéâtre d'anatomie en train d'ouvrir, évidemment, le ventre d'une belle femme nue?"[2]

The slightest turn of our angle of vision and we are presented with that other Renaissance body, the horrifying, decaying body of the woman as death, the sight/site of the Devil, of evil, of all that is ungodly in the human and spiritual commonwealth. The period that concerns us sees not only the birth of the body as light and as promise, but also the fear and mistrust of this body as the work of the Devil. Not only can we see this in poetry, the hags of Ronsard and d'Aubigné – those reversals into winter and death of those once-erotic bodies celebrated as youth and spring – but also in those visible signs of evil's presence in the world: the literal exposition, torture and destruction of recalcitrant bodies of countless peasant women. All showed on their bodies – bodies exposed to the sight, inspection and palpation of the priests, magistrates, and soldiers commanded to find the "Evil One" and destroy him and his servants – the supernumerary teat, the devil's mark, the bloodless warts, the proof, the visible sign that Evil was everywhere.

Let us not forget that the period of transition so seductively studied by Foucault, the period that joined and separated the Renaissance from the Classical age, this moment of passage between signifying systems, of changes in the order of the world, was a period of harrowing violence. This should not surprise us because we know that such passages are rarely navigated easily. Unfortunately, they always seem to be marked in blood, in the blood of those victims who do not seem to fit adequately into the symbolic systems that, at the very same time, are being thrown into disarray.[3] During the years that precede the flowering of French Classicism those pyres upon which thousands of bodies were rent and burned were set aflame throughout France and throughout Europe. These spectacular immolations serve to display to our gaze the "truth" of God, of the

Devil, the truth of our own hidden fears, the negative other of our adoration of and hatred for this beautiful/horrible new body.

In the following pages I would like to analyze one late, strange, transitional case of this passionate body, a case that was almost exactly coterminous with the initial flowering of Cornelian tragedy. I would like to see it functioning rather as the "other stage" of Classicism, a darker, more brutally ambivalent stage upon which is played out in much more violent scenarios the ritual sacrifice of desire to political necessity. I would have us witness this particular case of a spectacular theatricalization of the female body, and to see it as "a visible" language, whose strange semiosis can be useful, I feel, in helping us understand what was "at stake" in the forging of our precarious modernity, of, if I may use F. Barker's elegant title, our "tremulous private body."[4]

At the beginning of Louis XIII's reign, France, in its heterogeneity, was compared by Richelieu to "un corps monstrueux qui ... ne pourroit avoir ni substance ni durée ...'"; to a miscellaneous, chaotic body "qui ayant plusieurs têtes ne peut avoir un même esprit et qui, étant agité d'autant de divers mouvements qu'il est composé de differents sujets ne peut souvent être porté ni à connaître ni à souffrir son propre bien." It is perhaps not just of anecdotal interest that in almost the same breath with which he describes this monstrous body, he fixes a large part of the blame for this monstrosity on the Queen Mother – Marie de Medeci. Troublesome, constantly plotting, the Queen Mother remained an obstacle to political stability: "si l'on considère," he reminds the king, "que la Reine, votre mère, à la suscitation de quelques esprits envenimés, forma un puissant parti, qui vous affaiblissait, fortifiait beaucoup vos ennemis ..."[5] The Queen represents a form of political monstrosity, that preys upon the unity and strength of the king, and therefore of the body politic. The line separating monstrosity from maternity, a certain rhetorical excess from the fear of a certain femininity, is easily crossed by Richelieu. If only by rhetorical contiguity, he establishes a locus of indifference, a locus where the body politic meets and is confounded with the maternal, as the space of political confusion. In this confusion lies the (predicted) death of the state. In order for this body to "know" and to accept what is good for it, it must be purged and cleansed. To elaborate and shore up the foundations of Patriarchal monarchy this monstrous heterogeneity must be eliminated. First, the mother is literally expelled (Marie de Medici was forced into exile at Brussels); then the body is surgically amputated of those recalcitrant, divisive nobles, Montmorency, Marillac,

Cinq-Mars, whose partisan politics threaten the unity of the realm with dispersion; finally those purifying pyres are lit throughout the kingdom upon which are burned those other perverters of the common good, those evil mothers, the witches and devils who are everywhere whose ungodly work saps the body politic of its strength, and whose diabolical pact threatens all human order and hastens its downfall. In the general political scheme of things, what must be sacrificed, what must be tossed upon these burning pyres, are the recalcitrant, disruptive bodies of those witches, of those devil-possessed madmen whose heterogeneity must be eradicated, effaced. It is from this effacement that the triumphant "Absolutist state," and the new subject/citizens who are incorporated in it, emerge simultaneously. Their mutual constitution is both a renunciation and a sacrifice. Usually metaphorized in an individual or collective scapegoat, this sacrifice is internalized by the community and becomes its symbolic, constitutive nexus, a nexus of shared pleasure and guilt.[6]

It goes without saying that this renunciation is never unproblematic, is never not resisted, because what is in question is always the policing of the individual's most recalcitrant otherness, the body, always the ways in which this unsignifiable, decentering and always recalcitrant locus of conflictual impulses, of conflicted, contradictory semiotic systems, finds its repose not in difference but in ambivalence; not in the order of the One, but in the ambiguity of the many. It is for these conflicts, for these resistances, that the locus that is the body, that the body that refuses localization, will be the pawn in the bloody, violent scenes that subvert and subjugate the individual. This subjugation figures a theater of cruelty, a theater of pleasure, of jouissance, even, in which an entire economy of power and sexuality is invested for us as a strange, perverted "dialogo d'amore." A century before Sade the turmoil of the seventeenth century plunges us into a sado-masochistic dialectics of exquisite pain, from which "we" emerge. And this "we," or rather this "I," issues from the cauldron of change – much like Sœur Jeanne des Anges, of the Ursuline convent of Loudun, at the end of her translation from hysteric to mystic, with these words of ambivalent joy on her lips, with this cry/sigh of her own subjugation:

je ressens, en cette partie là, de si grandes douleurs que je ne vous saurais exprimer. Plus elles sont vives et plus je les désire ... En effet, je souffre avec beaucoup de plaisir et une douce impatience de souffrir d'avantage.

(*Auto*, p. 283)

Passion play: Jeanne des Anges

But this, of course, is Mother Jeanne at the end of her journey, after she has subdued her own recalcitrant body – after, that is, she has, in her own mimetic self-creation, done away with, sublimated her devils, and replaced them with her own internalized guilt/joy. We must leave her there, in order to come back to her once we too have briefly travelled her road, the road that took her from heterogeneity to homogeneity, from the universe of the analogous to the world of transparent representation.

Following in the footsteps of M. de Certeau, I have chosen to write about Sœur Jeanne des Anges, about her murderous "possession," about the indignities of her body, because her story strikes me as symptomatic of the transformation of French and European society at the end of the sixteenth and the beginning of the seventeenth century. In what follows I will be using Sœur Jeanne as a symptom, as a symbol of the transformation in the entire order of words and of things, that sweeps France out of the swirling veils of the "Baroque" and into the realm of Classical transparency. And it goes without saying that what is at stake in this symptomatology is the siting of the body, the spectacular "mise en scène" of the female body, focal point of the male gaze, vanishing point of the *Schaulust* – that desire to see/know that finds its foil in that other seventeenth-century stage upon which the Classical drama of Corneille and Racine is, at the very same moment, elaborating a similar dynamics of familial and social containment.

In just a few words, the setting of the Loudun scene, where I will be following in my description the details de Certeau sets forth in his book *La Possession de Loudun*. What is particularly striking in the Loudun affair, "le grand scandale de l'époque," is the extraordinary imbrication of the political, theological, medical and sexual.[7] De Certeau has shown us how the "site" of Loudun, the theater of this tragedy, is itself an ambivalent locus, one might say an erotogenic zone on the corpus of France. He presents the town as divided between a large Huguenot population in increasing conflict with a militant counter-reformation Catholicism, between those willing to obey the government's directives regarding its fortifications and those who, recalcitrant to the force of centralization, hostile to the "reforms" of Richelieu, resist the dismantling of the city's tower and protective walls. The lines of force are drawn up, and in that division we can detect the opposition between those partisans of the vision of a unified, integral body politic, a new *corpus mysticum* of the state, which, in the political writings of French theorists of the sixteenth century, is formed by the king's symbolic "espousal"

of his realm (the sexual connotations of appropriation and subjugation are evident); and those who eschewed this union, this subjugation, allying themselves with the anachronistic order of Renaissance
political separation, of territorial (parlementary) integrity, thus posing
(to a centralizing monarchy) the constant threat of centrifugal dispersion.[8] It will come, therefore, only as a slight surprise to find
that the "possessed," hysterical, body of the nuns becomes the point
of suture of these diverse forces working at cross-purposes, engaged
in a battle to the death. For the "body" is itself an ambivalent
locus of conflicting discourses – symbolic, imaginary, biological,
political – and thus always functions as a hinge of different semiotic
systems, joining and separating, negating and affirming, while remaining "itself" both within and without these systems, their point
of reference, their point of excess. At the very heart of the Loudun
controversy, a controversy that, like a vortex, sucks into its center, in
its spectacular mise-en-scène of the female body, all those discursive
orders – medical, sexual, juridical and theological – that form and
govern the world, we are presented with the convulsive bodies of
these nuns "possessed."

Hysteria, then, as a site of resistance, a site of conflict, not just
a conflict of a repressed sexuality (although it is that too), but an
irresolvable conflict of those codes that structure the body, that
structure its history and its production at the interstices of epistemic
transfigurations.[9]

When we look at the "possession" of Loudun we must remember
that we are not spectators in the amphitheater of the Salpetrière,
nor are we eavesdroppers *chez* Freud, 19, Berggasse: that is, "we"
are not yet "we," we are not that modern, split, censored, interiority
that is speaking, screaming, whispering and gesticulating in these
(female) bodies. No: "we" are situated in a radically other place, a
place where hysteria (if we must call it that) is the site of a conflict
that is about to create interiority as it moves towards that first
revolutionary split, that first outward sign of transformation, the
split between the private and a public space. In Loudun, however,
in 1632, in 1634, we pre-exist that division: there is as yet no clearly
defined public/private dichotomy, and therefore the split in the body
is not perceived to be a split in consciousness, but a "possession,"
the invasion of that bodily space by devils who, come from the outside world, come from Evil, must be ex-orcized, conjured-out, in
order for the body to discover its lost unity, which is always an
exteriority, situated in the hope of its suture in God.

It would seem to have been Jeanne de Belcier's fate to be marked by her body, and to have her body de-mark her being. From the tender age of three or four she bore on her body the sign of her own "difference," her own female "outrecuidance," a quality that was to remain with her throughout her life:

Elle se trouva en péril de choir et se blesser considérablement. Elle se fit un effort si violent pour se retenir qu'elle se disloqua l'épaule et se fit une contorsion aux reins, en sorte qu'elle demeura depuis le corps un peu de travers et une épaule plus élevée que l'autre.

(Fougeray, *Vie*, quoted in "Jeanne des Anges," essay by M. de Certeau in *Auto*, p. 344)

This bodily disfigurement was doubly traumatic: not only the cause of the withdrawal of her mother's love and the decision to hide her disfigured daughter in the convent, it also and by the same token deprived the child of a (hetero)sexual future: all pretenders to her hand were, by this same mother, given their *congé*. In her personal history, therefore, Jeanne's body marks an involuntary, unwanted, literally "traumatic" separation from the Mother and the immediate foreclusion of the possibility of a familial/sexual future. Jeanne's twisted body exiles her from any insertion within the semiotics of nobiliary kinship, exiles her from the possibility of power, from assuming her place as sexual "other" (in the dialectics of hetero-sexuality) and condemns her to a place of resistance in a female economy of the "same." An ambivalent locus of rejection and desire, the space of the convent, creates and draws into itself an unassimilable erotic charge. When the Devil first appears to Jeanne, he comes as the projection of her own unacceptable, unspeakable sexuality: he appears in the form of Urbain Grandier, the libidinous, scandalous priest, the priest who has written an elegant treatise against the celibacy of the clergy, the dangerous odd-man-out in the political life of Loudun. He comes to tempt her, to touch her, to whisper unclean thoughts to her:

Dans ce temps-là, le prêtre dont j'ai parlé se servait des démons pour exciter en moi de l'amour pour lui: ils me donnaient des désirs de le voir et de lui parler ... il ne manquait pas ensuite de venir la nuit dans notre maison et dans nos chambres pour nous solliciter au péché.   (*Auto*, p. 67)

But, as we know, the possession only started there. From Jeanne des Anges it spread throughout the convent where in the space of a few weeks there were more than fifteen nuns "possessed" by the Devil, and almost as many obsessed. The spectacle of a convent in total disorder quickly demanded the attention of both the ecclesiastical and secular authorities. The town is invested with their power, with their discourses, with their means and theories of expunging this "evil," this disorder that first and foremost manifests itself through and across these bodies, spectacular bodies, bodies giving themselves to sight in convulsions, in frenzied, uncontrollable movement, shouting, jumping, tearing, twisting themselves into blatantly scandalous erotic positions, and spewing forth even more scandalous blasphemies against God the Father, Jesus, the Virgin Mary – against, that is, the entire hierarchical, semiotic order that structures both this world and the next:

Toutes les dites énergumènes ont été agitées des plus violentes, plus extraordinaires et plus effroyables convulsions, contorsions, mouvements, cris, clameurs et blasphèmes qu'on puisse imaginer, étant impossible de les décrire, ni aucunement représenter, sinon en disant qu'il semblait à tous les assistants qu'ils voyaient en cette occasion toute la fureur de l'enfer.

(Lettre de Laubardemont, BN, fonds fr. 7618, ff. 50–51, quoted in de
Certeau, *La Possession*, p. 159)

quand il [Béhémot] occupait ma tête, je déchirais tous mes voiles, et ceux de mes sœurs que je pouvais attraper, je les foulais aux pieds, je les mangeais en maudissant l'heure que j'étais entrée en religion.   (*Auto*, pp. 71–72)

The possession of these nuns is a threatening symptom. It signals the breakdown of a corporate structure, only shakily in place, and its dispersion into chaos. This chaos, in the terms available to the society of the early seventeenth century, is speakable only as "evil," "unnatural," the Devil. Another way of putting this would be to say that the speaking bodies of the nuns, by revealing, thrusting into view, what a waning ideology has occulted, undo those cultural codes whose function it is to "naturalize" the production of the "effet de réel" (the illusion of the "natural") that tautologically underpins those ideological structures that interpellate the individual as subjected, as subject. As we know, for the world of the 1620s and 1630s, this subjectivity, a pre-bourgeois subjectivity is, in the words of Francis Barker, "but a condition of dependent membership in which place and articulation are defined not by an interiorized self-recognition ... but by incorporation in the body politic which is the King's body in its social form".[10] When, by standing on their heads, by kicking, jumping and screaming, the devils/nuns invert these codes, this body, its scaffolding, its entire infrastructure, is subverted, undone precisely at that point where the diverse signifying systems meet, in the individual body as it is defined and confined by discourse, by a discourse that contains it but which never entirely controls it; which can – as in the case of these nuns – be ex-orbited, fragmented and returned to the frightening world that predates interpellation as difference that pre-figures meaning, that refuses division. The interest with which the Loudun affair was followed in the highest circles of government (Richelieu personally financed the life of the convent) represented the attempted use of the scandal of the nuns as one more arm in the battle against protestant heretics (were they ever really sure of a positive outcome, the triumph of the "body of Christ" over the body of the nuns?) but also to insure, reassure themselves that their own hold on the world was not slipping, that the world was still theirs, not the Devil's.[11]

What is, however, even more intriguing is that the protocol of reassurance is always an acting-out of the body, an acting-out in public, in a "theater" of suffering and pain, which like all theater draws into its own production those socially fixed roles/positions of spectator/actor, of male/female, of possessed/clean, and confounds them. All the modern (and many of the contemporary) accounts that we have of the exorcism (that, let us remember, went on for six years, 1632–1638, the years that saw the triumphant if contested production of *Le Cid*) insist on the "spectacular" nature of these attempts to re-establish order:

Après le récit partout colporté, vint la reproduction dramatique: la salle, une église, était grande ouverte, le spectacle, annoncé chaque fois et légitimé par une procession solennelle où figuraient les possédées et leurs exorcistes; les spectateurs, au nombre de plusieurs milliers; la durée moyenne de chaque séance, de six à sept heures.[12]

The possession and exorcism of the nuns is a theater, a spectacle where the drama that is played out for the "thousands" of spectators come from all over Europe is the tragedy of rupture, the traumatic drama, the acting-out, at its weakest points of suture, of the failings of an old order of epistemology, and the troubled birth-pangs of a new one. What is at the very center of this spectacle is the "body," or rather the "bodies," not only the sight of the exposed, speaking body of the nuns, but the "corps à corps," the battle of the nuns (as body, as devil) and the priests: a battle which requires enormous strength and endurance, an almost athletic constitution, in which a strange, non-reciprocal symmetry acts out a cultural/sexual mating game of mastery and submission, or revolt and subjugation.

What might be at stake in the voyeurism/exhibitionism duality of the public exorcism is, on the one hand, the desire of the exorcist/public to "see" the other (= the devil); but since this other is always

73

a sighting/siting of the body, it is always also, in some sense, a sado-masochistic battle, the temptation and resistance of sexuality/spirituality. It appears to me that we might also equate it with the repetition of the "primal scene": that moment, according to freudian theory, when the child fantasmatically "discovers" sexuality, as a division and confusion of two differently sexed subjects.[13] The ritual of exorcism, an institutional ritual, both sets up and recuperates female resistance as a proof of an already-encoded essentiality of sexual difference. It is a primal scene that reconfirms difference as given to sight. Nevertheless, despite its ritual nature, despite its institutional confines, what is always threatening about this, what is demonic, is the possibility of the body's becoming totally exorbitant. But that is also, of course, the pleasure: the possibility that despite the conventions and control there is the knowledge – and the exciting knowledge – that the encoding is perhaps not infallible, that in its exhibition the body can and will break out, destroy, and destructure the system of representation, power and sexuality that inscribe it in a political-juridical subjugation. There is always the tension that evil, despite the assurance that it can never function without God's approval, despite, that is, the assurance by the institution of the Church that it will not get out of hand, will.

The pleasure and tension of these exorcisms as spectacle is the pleasure of teasing which puts into play the desire for seeing the Truth, for the confirmation that the structures that define the world and one's place in it as subject will endure, and the equally great temptation that they will not. That is, that the repression one lives and one likes will be in some sense shattered, done away with, in the convulsive dominance of the body, of its movements, its fragmentation, its pleasure/pain.

When the possessed nuns are at their most spectacular, when they are presented with the "consecrated body" of the host, when they writhe, blaspheme, spit, vomit and refuse to "incorporate" this body of the Lord in their own, they are effectively "de-symbolizing" the *corpus mysticum* that subjugates and subjects them. In a perverse way their own body, attempting to signify beyond the systems that would represent it and in which it is emmeshed, confounds all the discursive systems that create not only the space of the body, but also concurrently its sublimation as member of a more general political corpus, its "subjectivity" in the world.[14]

Despite this seeming "liberation" of the body, its unfettering from the constraints that would bind it, this ex-centricity is never free. It is constantly re-encircled, exorcised, palpated, judged by the entire community it disrupts. What we witness is a strange chassé-croisé of those dyadic oppositions that incorporate the human subject, of voyeurism-exhibitionism, of an elementary play of mastery and submission, of sado-masochism: dyadic oppositions which, in the frenzy of this spectacle (a spectacle that implies the innate reversibility of the roles/poles of any dialectic) are undone. From the sexed, gendered alignment of forces the spectacle presents us with at its beginning we descend into a vortex of fragmentation where there are no longer subjects as male or female, priest or possessed, but the spectacle of the confusion, the confounding and de-subjugation of the individual/body. An oscillation across the bodies of these women, bodies that both are and are not "them," bodies that fragment, and disperse any attempt at subjectivity in an alienation that can never be grounded "in" the body, whose origin is never an internal split, a "difference within" but is finally a difference without, grounded in an exterior reality – Devil or God. De Certeau, however, makes clear that in a strange perverted way we never know – in the encircling of, the laying-siege to, these bodies in excess, bodies that speak a language of fragmentation and disorder, bodies that refuse the limits of subjectivity – *who* is talking when Isacaaron, Béhémot, Asmodée, Léviathan, talk:

J'avais souvent l'esprit rempli de blasphèmes, et quelques fois je les proférais sans que je pusse faire aucune réflexion pour m'en empêcher ... Il se faisait de l'esprit de ces malheureux et du mien une même chose, en sorte que, par leurs impressions, je prenais tous leurs sentiments, j'éprouvais tous leurs intérêts comme si c'eut été les miens. (*Auto*, pp. 71–72)

Those systems of knowledge and power, that both subjugate and empower the subject they form, are themselves decentered by the very extravagance of the spectacle.[15] The body in its *Kreatürlichkeit* both reinforces the gaze of those who look on it (who must interpret it, must transcode it into whatever signifying systems are at their disposal) and forces a constant restructuring of that gaze, a constant displacement of the very semiotic fields that must readjust their own parameters to encompass what exceeds them.

Possession, then, or "hysteria" as a talking body, a body talking a language that refuses a subjectivity that would anchor that body, that would make it make sense, make order: the body talking what cannot be said. The locus of hysteria, the body, is a locus of conflict, of an irresolvable ambivalence; either, in our own terms, the ambivalence of a bi-sexuality that refuses the cutting interdiction of difference, resists the body's policing into those masculine or feminine codes that would enfold it and offer it to the gaze of the other as the already-there of sexual (political) difference; or, in the terms of the seventeenth century, of a psychomachia between good and evil, God and the Devil, a fight through and across these bodies that are both the site and symptom of a larger on-going political battle.

This is not to suggest that the contemporaries of the possession of Loudun all unquestionably saw this "disorder" as the proof of the Devil's existence. Many were the skeptics who accused the nuns of being mere impostors; many saw them as sexually frustrated "females" in desperate straits, deprived as they were of males:

Il vaudrait mieux dire Hystéromanie, ou bien Erotomanie ... ces pauvres diablesses de religieuses, se voyant enfermées entre quatre murailles, raffolent, tombent dans un délire mélancolique, travaillées par l'aiguillon de la chair, et, en réalité, c'est d'un remède charnel qu'elles ont besoin pour être parfaitement guéries.[16]

The medical corps had its own interpretation: actions such as these could be explained by "natural" physiological causes. There existed categories in medical discourse that explained this behavior, "diseases" – either epilepsy, melancholia or "hysteria." As for the last, hysteria, the seventeenth century saw it as it had been described by Galen, as a disease of the womb (which did not prevent the occurrence of hysteria in men: in either case the disease was caused by the retention of "semen" in the body). Curiously, however, this "disease," in common parlance bore another, more simple, more resonant name: it was called simply "the Mother".[17]

Hysteria, possession, fragmentation: the different parts of the body speaking a language that was scanned in screams, whispers, inarticulate gutturals, sighs, cries: a language, a body that returns, mimes a state of indifference, a state of dis-articulation, a state of the "Mother." Hysteria would then be, for the Baroque, a harking back to that state of indifference, to the pleasure/terror of the child/ mother unity that is both protective and deadly. In this the seventeenth century would seem to be eerily consonant with twentieth-century interpretations, which would see this "pre-Oedipal" attachment of the mother/child as the realm of a certain imaginary, an imaginary that persists, and resists, even after the intervention of a third, cutting term, the Law of the Father, the total separation of the infant from the mother and its insertion into the difference of sexuality, of language, of Law. It is from this initial ambivalent locus that each human child must make its way, must separate, if it is to survive as an independent being, condemned to live forever bereft, forever nostalgic for its ambivalence, but "free." This separation is navigated by the imposition/acceptance of the Paternal presence, as an interdictory, cutting law: the law of "No," that by splitting the Mother/child dyad establishes the necessary lack that impels the child into both language and sexuality. Certainly within the insecure confines of a Patriarchy establishing itself anew, the conflict between the lure of the indifference of the Mother and the division in the world of the Father comes down here, on the bodies of these nuns, not just to a crisis of sexuality, but to a turning point of politics, to a sexual politics that is deadly in its stakes and in its consequences.

The road out of the ambivalence of the Mother, out of hysteria, into language/sexuality is never traveled without wounding and scarring. We might see this journey towards "difference" as a sacrifice in which what is offered up on the altar of separation is never quite adequately sutured in the sacred return of the gift of desire. Who or what is the victim of this sacrifice? In the individual history of the subject, it would seem to be a certain (fantasy of) pleasure. In the political, in the construction of Patriarchal monarchy, it is a victim, a communal scapegoat, who is offered up on the altar of necessity in this ambivalent gesture of murder/appeasement. This human sacrifice marks and seals what, in all cases, appears to us as a strange and fearsome act of transference.

At the end of two years of exorcism, of scandal, of the body laid out and exposed in all its intimacy and abjection to crowds often numbering thousands, at the end of a trial that traps the errant priest in a mesh of accusations and counter-accusations, Urbain Grandier is convicted of consorting with the Devil. He is condemned to the "question ordinaire et extraordinaire," that is, to be tortured: first his legs are broken in several places, then he is paraded from church to church in order to "faire amende honorable"; finally, he is brought to the place of execution where a crowd of between six and ten thousand people is waiting for the final act of the tragedy. He is attached to the stake and the wood that has been previously exorcized is ignited:

Il témoigna en tout ne craindre nullement la mort ni ce qui suit après, mais craignait fort d'être brûlé vif et ne faisait autre chose que de prier qu'on l'étranglât, comme Mr de Laubardemont lui avait promis au cas qu'il se convertît. Il en arriva le contraire. Car le feu ou le diable coupa la corde en un instant et si promptement qu'à peine le feu était-il allumé qu'il tomba dedans et y fut brûlé vif sans crier. Seulement quelques-uns entendirent qu'il dit: "Ah, mon Dieu."[18]

But Grandier's death, while obviously eliminating an obstacle to the political order, did not put an end to the possession. The devils did not, with the burning of their earthly accomplice, stop tormenting the nuns. Although their "tormentor" had been broken, his body sundered and finally reduced to ashes, the nuns were not released from their bodies. If anything the possession kept up with exhausting, unceasing regularity. The moment of this failed transference marks, nevertheless, a watershed in the history of Sœur Jeanne's personal itinerary. For the death of Grandier does signal a moment of rupture, a rupture in the style of the exorcisms, in the way the body will be interrogated, will be interpreted, and finally will be repressed.

When the ecclesiastical authorities were confronted with the sham of their own procedures, when they realized that death could not free the sisters, they proceeded to bring in new, less conventional exorcists. It is at this stage that Père Jean-Joseph Surin enters on to the scene of Loudun and into the life of Jeanne des Anges. From this moment on, by his introduction of a new form of exorcism, a form that relies on frequent communion and private prayer, Jeanne is going to start down her road out of hysteria and into a new life as a "mystic," possessed no longer by the Devil but by God, a possession marked most notably by a radical repositioning of the body and of its language.

This second, radical stage of Jeanne's exorcism is fraught with obstacles, not the least of which is the Mother Superior's own delight in her possessed body. Nevertheless, with a perseverance that is nothing short of remarkable Father Surin radically restructured the locus and intent of exorcism, and accepts what we might call both the transference and counter-transference of the possessing, takes on to himself Jeanne des Anges's devils in a way that recalls not so much Freud's analytical situation as the gruelling, mutual "working through" of the patients and doctors at the Laborde clinic in France, or R. D. Laing's radical therapy in England.

To start with, Father Surin takes the nuns off the stage of public exorcism. He thus breaks the spectacular circle with its constant oscillation between public desire and demonic response, with its powerful public transference. He realizes that the possession, as public spectacle, is a reciprocal circle of desire between spectators and actors, in which the female body is interpellated by this excited audience as it plays out and upon its own fears and desires. Next, he is going to establish a new site of exorcism as an intimate, closed space of communion, a communion of Mother Jeanne and Father Jean-Joseph, in a language that is a strange sort of duet, a love song, the whispering, calling of one soul to another. From the former exorcism on the body, Father Surin works at an insinuating dialogue in the soul, in the introduction of the "word," of the idea of sin and of love, of guilt and repentance.[19]

This is a long, arduous, trying experience for both, priest as well as nun, Father as well as Mother, Sister as well as Brother. The two articulable poles of their dialogue, of their dialectics, create them each as subject and object of desire. However, in a first time, this division remains blurred: their collusion with and in hysteria indicates a sharing of an as yet inarticulable division into fixed and yet effaced familial positions:

Cela arriva un jour que M. le duc d'Orléans, frère du roi, était à l'exorcisme; car il vit que la Mère étant délivrée pour quelque temps, je fus ... [possédé à sa place]. Pendant que j'étais tourmenté, un des assistants parlait à la Mère qui était fort tranquille, et l'exorciste ayant commandé au démon de me quitter, le visage de la Mère changea aussitôt me voyant soulagé, je me relevai pour aller poursuivre mon ennemi qui occupait la Mère et l'ayant chassé pour quelque temps, nous demeurâmes paisibles tous les deux.[20]

In this new intimate site of transference the devils are re-routed through the bodies that in this dialogue are positioned for the first time, and not without considerable resistance, in an opposition that subjects each of the participants to a role that structurally can no longer be avoided. In the "parloir" of this new exorcism, the seductive transference becomes a confrontation of the "two": sister/brother, Mother/Father, man/woman. If hysteria is the inability of the subject to situate him/herself "correctly" in a positional schema of (hetero) sexuality, the first major step in overcoming that inability is to impose the possibility of this positioning even as this positioning is both confused and then sorted out. The two articulated bodies are re-inscribed in this locus that mirrors, produces a strange, familial scenario. At the same time it is important to notice the congruence of this creation of a "familial" positioning with what has become the first "private space" of the Loudon scandal. It is with this co-terminous creation of both a separate private space and a dyadic positioning that traces the ghostly confines of a family romance that the "hysterical," that is "floating," desire can be bound in a new scenario of political and sexual signification.

This scenario, a sexual exchange and positioning, works out of the possession/hysteria and into the acceptance of "difference" as the Law of the Father. This privatization of the body is reinforced by the continual reliance on the ceremony of "frequent communion," the acceptance and "incorporation" of the host. Frequent communion, that is, the internalization of the body of the Father, the imposition of the Father as Law and as Love (object of desire), becomes slowly but surely the way out.

This incorporation of the paternal body is the most highly invested of all catholic rituals and the one that had met with the greatest resistance on the part of the devils.[21] When the Holy Sacrament is presented to the nuns their possession reaches paroxysmic proportions:

> Après quoi l'exorciste [le père Lactance] a contraint le diable [Jeanne des Anges] d'adorer le saint Sacrement et l'a fait mettre en toutes les postures qu'il a voulues, en telle sorte que tous les assistants en ont été comme ravis d'admiration, et même en ce que, par sa parole, il a fait mettre ce corps le ventre contre terre, la tête relevée en haut, les bras et les pieds tournés en arrière, joints et enlacés ensemble, et les a fait pareillement déprendre et remettre. (de Certeau, *La Possession*, p. 156)

Although, at first, Father Surin meets with no less resistance, nevertheless something gradually changes. After much struggle, the devils who remain rebellious to the "body" of God are vanquished and one by one leave the body of Sister Jeanne. Their leaving the body is memorialized in a strangely ostentatious fashion: they inscribe on her hand the names of Jesus, Mary, Joseph and François de Sales: signs of the presence of God, but also reminders of that same presence having been the locus of the Devil ("Figures portent absence et presence ..." as we have been taught):

> Il se passa plusieurs choses qui sont marquées dans les procès-verbaux, mais la principale, fut la sortie l'Isacaaron qui se fit en cette sorte: le père Surin entendant les horribles blasphèmes que ce maudit démon vomissait contre Notre-Seigneur et la Sainte-Vierge, et qui faisait trembler tous les assistants, il lui commanda d'adorer le très Saint-Sacrement et de faire amende honorable à la Sainte-Vierge. Il est quasi impossible d'exprimer les violentes résistances que cet esprit superbe fit à ce commandement; je dirai seulement qu'il fut contraint d'y obéir.
>
> Il demanda pardon à la Sainte-Vierge et déclara que sa puissance le contraignait de sortir tout maintenant à ses pieds et de quitter mon corps. En disant cela, il imprima en même temps le nom de Marie sur la main au-dessus de celui de Joseph ... Il se trouva plus de cent personnes à cette sortie. (*Auto*, p. 181)

The sign of Jeanne's "cure," the exit of her devils, reveals itself to be the body's own submission to the Name, to language. As the body leaves the space of hysteria, as it works out of hysteria as the indifference of a language without subjectivity, it signals itself as inscribed, subjected to the linguistic corpus. Why are the inscriptions on her hand so important – not only as the fetishistic object of devotion and exhibition (she will parade her arm throughout France where it will be seen by thousands of curious spectators) but as the "sign" of her re-inscription in the signifying order of seventeenth-century political existence? First, these stigmata signify the disappearance of the body, its repression as a recalcitrant, maverick, threatening other. Then, not only do the Holy names appear as a miracle, a sign that this body/soul has been saved by and for God, they also appear in a proper familial/hierarchical disposition:

Le jour de sainte Thérèse, ... le père Surin, quoique très languissant, ayant dit la messe, il apporta le Saint-Sacrement à la petite fenêtre de la grille pour me communier. Comme il disait ces paroles "Corpus Domini Nostri Jesu Christi" je fus tourmentée extraordinairement. J'eus une furieuse contorsion qui me plia en arrière; mon visage devint effroyable. Dans ce moment, le Père vit très manifestement se former sur ma main le nom de Jésus, au-dessus des noms de Marie et de Joseph, en beaux caractères vermeils et sanglants. Le nom de François de Sales fut ensuite formé sans que le Père s'en aperçut; quelques religieuses qui en étaient proches virent se former celui de François de Sales. Il est à remarquer que le nom de Joseph ayant été écrit le premier par Balaam sur le haut de ma main, il descendit peu à peu pour faire place à celui de Marie qui fut formé par Isacaaron, et ces deux noms descendirent encore pour faire place au nom de Jésus qui fut marqué par Béhémoth.

Ce démon étant sorti, je reçus le corps de Notre-Seigneur et, depuis ce temps là, j'ai toujours été quitte des opérations des démons.

(*Auto*, p. 204–205)

Jeanne's body signs its own subjection not only to the celestial hierarchy but, of course, to this hierarchy as family, and to her own reinsertion, reinscription into order. In this way her body ceases to speak its de-subjugating language, but is inscribed in a discursive system that effectively effaces its presence. Only her hand remains, a hand that is offered to veneration as the sign of her being in a privileged relation to God, His presence in the world:

L'on me mit dans une salle basse où il y avait une fenêtre à hauteur d'homme qui répondrait à une cour de la maison. J'étais assise, le bras sur un oreiller, et ma main était étendue hors de la fenêtre, pour être vue du peuple. Les personnes de la première qualité ne purent entrer dans cette salle parce que le peuple en occupait les avenues. On ne me donnait pas le loisir d'entendre la messe ni de prendre mes repas. (*Auto*, p. 218)

Her body has ceased to be visible; only this hand remains, an external symbol of an internal state of grace. This state of grace has been achieved by a strategic reversal whereby the figure of a "loving" God has replaced the figure of the Devil. This reversal into opposites becomes perfectly understandable if we transcode it into the dichotomies Freud theorized when he spoke of the inherent ambivalence of the image of the Father: "It requires no great analytic insight to divine that God and the Devil were originally one and the same, a single figure which was later split into two bearing opposite characteristics."[22] Once again, what we seem to be confronted with is the resolution of an untenable ambivalence by the movement towards one of the poles (the socially encoded "correct" pole) that meshes with the entire paradigmatic chain of signifiers inscribing Jeanne in the space of the feminine as that "feminine" is declined as love, as submission, as passivity. At the same time this movement out of ambivalence, this restructuring of the subject in a signifying chain that is there to situate it, produces another significant reversal: what has been experienced as the suffering of the body, that is, the visible, exterior signs of the body possessed, is, by the expulsion of the figures of that suffering (the devils as physical, or as allegories of pain), now internalized as a new scenario of passion. From a body racked by devils, devils who disperse, fragment and de-subject her in the sight of the world, from a body unable to separate from "the Mother," Jeanne now becomes on the inner stage of her mystical voyage towards union with God the subject/object of divine love. This love of/for the Father subjects her to a passion that centers her sense of herself upon the image of her own exquisite surrender to the passion of Christ. This passion is now marked not on the outside but on her heart:

Environ les trois heures du matin, il [her angel] se présenta à moi et me dit: "C'est à présent que le ciel et la terre sont dans l'étonnement de voir un Dieu qui souffre et pâtit pour ses créatures; ... voyez si vous voulez être du nombre de ceux qui l'abandonnent, ou bien si vous voulez l'accompagner." Je lui ai répondu: je veux suivre mon Sauveur, je lui en demande la grâce. Il m'a répondu: "Votre Souverain a accepté vos désirs, vous ressentirez au dedans de vous une partie des douleurs qu'il a portées dans sa Passion, et, pour comble de ses miséricordes, il imprimera sa croix sur votre cœur; tenez cette faveur fort secrète." (lettre, 20 avril 1645, quoted in *Auto*, p. 272)

One could easily go on to speak of Jeanne's great talent for mimeticism rather than mysticism, her obvious imitation of Teresa of Avila's description of her own relation with her angel. Jeanne's heavenly visitor appears to her in the guise of a beautiful young man, about eighteen (sometimes fifteen, p. 269) years old, with blond hair and radiant eyes, holding in his hand a "long, thick and shining candle." ("Cet ange avait un vêtement blanc comme neige, tenant en main un cierge blanc, fort grant et fort gros et fort allumé," *Auto*, p. 196). This would, however, miss the point, because what is important is not how obviously Jeanne des Anges is involved in a repetition of a cultural model, but how her version of that model re-inscribes that representation as one more twist of a subjugation and subjectivization that is inseparable from the masochistic pleasure that subjugation represents.

Sœur Jeanne takes on to herself the "passion" of Christ, a passion in the true sense of the word, both a suffering and a pleasure, and in this new internalized ambivalence, a pleasure/pain, she is both subjugated to the Law of the Father, and in this subjugation becomes a subject: it is this routing through masochism that enables her to articulate the "I" of authoritative and authorial self-representation.

Sœur Jeanne has a passion for passion. Her descriptions of the imprinting on her heart of the different symbols of Christ's crucifixion (cross, nails, sponge, hammer, lance etc.) is accompanied by her constant self-description as a victim/object of divine love:

Il me semble, par les choses qui m'arrivent au renouvellement des marques que je porte sur la main, que c'est un effet de ce que m'a dit mon bon Ange, que Notre-Seigneur imprimerait sur mon cœur les armes de sa Passion, car je ressens, en cette partie là, de si grandes douleurs que je ne vous saurais exprimer. Plus elles sont vives et plus je les désire; et, quelques plaintes que la nature fasse, je ne me puis m'empêcher de conjurer Notre-Seigneur d'avancer son œuvre et de me rendre semblable à lui en douleurs ...

(lettre, 14 sept. 1645, in *Auto*, p. 282)

An acceptance of the Law of the Father, according to psychoanalytic theory, is always, symbolically, an acceptance of castration, but the question now arises: what does it mean for a woman to be "castrated"? How can castration be symbolically written on the body of a woman? For a woman to "accept castration" would mean to accept an "après coup" of an always-already-there of maternal deception, of the (fantasized) abandonment, separation of/from the mother. At the same time (in a masculine economy), this "acknowledgement" of an inherent lack, of a "degradation," could only be converted into a (female) subject by the concomitant internalization of this lack as an original fault, as a "sin." A woman then could only love in this economy at the site where that sin is both constantly reiterated and effaced, in the masochistic passion of sacrifice and redemption.[23]

Yet, by accepting "masochistic" pleasure as a site/sign of her being "chosen," Sœur Jeanne inscribes her passion within a system that marks her self as an ambivalent, still incomplete, subjugation, subjected to a male model – even as this model is made to seem abject, made to seem in some way, by its spectacular difference, feminized-maternal, a source of unlimited love (Christ on the Cross).

In his *The Tremulous Private Body*, Francis Barker, trying to define the radical transformation in subjectivity that occurs during the seventeenth century, argues that:

The political upheaval of the mid-century established a new set of connections between subject and discourse, subject and polity and in so doing altered fundamentally the terms between which these mutually constitutive relations held. In the space of a relatively few years a new set of relations between state and citizen, body and soul, language and meaning was fashioned.[24]

I would argue that this restructuring of language, of signification of the space and site of the body, and of its pleasure is inherently masochistic ("Au dedans de moi-même, je sentais, une si grand joie de ce qu'il me semblait qu'il opérait en moi ses opérations douleureuses par un effet de son amour", (*Auto*, p. 287). In the curious case of Jeanne des Anges's possession and deliverance, her body traverses the epistemic changes that were occurring first as the site of a "sympathetic" fragmentation, then in the body's own effacement in transparent representation – the body as the sign of God. In the strange way her body functions first as a troubling presence – the body *en soi* – to become an absence, its disappearance, incorporation as masochistic mysticism. This move from presence to absence, from hysteria to mysticism, traces a move from exteriority, from public spectacle to private "inner-scene," and in this tracing engages, I would argue, the production of modern subjectivity.

What is finally interesting in the case of Jeanne des Anges is her "liberation" from the devils and her "subjugation" to God. There is in this liberation and inscription a strange change and an even stranger repetition: it is as if the expulsion of the devil had to be marked by a bodily reminder – the stigmata that remain with her, that are constantly "renewed" by her angel, a reminder that constantly recalls the recalcitrance of the body; its mark as what exceeds order even as it represents order; the visible sign of the excess that can always well forth. Nevertheless this very presence on the body

betrays the change that has taken place, betrays the submission of
the body to its other, to its status of no longer representing its own
"naturalness" – that is, a language of the body, but now the body
inscribed in order, in a hierarchy of meaning that is always the
meaning of loss, of castration, and of castration's representation in
the semiosis of subjectivity, in the "I" formed in the sliding chain
of signification that defines its subjugation/subjectivization even
as it undermines it.

On another level, what we also see, if we wish to consider it in
those terms, in the "history" of Jeanne des Anges is the gradual
but inexorable "sea change" of epistemic systems. Moving across the
body of this woman from the order of analogy, from the body as
surface of disarticulated meaning, to the wrenching control brought
about by the internalization of the physical, its expulsion in/as
referentiality, we perceive the triumph of the sign (the "stigmata"),
the triumph of the "name." I would argue that this triumph of the
"signifier" is the triumph of the "Family" (Father, Mother, Child)
as the Oedipal schema. Is it only a coincidence that in her last visions,
Jeanne des Anges sees and speaks with "la Mère de l'*Incarnation*,"
that once she is firmly situated in the difference of the Father, the
Mother can return "incarnate"? The body is no longer free-floating,
but is now anchored, controlled, hierarchized in a subjugation to
an order that is (becoming) at once social, political and sexual: the
body there but no longer showing itself, no longer there but become
in its interiorization, in the guilty masochism of its own internal
policing, in its pleasure and guilt, the transparent signifier of the
Law, the absent locus of love. It is in this new space of the representation that the modern, post-Renaissance subject is born, born in the
constant desire for its own further/final effacement, an effacement
in which it will become one with the Law that circumscribes it, that
subjugates it – and in thus doing, gives it an ultimate, transcendent
grounding.

By a curious twist of fate, a final imbrication of Jeanne des Anges
with the history of Classicism situates her, her "passion," at the
intersection of the old order of the Baroque and the "birth" of the
new order of Absolutism. In one of her more extravagant, final
visions, Jeanne, ill, is visited by St. Joseph:

Je vis aussi saint Joseph en forme et figure d'homme, ayant le visage plus
resplendissant que le soleil, avec une grande chevelure. Sa barbe était à poil
de châtain; il me parut avec une majesté bien plus qu'humaine, lequel

appliqua sa main sur mon côté droit où avait toujours été ma grande douleur. Il me semble qu'il me fit une onction sur cette partie, après quoi je sentis revenir mes sens extérieurs et me trouvai entièrement guérie.

(Auto, p. 196–197)

The five drops ("assez grosses") of St. Joseph's divine balm are discovered on her inner garment, which is immediately cut up into a swatch that becomes the most precious of holy relics in her community's possession. Besides smelling "parfaitement bon" *(Auto,* p. 223) – as Richelieu, to whom she shows the cloth, says – St. Joseph's balm is particularly soothing for women in labor. When Jeanne who, faithful to her vow to travel to the tomb of François de Sales in Savoy for her final exorcism, stops at the palace of St. Germain-en-Laye to visit with Louis XIII and Anne of Austria, the pregnant queen, fearing the pains of childbirth, asks her for a piece of the miraculous relic:

La Reine désira encore que je coupasse un morceau de la chemise, où l'onction était, pour obtenir de Dieu, par les prières de saint Joseph, un heureux accouchement. *(Auto,* p. 235)

Jeanne refuses to divide the cloth, but does consent to lend it to the queen at the moment of labor. After her triumphal voyage across France to Annecy and the final, successful exorcism at François's tomb, Mother Jeanne returns to Paris just in time for the queen's lying-in. And it is with the help of Jeanne's holy relic lying across her belly that Anne of Austria brings forth into the world the dauphin France had so long awaited. In an odd twist of fate, Louis XIV makes his entrance on to the stage of world history by and through the legacy of Jeanne des Anges and her troubled, passionate possession.

4

RODOGUNE: SONS AND LOVERS

Nous n'avons point de cœur pour aimer ni haïr
Toutes nos passions ne savent qu'obéir.
(III, iii, 869–870)

Traditionally *Rodogune* has been seen to mark a turning point in the Cornelian canon.[1] It incorporates the lessons of the past while already indicating a new path to follow. This new direction turns out to be a detour, a sexual deviation. From here on the women become the standard bearers of the "will to power," of the renunciation and singleness of purpose that, up until *Rodogune*, had been the lot of Corneille's heroes. The men are mired in metaphysical dilemmas which gradually reduce them to positions of indecision, passivity and ultimately impotence.[2]

Rodogune stands at the crossroads of two worlds, and at this nexus of ambivalence men are unsexed and women are virilized. The essential traits defining sexual difference, the separation of the Cornelian world into the well-ordered camps of masculinity and femininity, are blurred. It is from the blurring of these "natural" positions, from their perversion, that the monstrous – of which *Rodogune* is perhaps the best example – is born and triumphs.

Curiously, this monstrous play is, Corneille tells us, his favorite:

On m'a souvent fait une question à la cour: quel était celui de mes poèmes que j'estimais le plus; et j'ai trouvé tous ceux qui me l'ont faite si prévenus en faveur de *Cinna* ou du *Cid*, que je n'ai jamais osé déclarer toute la tendresse que j'ai toujours eue pour celui-ci, à qui j'aurais volontiers donné mon suffrage, si je n'avais craint de manquer, en quelque sorte, au respect que je devais à ceux que je voyais pencher d'un autre côté.

(*Examen*, p. 350)

The reasons for his preference, Corneille says, are double. On the one hand, from the point of view of a professional playwright he is most satisfied with his play's construction. There is a certain perfection of technique, coupled with a perfection of subject matter, which makes this perhaps the most beautiful of all his plays:

certainement on peut dire que mes autres pièces ont peu d'advantages qui ne se rencontrent en celle-ci: elle a tout ensemble la beauté du sujet, la nouveauté des fictions, la force des vers, la facilité de l'expression, la solidité du raisonnement, la chaleur des passions, les tendresses de l'amour et de l'amitié. (*Ibid.*, p. 353)

Furthermore, *Rodogune* not only incorporates all the diverse charms of the plays that preceded it, it presents these charms in a form whose harmony is consistently respectful of Classical precepts:

cet heureux assemblage est ménagé de sorte qu'elle s'élève d'acte en acte. Le second passe le premier, le troisième est au-dessus du second, et le dernier l'emporte sur tous les autres. L'action y est une, grande, complète; sa durée ne va point, ou fort peu, au delà de celle de la représentation. Le jour en est le plus illustre qu'on puisse imaginer, et l'unité de lieu s'y rencontre en la manière que je l'explique dans le troisième de mes discours, et avec l'indulgence que j'ai demandée pour le théâtre. (*Ibid.*, p. 353)

What we have, then, in *Rodogune* is a work of art that in its perfection presents itself to us as what Nietzsche would later describe as one of the highest examples of "Apollonian" culture.[3] Nietzsche reminds us, however, that this form of art which he calls "naive" (i.e. a perfect harmony between man and the world) is an illusion which is only achieved at the expense of some great, hideous crime. Apollonian art

always must first overthrow an empire of Titans and slay monsters, must have triumphed over an abysmal and terrifying view of the world and the keenest susceptibility to suffering through recourse to the most forceful and pleasurable illusions.[4]

One of the first things we will have to consider in our reading of *Rodogune* is the illusion of its perfection, an illusion built precisely upon a subject (perversion) that would seem to be beauty's contradiction. How, in other words, do the beautiful and the monstrous coexist in the tragedy? How do form and content collaborate and what does this collaboration mean for the (mutually exclusive) definitions of these two terms? A second question, more difficult to answer, would involve the impossibility, given the collaboration of the antithesis beautiful/monstrous, of either of those two concepts existing independently of the other. How would either of the two terms, and the chain of antithetical oppositions that they spawn, be grounded in any metaphysical essence that could exist outside of their representation as spectacle? Is there any way for us to extricate ourselves from a beauty/horror that we are told is monstrous? Is it possible to situate ourselves in a world where the beautiful is not already contaminated by, is not already part of, the terror?

Perhaps we might begin to answer these questions by returning to Corneille's second reason for preferring *Rodogune* to his other works. Unlike his first explanation, this reason is emotional: it is undefinable, a certain "je ne sais quoi" attaches the poet viscerally to his poem:

Cette préférence est peut-être en moi un effet de ces inclinations aveugles, qu'ont beaucoup de pères pour quelques-uns de leurs enfants plus que pour les autres; peut-être y entre-t-il un peu d'amour propre, en ce que cette tragédie me semble être un peu plus à moi que celles qui l'ont précédée, à cause des incidents surprenants qui sont purement de mon invention, et n'avaient jamais été vus au théâtre; et peut-être enfin y a-t-il un peu de vrai mérite qui fait que cette inclination n'est pas tout à fait injuste.

(*Ibid.*, p. 353)

Corneille's explanation for his inexplicable predilection is couched in curious (if traditional) metaphors of paternity and engendering. Certainly, the use of these metaphors to describe a tragedy whose force comes from the perversion of maternity cannot be entirely jejeune. Rather, it must be directly connected with the central dilemma of the play the metaphors attempt to represent, and must bring us, through its metaphorical detours, into the very heart of the tragic.

Although Corneille claims to prefer *Rodogune* principally because it is his "unique" creation, he begins both his *Avertissement* (1647) and his *Examen* (1660) by quoting another author (Appianus Alexandrinus) and another work (*Les Guerres de Syrie*) as the origin of his play. From the beginning, as is his custom, Corneille refers to history as the inspiration for tragedy. The two genres would exist in a symbiotic relation where the one (history) narrates the events that the other (tragedy) re-presents. However, after the long quotation from Appianus Alexandrinus Corneille tells us that, in effect, his tragedy is not really a recasting of this history. For various reasons, Corneille has taken the liberty of accommodating historical facts to the specific dictates of the theater. He changes the characters, the chronology, and more important still, the particular events of the historical narration:

Voilà ce que m'a prêté l'histoire où j'ai changé les circonstances de quelques incidents pour leur donner plus de bienséance.   (*Avertissement*, p. 350)

J'ai cru que, pourvu que nous conservassions les effets de l'histoire, toutes les circonstances ... étaient en notre pouvoir. (p. 351)

J'ai déguisé quelque chose de la vérité historique. (pp. 354–355)

Je l'ai même adouci [l'effet dénaturé] tant que j'ai pu en Antiochus que j'avais fait trop honnête homme dans le reste de l'ouvrage, pour forcer à la fin sa mère à s'empoisonner elle-même. (pp. 350)

These "events" that Corneille takes the dramatic license to change seem, the more he talks about them, to be unreliable. History is denied veracity. It is divested of its status as origin. The more Corneille quotes other sources (the first book of Maccabees, Justinius, chaps. 36, 38 and 39, and Josephus' *Antiquités judaïques*), the more it becomes evident that *Rodogune*, as tragedy, does not have an origin in history because no historical version can be found that is not immediately contradicted, changed, augmented or diminished by another.

What started as a grounding for the independence of rhetorical genres quickly turns in the *Avertissement* and *Examen* into the blurring of these genres. The very question what is history and what is tragedy, what past action and what present fiction, becomes corrupted as history and tragedy mutually contaminate each other to become no longer independent entities but hybrids – one could almost say "perversions," monstrous reflections of each other:

Je dirai plus: quand cette proposition serait tout à fait condamnable en sa bouche [cf. Rodogune's ultimatum to the princes] elle mériterait grâce et pour l'éclat que la nouveauté de l'invention a fait au théâtre et pour l'embarras surprenant où elle jette les princes et pour l'effet qu'elle produit dans le reste de la pièce qu'elle conduit à l'action historique.

(*Ibid.*, p. 355)

The *Avertissement* and *Examen* negate the founding of the play in a particular text that the spectacle would reproduce in the present. Perversely any notion of grounding/origin, any stable matrix, is undermined and Corneille alone remains as the progenitor of this scandalous offspring.

By describing himself as the "father" of his poem, however, Corneille remains in another, equally equivocal metaphorical situation. The metaphor claims for himself, as gender, a specificity that was denied to genre. Corneille claims *Rodogune* as his own, the product of his "invention." However, by metaphorizing this birth as a masculine prerogative, Corneille alludes to and elides what he cannot perhaps admit to himself and less to his public: by giving birth Corneille has become "monstrous," he has unsexed himself. He is as much mother as father. By both affirming and denying his own participation in a (metaphorical) act that is the domain of the female, Corneille blurs those lines of sexual difference that are at stake in the tragedy he has produced. What, however, seems unavoidable for Corneille, as it is for us, what the prefaces set in motion even as they attempt to contain it, is a certain atmosphere where monstrosity (the hybridization of genres and genders) is not the exception but the rule, where it is, almost, "natural."

At first glance nothing could be more perfect in its symmetry than the tragic confrontation in *Rodogune*. On whatever level we choose to dissect the play we always return to a dyadic opposition that divides, along political and sexual lines, innocence and evil, male and female, nature and love. On the most obvious level of sexual difference, Séleucus and Antiochus confront Rodogune and Cléopâtre as they all play out this "partie carrée de l'assassinat."[5] Not only is the sexual symmetry perfect in its simplicity, but the imbrication of the sexual and political reflects this perfection in the chiasmatic dilemma faced by all the participants of the tragedy: to Cléopâtre's ultimatum that the crown be given to that son who will eliminate Rodogune responds, in perfect doubling, Rodogune's imperious bargain to offer herself to that brother who will do away with the Queen. The two brothers are trapped within a classic and Classical double-bind. In either case they are imprisoned in a structure which is closed in upon itself and which, because of this closure, reduces them to total passivity.

For the first time in Cornelian theater men are completely enveloped in a universe that (despite its historical framework) offers them no real hope of escape. No heroic action is possible. The passions that structure their world seem to exclude them: they have come back to their mother who represents a world cut off from any structuring male order. It has been turned topsy-turvy in the chaos of female usurpation. Masculine genealogy has been subverted, not only because the King has been eliminated, but even more so because the birth of twins — a monstrous female production — throws it into disarray. The perfect symmetry of the play proves to be structured from the outset by an absence (of the Father) and a perversion. This perversion of the "natural" political and sexual order can only produce monsters that are all the more terrifying because so uncannily familiar and yet so different. All the normal divisions that have so comfortingly prevailed in the universe of Cornelian tragedy are retained, and yet by their simple reversal they plunge us immediately into a world of transsexual deformations where mothers and mistresses are devouring gorgons and where young men are reduced to whimpering castrati. It is this simple exchange of sexual essences that leads us into the very crux of the tragic, where the horrifying alternative of matricide or infanticide is made to appear as the only natural choice available to characters forced to live the untenable.

When the play opens this discord is not evident. On the contrary, the first words we hear announce an end to strife and contention. The crises that had rocked Syria are resolved. The dark night of war is over and a new day of harmony and peace is dawning:

> Enfin, ce jour pompeux, cet heureux jour nous luit,
> Qui d'un trouble si long doit dissiper la nuit.
> Ce grand jour où l'hymen, étouffant la vengeance,
> Entre le Parthe et nous remet l'intelligence,
> Affranchit sa princesse, et nous fait pour jamais
> Du motif de la guerre un lien de la paix.
>
> (I, i, 1–6)

The tragedy starts as an epithalamium. The first words are a paean of hope. However, despite the promising tone of Laonice's initial speech it immediately becomes apparent to us, familiar as we are with the dissonant echoes the word "hymen" carries in all of Corneille's plays, that marriage is a highly ambivalent, most often dangerous, act.[6] The marriage that is about to be celebrated does, on the one hand, represent reunion and harmony, but on the other, it is also the harbinger of revolution and disruption. In this most manichean of dramas the marriage that serves as the motivating nexus of dramatic action drags into its center not only forces of gratification and hope, but also, and more important, negative impulses of frustration and aggressivity.

This wedding that is meant to confirm a treaty of peace between two warring states does so by introducing a profound restructuring of political power. Before the play begins, Rodogune, captive, is little more than a slave. The marriage will elevate her to the rank of sovereign:

> Rodogune, par elle en esclave traitée,
> Par elle se va voir sur le trône montée.
>
> (I, i, 19–20)

By the same token, Cléopâtre relinquishes her supreme authority and becomes Rodogune's subject.

More important than this reversal in the roles of the two female protagonists, more radical, will be the effect of this marriage on the two princes. Up until this day their twinship, the present cause of anxiety and tension, has been lived by them in perfect symbiosis. The two men, mirror images of each other, have been reared with a complete unity of spirit and affection that has proven impervious to discord or doubt. Raised far from the troubled court of Syria, in Egypt, the princes have been brought up in harmony.[7] Now, however, this entente is threatened by a nascent sexual jealousy and the threat of a more radical separation. The brother who is declared the elder wins both the crown and the princess: on him will devolve both sexual and political authority. The other will be left bereft:

> Ce grand jour est venu, mon frère, où notre reine,
> Cessant de plus tenir la couronne incertaine,
> Doit rompre aux yeux de tous son silence obstiné,
> De deux princes gémeaux nous déclarer l'aîné:
> Et l'avantage seul d'un moment de naissance
> Dont elle a jusqu'ici caché la connaissance,
> Mettant au plus heureux le sceptre dans la main,
> Va faire l'un sujet, et l'autre souverain.
>
> (I, i, 7–14)

The situation of the two brothers presents them as helpless victims of a sexual/political imbroglio in which their fate, a new birth in "difference," is entirely in the hands of women. In the female world to which they have been summoned, a world where the father has vanished, the only masculine presence available to them is their own reciprocal reflection. Deprived of a paternal image, they can only gaze at each other for that reassuring reflection of an "integrity" that is threatened by both their mother and their mistress.

In the world of the Syrian court, a world dominated by a menacing, essentially foreign mother and an equally unknown lover, they must maintain their union as the only defense possible against a complete alienation in the order of metonymical (matrilineal) descent that has been substituted for the legal order of Patriarchy. Cléopâtre (to whom we shall return in a moment) has substituted herself as the sole point of reference for any devolution of power. In this way, contrary to all the rules that have pertained in the Cornelian universe, metonymical displacement, the sign of the female, attempts to eradicate the "metaphoric" displacement of paternity as the legal grounds for political power in the world of the play. This unnatural act – both a regicide and a patricide – threatens the integrity of the princes. If they accept the Mother's law, that is, if they follow her dictates, "imitate," her:

> Mais si vous me devez et le sceptre et le jour,
> Ce doit être envers moi le sceau de votre amour.
> Sans ce gage ma haine à jamais s'en défie:
> Ce n'est qu'en m'imitant que l'on me justifie
>
> (II, iii, 665–668)

they are condemned to their disappearance as men. By being like the mother, rather than their (unknown) father, they are emasculated, becoming mere eunuchs to Cléopâtre.

Furthermore, the marriage that they are presented with also threatens to separate them from each other. This separation of one twin from the other sunders them, and introduces into identity a difference that can only be experienced by them as an alienation of their own being, as death.[8] When the princes turn in horror from their mother to their mistress they are once again presented with a threat to their integrity that is too great for them to sustain. Despite the love of both princes for her, Rodogune also condemns them to dispersion.

Rodogune's ultimatum is so shocking (perhaps the most shocking proposal in all of Corneille's theater) because it presents the ambivalence of the infant's relation to its all-powerful mother, its desire to destroy this mother, as a real political possibility. Corneille himself is so struck by the scandal of Rodogune's bargain that he feels himself obliged to make excuses for it:

Elle avoue elle-même à Antiochus qu'elle les haïrait, s'ils lui avaient obéi; que, comme elle a fait ce qu'elle a dû par cette demande, ils font ce qu'ils doivent par leur refus; qu'elle aime trop la vertu pour vouloir être le prix d'un crime et que la justice qu'elle demande de la mort de leur père serait un parricide, si elle la recevait de leurs mains.   (*Examen*, p. 355)

So monstrous does this crime appear to Corneille that he cannot even use the proper word that describes it: "matricide" is never used by him, only the more generic "parricide." The ultimatum is so scandalous that it must be denied, covered up, transformed. Curiously, almost all modern commentators on the play reiterate Corneille's apology.[9] No one wants to think that Rodogune really means what she says. The princes, however, do believe her, and despite Corneille's denegation, it is this ultimatum (as he is quick to admit one paragraph later on)[10] that motivates the dramatic action of the rest of the play.

When the two brothers, each burning with desire ("Jugez mieux du beau feu qui brûle l'un et l'autre") are confronted with Rodogune and her bargain, their ardor is quickly dampened:

Rodogune: *sons and lovers*

Quoi, cette ardeur s'éteint! l'un et l'autre soupire!

(III, iv, 1039)

Face to face with the flames of Rodogune's taboo passion, her blood lust ("J'écoute une chaleur qui m'était défendue ..."), the brothers retreat. It seems, nevertheless, that the negation of this desire represents a more complicated, if not more highly invested, involvement of the brothers in the matricide they flee.

Both women propose the other's murder as an act of (justifiable) revenge. Each claims to be acting in the name of the (dead) Father:

CLEOPATRE   Le sort de votre Père enfin est éclairci:
Il était innocent, et je puis l'être aussi.
Il vous aimait toujours et ne fut mauvais père
Que charmé par la sœur ou forcé par le frère;
Et dans cette embuscade ou son effort fut vain,
Rodogune, mes fils, le tua par ma main.
Ainsi de cet amour la fatale puissance
Vous coûte votre père, à moi mon innocence;
Et si ma main pour vous n'avait tout atténté,
L'effet de cet amour vous aurait tout coûté.
Ainsi vous me rendrez l'innocence et l'estime,
Lorsque vous punirez la cause de mon crime.

(II, iii, 625–636)

RODOGUNE   J'écoute une chaleur qui m'était défendue;
Qu'un devoir rappelé me rend un souvenir
Que la foi des traités ne doit plus retenir.
Tremblez, princes, tremblez au nom de votre père:
Il est mort, et pour moi, par les mains d'une mère.
Je l'avais oublié, sujette à d'autres lois;
Mais libre, je lui rends enfin ce que je dois.

(III, iv, 1016–1022)

It is no secret that the princes are caught at the interstice of a jealous crossfire. What is really at stake in this war of Amazons is not so much the present, the crown and the right to rule, as the past. Each woman must justify her position in relation to the (dead) king. What this means for the princes is, of course, that regardless of the woman they chose to defend, they are always in the position of having to situate themselves not as men, but as children in the Oedipal constellation they inscribe in relation to their dead Father. In this Oedipal constellation the brothers are always destined to a position of inferiority; they are always an inadequate replacement for a fantasmatic object.

The princes, however, deprived of any "male" model, deprived

95

(that is) of their entry into the world of the Law, cannot imitate their father; nor can they, without condemning themselves to total destruction, imitate their mother. They are left precisely at the crossroads of Mother and Father, a product of both, neither of which can be abandoned without risking their own annihilation.

Rodogune's ultimatum is finally more monstrous than Cléopâtre's because in her drive to recapture the object of her desire/lust she must plunge both princes into a murder that would be both a matricide and a suicide. In order for the princes to be desirable to her, Rodogune wants them to pass through the annihilation of the mother/rival and to assume the place of the Father, which is forever denied them.

In either case, when confronted by the desire of the mother or of the mistress, both princes recoil in horror. They turn away from the women and back to themselves. This is the only way they can maintain, in their mutual reflection, a mimetic position that allows them an integrity and defends them against the disintegration that would be their lot in the domain of female revenge.

In order not to be separated, in order not to fall victim to an emasculation that would spell their end, the two brothers constantly seek to reaffirm their own specular relation. Rather than just comfort each other with empty words, the brothers decide to solemnly ask the gods to protect an affection which is as exclusive as it is reciprocal:

ANTIOCHUS J'embrasse comme vous ces nobles sentiments
    Mais allons leur donner le recours des serments,
    Afin qu'étant témoins de l'amitié jurée
    Les dieux contre un tel coup assurent sa durée.
SELEUCUS Allons, allons l'étreindre au pied de leurs autels
    Par des liens sacrés, des nœuds immortels.
(I, iii, 205–210)

Listening to the brothers' heated affirmation of love and devotion, we have the strange impression of being present at the exchange of vows that takes place during a marriage. The words they use ("sworn affection", "sacred and immortal bonds") echo the exchange of promises at a wedding. There is even, "en sourdine," the introduction of the sexual embrace ("étreindre") that echoes, in the last lines, the "embrasser" of the first.

The only marriage that takes place in *Rodogune* is the brothers'. Left to their own devices, the brothers seek refuge against the ragings of female passion in the security of a homosexual union. This union is the only response left to them to defend themselves against being reduced to mere objects alienated from their own place in a (perverted) Paternal order. It is not the least of the tragedy's inversions that the only sexual relation free of perversion, the only nuptials that are innocent of scheming and blood, is the union of the two brothers. It is a union which protects them from the two women even as it prevails over Death:

> Allons, et soyez sûr que même le trépas
> Ne peut rompre des nœuds que l'amour ne rompt pas.
> (II, iv, 757–758)

Although the princes are identical they are not equal. Within the couple they form there is an essential metaphoric split that separates them from each other. It is the difference of this ill-defined scission that proves fatal to one and "beneficial" to the other. In this play the political machinations of the court, the intrigues that are constantly woven and unwoven, call for an almost sixth sense of intuitive awareness that allows survival within the context of these continuously changing dispositions. The metaphors that Corneille uses to indicate this intuition are particularly appropriate to the changing ambivalence. The predominance of visual images, those metaphors of blindness and insight, are particularly well suited to underline the constant oscillation of desire and politics in the internal dynamics of the tragedy.[11]

The world of the play is divided between those who have keen insight and those who don't. Laonice, for instance is presented as both kind-hearted and yet naively incapable of seeing what is really going on around her:

> Pour un esprit de cour, et nourri chez les grands,
> Tes yeux dans leurs secrets sont bien peu pénétrants.
> (II, ii, 441–442)

Of the two brothers, Séleucus is both more quick-tempered and endowed with keener vision than Antiochus. Paradoxically the insight places Séleucus along the same axis as his mother and makes him, in the couple he forms with Antiochus, more active, less given to indeterminacy, more "virile." In this play, "seeing" is a penetrating, interpretive gesture. It is a metaphor for phallic power, for political acumen, for masculinity.

Séleucus "sees" what both his mother and Rodogune attempt to hide from the brothers, the price he must pay for the throne and for a wife:

> Dans mon ambition, dans l'accident de ma flamme,
> Je vois ce qu'est un trône, et ce qu'est une femme.
> (III, v, 1083–1084)

He also sees through the hypocritical discourse of his mother and his mistress:

> Vous pardonnerez donc ces chaleurs indiscrètes.
> Je ne suis point jaloux du bien que vous lui faites;
> Et je vois quel amour vous avez pour tous deux
> Plus que vous ne pensez, et plus que je ne veux.
> (IV, vi, 1467–1470)

Séleucus' piercing vision allows him to look on female secrets, on the dark side of Cléopâtre and of Rodogune and to see their monstrous natures. Curiously, Séleucus' phallic gaze is returned by the lethal stare of both his mother and lover: when Séleucus spies on the secret side of his women they, Medusa-like, kill him. His gaze into femininity proves fatal.

Antiochus, on the other hand, refuses to look, and refuses to see. To Séleucus' unmediated vision he prefers to interpose a (metaphoric) veil. When he is called upon to look into the crimes of his parents, he chooses instead to look away:

> Sur les noires couleurs d'un si triste tableau
> Il faut passer l'éponge, ou tirer le rideau.
> Un fils est criminel quand il les examine,
> Et quelque suite enfin que le ciel y destine,
> J'en rejette l'idée et crois qu'en ces malheurs
> Le silence ou l'oubli nous sied mieux que les pleurs.
> (II, iii, 593–598)

Antiochus refuses to gaze on his parents' nakedness, refuses, that is, a confrontation with a taboo whose infraction would be coterminous with Death.

Antiochus prefers blindness to insight. In order not to see his mother's (and therefore his own) shame, he draws a veil of tears over his eyes:

> Pleurez donc à leurs yeux, gémissez, soupirez,
> Et je craindrai pour vous ce que vous espérez.
> (III, vi, 1101–1102)

Antiochus' refusal to look, his refusal to see the truth, his constant refuge in tears and sighs, places him squarely within the traditional camp of femininity in the Cornelian universe. On the other hand, Séleucus' clairvoyance places him on the side of the men. In this play, however, with its doublings and reversals of traditional roles, Séleucus' vision is even more dangerous, for here not only does he see his mother's nakedness, he shares it also. In *Rodogune* insight

is a possession of the women. It is part of their force and their major
arm of defense against each other. Cléopâtre, for instance, is constantly reminding us that the political choices she has made all her
life have been visually determined:

> Pour vous sauver l'Etat que n'eussé-je pu faire?
> Je choisis un époux avec des yeux de mère.
> (II, iii, 539–540)

> Je vis votre royaume entre ces murs réduit.
> (II, iii, 533)

She is constantly calling upon her entourage to use their eyes, to
"see" what she sees:

> Mes enfants, prenez place. Enfin voici le jour
> Si doux à mes souhaits, si cher à mon amour,
> Où je puis voir briller sur une de vos têtes
> Ce que j'ai conservé parmi tant de tempêtes.
> (III, i, 521–524)

And she is constantly seeing for the princes:

> Dites tout, mes enfants: vous fuyez la couronne,
> Non que son trop d'éclat ou son poids vous étonne:
> L'unique fondement de cette aversion,
> C'est la honte attachée à sa possession.
> Elle passe à vos yeux pour la même infamie ...
> (II, iii, 615–619)

Finally when she dies, it is again her eyes that reveal her treachery:

> Seigneur, voyez ses yeux
> Déjà tous égarés, troubles et furieux ...
> (V, iv, 1805–1806)

Rodogune, as befits a rival, is also marked by clairvoyance. She
sees, as in the situation in V, iv just quoted, better and faster than
Antiochus. She is constantly telling the princes to open their eyes
and see their mother's monstrous nature. Finally her own eyes lead
her back to the ritual scene of her (promised) husband's murder,
the scene that scatters her desire, fragments her being, and prepares
her impossible love for the sons:

> Rapportez à mes yeux son image sanglante,
> D'amour et de fureurs encore étincelante
> Telle que je le vis, quand tout percé de coups
> Il me cria "Vengeance! Adieu, je meurs pour vous."
> (III, iii, 859–862)

Clearly then, Antiochus' refusal to see, his facility to veil his eyes, places him, by his refusal to share in the visual gifts of the women, in a (perverted) order that refuses femininity in this drama. This strangely paradoxical affirmation of a masculinity is maintained by him until the very conclusion of the tragedy and accounts not a little for its very ambivalent, non-resolved ending. Séleucus, who has gazed on both his mother's shame and Rodogune's perversity, is killed as he flees back into the world of men (the blindness of his brother); he dies in the shadows:

> Je l'ai trouvé, seigneur, au bout de cette allée
> Où la clarté du ciel semble toujours voilée.
> (V, iv, 1611–1612)

Séleucus dies by his mother's hand, and this death is described metaphorically as his loss of sight:

> Avec assez de peine [he] entr'ouvre un œil mourant
> Et ce reste égaré de lumière incertaine,
> Lui peignant son cher frère au lieu de Timagène ...
> (V, iv, 1638–1640)

Antiochus, hearing of his brother's death, is plunged further into incertitude. Not knowing whom to suspect and whom to fear, he characteristically refuses to look at either his mother or his fiancée. He prefers to blindly continue the ceremony that has already started, convinced that it will lead him to his own death. It is in this abyss (which he refuses to contemplate) that he hopes to escape from the chaos of the women and return to union with his brother:

> Je ne veux point juger entre vous et ma mère.
> Assassinez un fils, massacrez un époux,
> Je ne veux me garder ni d'elle ni de vous.
> Suivons aveuglément ma triste destinée:
> Pour m'exposer à tout achevons l'hyménée.
> Cher frère, c'est pour moi le chemin du trépas:
> La main qui t'a percé ne m'épargnera pas;
> Je cherche à te rejoindre, et non à m'en défendre.
> (V, iv, 1768–1775)

It is only by plunging on blindly into this marriage that Antiochus can hope to escape from the impossible double-bind of the women. The closer he comes to choosing one over the other the more he is confronted with the displaced truth he cannot, should not, see: the truth of the woman, her power and her force is her "absence," her *béance*, the fact that she is an abyss into which Antiochus is drawn:

Rodogune: *sons and lovers*

Pour moi qui ne vois rien dans le trouble où je suis
Qu'un gouffre de malheurs, qu'un abîme d'ennuis ...
(V, iv, 1801–1802)

It is this fall into the abyss that both tantalizes and horrifies Antiochus with the image of his own dispossession.

The division in the play that opposes politics and sentiment along a separation of sex inscribes Rodogune and Cléopâtre, whatever their rivalry, along the same axis as reflections of each other. Ironically both must feign a submission to men in order to more strategically dominate. It is through a surreptitious submission to the males that both women, like queen bees surrounded by drones, wield the most power. Once Cléopâtre's first husband is done away with, she chooses as mate a brother-in-law who reigns but cannot rule:

> Il occupait leur trône, et craignait leur présence,
> Et cette juste crainte assurait ma puissance.
> Mes ordres en étaient de point en point suivis
> Quand je le menaçais du retour de mes fils:
> Voyant ce foudre prêt à suivre ma colère,
> Quoi qu'il me plût oser, il n'osait me déplaire;
> Et content malgré lui du vain titre de roi,
> S'il régnait au lieu d'eux, ce n'était que sous moi.
> (II, ii, 455–462)

Rodogune, too, although in a radically different political situation, is in an identical bind in relation to the men of her entourage. More powerful than they, she too must rely on them for a validation that is only a reflection of the desire she inspires in them. By their own admission their protection of her is a sham. They are in fact powerless, impotent:

> J'aurais perdu l'esprit si j'osais me vanter
> Qu'avec ce peu de gens nous puissions résister.
> Nous mourrons à vos pieds, c'est toute l'assistance
> Que vous peut en ces lieux offrir notre impuissance.
> (III, ii, 825–828)

Rodogune confronts us with the uncomfortable realization that finally men are expendable. Their only function in the play, the only act that they can perform, is to die. All the men in this tragedy are sacrificial victims on the altar of some destructive female deity. *Rodogune* is the mise-en-scène of all masculine fantasies of the devouring Mother who destroys her children. Both women are opposite but complementary images of the goddess to whom the

101

men either sacrifice themselves or are sacrificed. In front of these two furies the men in *Rodogune* are rendered powerless, impotent, and are finally eliminated. It is clear that in this play the women, be they mother or lover, are essentially one, and this "one" leads us to associate them to the horrifying fantasy of Death.

Although "biologically" identical, the two women are distinguished in their political positions, which pit them against each other. The "hive" of the Syrian court cannot tolerate two queens. There is no compromise possible for either. At the same time it is this strategic impasse that exacerbates a rivalry whose roots go much deeper than the present political situation and reach down into the fantasmatic territory of desire, where the central, absent image of the Patriarch, figures as the motivation of their passion and their rivalry. In *Rodogune* the political is always imbricated in the sexual and the sexual in the political.

Physically and metaphysically Rodogune is trapped in Syria. As a prisoner of war, she is the victim of a treaty that restores her to freedom and makes her a queen of a world that she has been raised to serve. She has no other alternative. Even when threatened with death, Rodogune has no choice but to remain where she is. For her the universe is reduced to the confines of Séleucie:

> C'est ici qu'il vous faut ou régner ou périr.
> Le ciel pour vous ailleurs n'a point fait de couronne;
> Et l'on s'en rend indigne alors qu'on l'abandonne.
>
> (III, ii, 818–820)

It is at this point, the traditional point of no return where the Cornelian hero defines himself, that the similarity between the two female protagonists ends and the difference in the way they achieve their political ends emerges. It is in their different manners of achieving their goals that the circle uniting sexuality and politics is made to close in on itself.

The essential split that separates Rodogune from Cléopâtre, that introduces into this division of the same a difference of quality, is metaphorized throughout the tragedy by the ambivalent criss-crossing of the terms "nature" and "love". This division follows a metaphysical distinction that would separate each woman as two distinct versions of femininity, either a maternal or a sexual object. Needless to say, here again the play presents this split as a question of one or the other; the possibility of the interrelation of these two poles, their mutual contamination, is precisely what this separation denies.[12] This division, the product of one of the most highly invested of

102

taboos – the taboo of mother–son incest – is as unreliable for the unconscious as it is radically important for the representational system whose function it is to reproduce a normalizing, and thus prescriptive, narrative of sexuality. It is precisely the impossibility of maintaining this separation (even in metaphor) that forms the central conundrum of desire and loathing that is at work in *Rodogune*. The play schematizes this impossible antithesis by its (rather traditional) division of the femininity into an older (jealous) Mother, the phallic monster ready to sacrifice and devour her offspring, and the less threatening young, virginal maiden-prisoner.

Cléopâtre's entrance on stage clearly and immediately associates her with Corneille's first example of the phallic mother – Medea. Although her entrance is preceded by a long narrative in which Laonice attempts to excuse her queen's past crimes, Cléopâtre's first lines, more by their incantatory quality than by what she actually says, establish her as new incarnation of the sorceress. Her first lines take her out of history and plunge her back into the darker mythic regions of fantasy and magic:

> Serments fallacieux, salutaire contrainte
> Que m'imposa la force et qu'accepta ma crainte,
> Heureux déguisement d'un immortel courroux,
> Vains fantômes d'Etat, évanouissez-vous!
> (II, i, 395–398)

In the time it takes to speak these first lines, Corneille succeeds in blending history and myth in the person of Cléopâtre. She appears as the re-embodiment of the demonic. With one dramatic gesture, Cléopâtre emerges as the horrifying project of an all-powerful malevolent "fury". This fantasmatic female, who has been successfully banished from Corneille's theater ever since Medea flew off in her dragon-drawn chariot, returns here once again in full force.[13]

This monster/mother is invested in all the contradictory echoes that resound in her inscription within the metaphor "nature." As a witch/sorceress, Cléopâtre is presented as a representative of matter, of the physical, those forces of the universe which she embodies and controls. Simultaneously, however, this "nature," is immediately essentialized and desired as a metaphysical trait. "Nature" becomes a metaphor for maternal affection, for the emotional link that (supposedly) ties mother to child in a bond that ignores negativity. By this slippage between the physical and metaphysical Cléopâtre is presented as an ambivalent nexus connecting the sexual to the political in this drama. This ambivalence makes it impossible for the play to distinguish the one from the other. On the one hand, as sorceress she is connected to those forces of the universe that mock man as they destroy him. On the other, as "mother" she is endowed with all those positive attributes of maternity that society strategically and aggressively idealizes in/as women. It is this refusal to admit to hostile or aggressive feelings either in the mother or the infant that is disguised and denied in the "maternalization" of women as metaphor. It is precisely the return of these repressed, ambivalent feelings that we witness in the play. They appear to us in their emergence as the monstrous perversion of Cléopâtre.[14]

Rodogune, on the other hand, is presented as the opposite extreme of Cléopâtre; she is, in her own definition of herself, "passion-less":

> Plus la haute naissance approche des couronnes,
> Plus cette grandeur même asservit nos personnes;
> Nous n'avons point de cœur pour aimer ni haïr;
> Toutes nos passions ne savent qu'obéir.
>
> (II, iii, 867–870)

Rodogune appears, in her passivity, not as a subject but as an object. To Cléopâtre's obvious incarnation of force and aggressivity responds Rodogune's (structurally defined) selfless vulnerability. It is as this perfectly absent, and therefore unthreatening, blank, this vacant space exposed to the eyes of all the males in the play, that Rodogune reflects the desire she inspires in the men. She is, most naturally, a perfect "love object," a mere reflection of desire.

In this split that divides the representation of woman Rodogune has, in her duel with Cléopâtre, an advantage that she will know how to use. Both brothers fall in love with her as soon as they lay cyes on her:

> Sitôt qu'ils ont paru tous deux en cette cour,
> Ils ont vu Rodogune, et j'ai vu leur amour.
>
> (I, iv, 289–290)

Their love is expressed by them as a preference, a preference which is experienced as a victory of passion over nature, over, that is, their "natural" ties to the mother:

> Notre seul droit d'aînesse est de plaire à vos yeux;
> L'ardeur qu'allume en nous une flamme si pure
> Préfère votre choix au choix de la nature,
> Et vient sacrifier à votre élection
> Toute notre espérance et notre ambition.
>
> (III, iv, 914–918)

Rodogune: *sons and lovers*

The brothers continue to articulate their dilemma as a choice. They continue to see a clear division between Love (Rodogune) and Nature (Cléopâtre):

> Les plus doux de mes vœux enfin sont exaucés.
> Tu viens de vaincre, amour, mais ce n'est pas assez:
> Si tu veux triompher en cette conjoncture,
> Après avoir vaincu, fais vaincre la nature;
> Et prête-lui pour nous ces tendres sentiments
> Que ton ardeur inspire aux cœurs des vrais amants,
> Cette pitié qui force, et ces dignes faiblesses
> Dont la vigueur détruit les fureurs vengeresses.
> Voici la reine. Amour, nature, justes dieux,
> Faites-la-moi fléchir, ou mourir à ses yeux.
>
> (IV, ii, 1251–1258)

Throughout the play Antiochus will continue to keep his women separated, to divide them into the camps of the erotic and the maternal. This impossible division does not dupe his ill-fated twin. Séleucus realizes that despite these apparent differences, Rodogune and Cléopâtre are more alike than different:

> Dans mon ambition, dans l'ardeur de ma flamme,
> Je vois ce qu'est un trône et ce qu'est une femme,
> Et jugeant par leur prix de leur possession,
> J'éteins enfin ma flamme et mon ambition.
>
> (III, v, 1083–1086)

Rodogune would be totally without dramatic interest if she were only confined to the empty space of a passive love object. However, instead of remaining in the stance of her role, Rodogune becomes aware of the political potential of her own erotic appeal. The strategic use she makes of herself as the projection of another's desire enables her to control that desire to her own dynastic ends. Several commentators have pointed out that both Rodogune and Cléopâtre are politically more astute than either of the princes.[15] The situation that the princes attempt to create out of their own passivity, their preferring passion to the throne and their willingness to sacrifice the throne for Rodogune, is, from Rodogune's point of view, a false dilemma. She cannot not reign. She cannot not marry the heir to the throne.[16]

Rodogune, to survive, must play the only card available to her. She must be the erotic object the princes want her to be. Oronte makes it clear to her that this sexual choice is also the only "political" option she has:

> Mais pouvez-vous trembler quand dans ces mêmes lieux
> Vous portez le grand maître et des rois et des dieux?
> L'amour fera lui seul tout ce qu'il vous faut faire.
> Faites-vous un rempart des fils contre la mère;
> Ménagez bien leur flamme, ils voudront tout pour vous.
> ...
> Craignez moins, et sur tout, madame, en ce grand jour
> Si vous voulez régner, faites régner l'amour.
>
> (III, ii, 829–833, 841–2)

At first shocked by the suggestion of her military advisor, Rodogune quickly realizes that her pandering to the erotic fantasies of the brothers, offering herself as their object, is her only possibility of winning the duel with their mother. Like Corneille's other heroines (Pauline, Chimène, Emilie), Rodogune realizes her greatest power resides in her refusal of her own sexuality, in repressing her desire in order to reflect the desire of the other:

> Je croirai faire assez de la daigner souffrir:
> Je verrai leur amour, j'éprouverai sa force,
> Sans flatter leurs désirs, sans leur jeter d'amorce;
> Et, s'il est assez fort pour me servir d'appui,
> Je le ferai régner, mais en régnant sur lui.
>
> (III, iii, 850–854)

Here Rodogune rejoins Cléopâtre by using the same tactics to the same end. Love and nature, mother and mistress, meet, and the division that separated the women into two distinct and fictitious camps collapse into each other. It is from this juncture, the confusion of nature and passion, that the female monster emerges.

And yet Rodogune *is* different from Cléopâtre. There is a profound and perverse distinction that marks the two rivals and that defines the one as actually more monstrous, because more perverse, than the other. Cléopâtre and Rodogune are engaged in a battle for sovereignty. In the final analysis the ultimate question concerns who will be queen and who slave, who will live and who die. In the strange chassé-croisé of inversion that this play represents, the question of sovereignty is a question of who, in this universe of Amazons, is most masculine – that is, which of these two women is less "lacking," more given to sublimation, to a wholeness, and less condemned to the realms of the "in-between."

The essential and fatal distinction that separates Cléopâtre from Rodogune is that of an internal split that makes Cléopâtre susceptible to desire and renders Rodogune invulnerable. From the very beginning of the tragedy Cléopâtre presents herself as motivated by a monolithic drive not to be a subject, nor to be subjugated to another. This desire is metaphorized in her adulation of the throne-crown — "Délices de mon cœur," a phrase one would more commonly associate with a mother's expression of love for a child rather than for a scepter.

It is here perhaps that Cléopâtre can be seen to deviate from those prescriptive, and thus normative, narrations that have tended to represent women within a patriarchal definition of the maternal. This representational imperative has been traced, in our own century, most forcefully by Freud in his description of the "normal" path the little girl must travel to become a non-neurotic heterosexual woman.[17] In his analysis, Freud states that the "normal" evolution of the young girl toward adulthood depends on the transference and sublimation of her "penis envy." This would be successfully accomplished by her bearing and rearing of a (male) child. In her love for and deference to the child, the woman (so the narration goes) both recognizes and compensates for her feelings of inferiority in relation to men. If we were to hazard the transference of Freud's hypothesis to Corneille's heroine, it would seem that in Cléopâtre's case there has been a displacement of this "normal" path from her children on to the throne; the throne becomes the fetishistic object concealing and revealing Cléopâtre's refusal of (symbolic) castration.[18] Wishing to keep the throne, as a symbol of political and thus sexual sovereignty (integrity), in her possession reveals a strange (if occulted) desire; it both affirms and denies that she is and isn't "castrated," that she has and hasn't the power and integrity she envies.[19] Those metaphors (the "crown" and the "throne") for the power and presence of the king serve as the fetishistic screens of Cléopâtre's (perverted) desire. Having them, she is not subject but rather sovereign (whole). She is one with the father/king because she is in his place and clothed in his attributes. At the same time by the very fetishistic valence of her quest there constantly works the doubt that she really does possess those attributes. When Cléopâtre is confronted with the return of her sons, when (that is) the Phallus, as the populace wants and recognizes it — "Le peuple épouvanté, qui déjà dans son âme / Ne suivait qu'à regret les ordres d'une femme ..." (I, i, 47–48) appears outside of her person as the floating signifier ("cette couronne flottante") of her lack, she continually attempts to destroy that signifier, to deny what she sees, to eliminate any obstacles that contradict her fetishistic projections.

Despite devouring the males who surround her she is not immune to the constantly recurring anxiety that she is not sovereign. The essential lack that inheres in her rises to the surface most forcefully not in the men whom she can easily master, but in Rodogune. Cléopâtre's dominant goal in this play is to retain the crown because it represents her sovereignty in front of Rodogune. Her retention of the crown is the constant reminder that she has mastered and replaced Rodogune's lover, her own unfaithful husband.

Despite her "passive," disempowered status, Rodogune elicits that most destructive and revealing fissure of dependency in Cléopâtre: jealousy. Cléopâtre is jealous of Rodogune because Rodogune appears to her as an entity closed in on itself, an entity that inspires desires in others but appears, in its narcissistic self-contentment, impervious to desire. Rodogune exists as the object of the desire of all the males, but perhaps most important, she is (was) the object of Cléopâtre's own husband's desire, and now of her sons'. Within the very circle of males Cléopâtre needs to dominate in order to be sovereign, Rodogune appears to have already ensconced herself as the totality Cléopâtre envies and wants. Cléopâtre's hatred is the aggressive component of that same desire, a desire that is so strong that it destroys the façade of strength and virility Cléopâtre affects and constantly reminds her, by the force of her own hostility, that she is precisely not what she wants most to be – absolute, free from desire. On the contrary, more than any of the males in the play, Cléopâtre appears as subject, subjugated to her fantasies of integrity, and to her erotic ambivalence that would make of her both man and woman, that would give her complete control over her husband, her sons and Rodogune. Finally, she is subjected to an erotic force that is constantly, tantalizingly beyond her control. The farther Cléopâtre ventures into the realm of sovereignty, the more she is brought face to face with her own subjection to her lack, to Rodogune.[20]

Despite her role of subjective victim, Rodogune, unlike Cléopâtre, never varies. She remains, throughout the play, one, in both her erotic and her political adventures. From the beginning of the drama to its end, Rodogune's desire is the same as Cléopâtre's: she wants to be queen, she wants to reign. Unlike Cléopâtre, however, Rodogune will reign not by suppressing the men who stand in her way, but by exploiting them. More forcefully than Cléopâtre, Rodogune can dompt the men she meets on her road to the throne because she never allows her erotic desires to diverge from her political aims. This is the message she gives Laonice:

Rodogune: *sons and lovers*

> Quelque époux que le ciel veuille me destiner,
> C'est à lui pleinement que je veux me donner.
> De celui que je crains si je suis le partage,
> Je saurai l'accepter avec même visage;
> L'hymen me le rendra précieux à son tour,
> Et le devoir fera ce qu'aurait fait l'amour,
> Sans crainte qu'on reproche à mon humeur forcée
> Qu'un autre qu'un mari règne sur ma pensée.
>
> (I, v, 373–380)

It is this same message that she repeats to Antiochus:

> L'orgueil de ma naissance enfle encor mon courage,
> Et quelque grand pouvoir que l'amour ait sur moi,
> Je n'oublierai jamais que je me dois un roi.
> Oui, malgré mon amour, j'attendrai d'une mère
> Que le trône me donne ou vous ou votre frère.
>
> (IV, ii, 1228–1232)

Rodogune articulates what the brothers have never understood: first the throne, then a husband.

I do not want to suggest that Rodogune is without sexual desire, that she does not love. Her passion, however, is remarkable in that it is "transcendental," masculine: it utilizes love as politics. The object of Rodogune's desire is always the throne, but the throne metaphorized in the King. In a sense, however, the fact that this king has been eliminated from the scene before the play begins – eliminated, therefore, since forever for the purposes of representation – he becomes a vanishing point controlling all desire in the play, both sexual and political, in its fantasmatic (that is, imaginary) dimension. What Rodogune accepts and what Cléopâtre cannot accept is that we can only approach this object asymptomatically; it is always a receding ideal. It is never within our grasp. Rodogune knows that we can only settle for its image, its metaphor in the world. In this sense she accepts her "castration" in the symbolic register and is thus, we might say more than Cléopâtre, capable of situating herself within the Law.

From the start Rodogune tells us that she is not indifferent to the two brothers, or rather that in their identity she, for reasons she cannot explain, introduces difference:

> Comme ils ont même sang avec pareil mérite,
> Un avantage égal pour eux me sollicite;
> Mais il est malaisé, dans cette égalité,
> Qu'un esprit combattu ne penche d'un côté.

109

Il est des nœuds secrets, il est des sympathies,
Dont par le doux rapport les âmes assorties
S'attachant l'une à l'autre, et se laissent piquer
Par ces je ne sais quoi qu'on ne peut expliquer.
C'est par là que l'un d'eux obtient la préférence ...

(I, v, 355–363)

This secret and inexplicable passion that radically separates the two princes does so in a particularly decisive way for the evolution of Rodogune's erotic history and for the political resolution of the dilemma facing the princes.

Let us remember that Corneille, by killing off Séleucus, resolves his dilemma; he never has to inform his audience which of the two brothers was born first – which, in other words, in the genealogical imperative of Patriarchy bears the first and decisive mark of the father:

la mort de Séleucus m'a exempté de développer le secret du droit d'aînesse entre les deux frères, qui d'ailleurs n'eût jamais été croyable, ne pouvant être éclairci que par une bouche en qui l'on n'a pas vu assez de sincérité pour prendre aucune assurance sur son témoignage.

(*Examen*, p. 356)

This mark, however, is recognized and validated not by the sons' mother but by a surrogate mother: Rodogune, new wife of the Father. It is she who recognizes Antiochus as the metaphoric substitute (the image) of the dead King:

Je brise avec honneur mon illustre esclavage;
J'ose reprendre un cœur pour aimer et haïr,
Et ce n'est plus qu'à toi que je veux obéir.
Le consentiras-tu, cet effort sur ma flamme,
Toi, son vivant portrait, que j'adore dans l'âme,
Cher prince dont je n'ose en mes plus doux souhaits
Fier encore le nom aux murs de ce palais?

(III, iv, 880–886)

Antiochus is the living replica of the King. In the ideology of absolute monarchy, the King, we know, never dies; the essence of kingship is immediately passed on from one king to the next without any interruption.[21] Rodogune recognizes the difference between the brothers and articulates it because she alone knew and compared the images of the old and new kings:

Pour rendre enfin justice aux mânes d'un grand roi,
Rapportez à mes yeux son image sanglante ...

(III, iii, 858–859)

These two images reflect each other. A new identity of males nullifies the identity of twinship, that monstrous error of usurping femininity, and re-establishes patrilineal descent. The new image also reflects Rodogune's desire, that unswervingly recognizes and names her mate, through whom and by whom she accedes to the sovereignty for which she is destined. In a sense Rodogune loves neither of the men; she loves the King who makes her queen.

The last scene of the tragedy plays out for a final time, and in one more reversal, the triumph of Rodogune. The desire that has led her through the turmoil and storms that raged about her to the throne is once again threatened with frustration as the bridal cup, floating as uncertainly as the crown, passes from hand to hand in an as yet unresolved ritual of death and marriage. To the perfect sexual symmetry of the two pairs Séleucus–Antiochus/Rodogune–Cléopâtre, the murder of Séleucus has introduced a disorder that the Cornelian universe cannot tolerate. It is this disorder that is finally expelled by the elimination of Cléopâtre.

Antiochus, as usual, is neither willing nor able to see the writing on the wall. He remains trapped in his own passivity, his own blindness. Unable to judge between his mother and his fiancée, Antiochus participates in his own execution: he almost kills himself. It is Rodogune who, more vigilant than he, stops him from drinking from the poisoned cup. By pointing to Cléopâtre's death throes, she stops the marriage. Even when he is presented with the irrefutable proof of his mother's guilt, Antiochus prefers not to believe it. He cannot accept her total fall out of "nature," nor the consequent idea that there is no "nature" where he might find a protective haven. He pleads with Cléopâtre not to abandon him, but to love him:

> Ah! vivez pour changer cette haine en amour.
> (V, iv, 1825)

His desperate invocation is a plea that she conform to the idea he needs of maternity and thus of femininity. It is an idea that is necessary to his own self-image as a man, an idea that subtends an entire masculinist projection of the world. It is upon this vision of a "natural" maternal love that his survival in the world depends. But Cléopâtre, at least true to herself, refuses this appeal to a "nature" she execrates.

She dies, and by eliminating herself she is responsible for restoring a new symmetry, for clearing away the conflicting doubles that dogged both Antiochus and Rodogune. Finally Cléopâtre is responsible for the normalization, the heterosexualization in and through marriage with which the play concludes. Rodogune and Antiochus are left alone on stage to face the future together.

This future is, however, clouded. As we mentioned at the beginning of the chapter, no other of Corneille's tragedies ends on such a pessimistic note, a note of such ambivalence. There has been a complete reversal in the course of this tragedy: what started out as "ce jour pompeux" ends in mourning:

> Et vous, allez au temple
> Y changer l'allégresse en deuil sans pareil,
> La pompe nuptiale en funèbre appareil.
> (V, iv, 1890–1892)

The note of ambivalence that has been associated with the wedding from the play's beginning is echoed with greater force at the tragedy's end. It is as if this marriage were a sacrifice in which the new Cornelian couple, a weak, ambivalent king and a strong determined queen, offer their negativity on the altar of a Patriarchal system that has been perverted. Cléopâtre's curse:

> Puissez-vous ne trouver dedans votre union
> Qu'horreur, que jalousie, et que confusion!
> Et pour vous souhaiter tous les malheurs ensemble,
> Puisse naître de vous un fils qui me ressemble!
> (V, iv, 1821–1824)

resounds in the empty theater long after the curtain falls. It warns us that, in the future, this perverted couple, a monstrous inversion of Classicism's sexual and political precepts, will produce only new and more ominous offspring.

5

MOLIÈRE'S *TARTUFFE* AND THE SCANDAL OF INSIGHT

Alors, le regard cherche, nous regardons de tous nos yeux dans
le seul but de, enfin, ne plus voir, mais être.[1]

Car si le visible ne s'épuise ni en une visée transcendente, ni en
une pensée proximale d'un espace partes extra-partes s'il est
prégnant de l'invisible, "Voir c'est ne plus être." ... plus on
voit, moins on est, plus on est moins on voit.[2]

Unquestionably *Le Tartuffe* is Molière's most scandalous comedy.
From its creation at Versailles as part of the royal festivities known
as the "Plaisirs de l'Ile Enchantée" in May of 1664 to its withdrawal
from the stage and the royal government's refusal to allow its public
performance for a period of several years, the play, in its different
versions, ignited a debate rarely paralleled in the annals of the French
stage. During the period of its prohibition, Molière, his supporters
and enemies engaged in heated controversy over the real or imagined
attack on piety and "dévots," and over the social, moral and ethical
role of the theater in society. Until its rehabilitation in 1669, the play,
perhaps more than any other of the seventeenth century, generated
a dizzying whirlwind of charges and countercharges that clearly
situates it as the focal point of an entire epistemological dilemma,
of a sensitive, overly charged threat to all social order, to, even (if
we listen to the ravings of Pierre Roullé) the invasion of the well-
ordered world of ecclesiastical and monarchal order by the "satanic":
Molière was accused of being "un démon vêtu de chair et habillé en
homme ..."[3]

The nature of this scandal, the way it polarized opinion in the
small but acutely politicized world of the court and of the Parisian
intelligentsia, may strike modern readers (as surely as it appears to
have struck Molière and his supporters) as exaggerated, but queasily
disturbing. What was really at stake in this uproar? Was it merely
a cabal of religious and political fanatics bent on destroying a playwright who catered too intimately to the whims of a young, undocile

113

king? Or, on the other hand, is it possible that such men as Lamoignon and Péréfixe, the archbishop of Paris, actually saw through the "appearances" of religious scandal to a more profound, more unsettling, less containable disruption that the comedy sets in motion?

Molière claims in his preface that it is not possible to confuse the truly pious with his hypocrite, since, as he states, he has taken all necessary precautions lest this confusion occur:

j'ai mis tout l'art et tous les soins qu'il m'a été possible pour distinguer le personnage de l'Hypocrite d'avec celui du vrai Dévot. J'ai employé pour cela deux actes entiers, à préparer la venue de mon scélérat. Il ne tient pas un seul moment l'auditeur en balance; on le connaît aux marques que je lui donne et, d'un bout à l'autre, il ne dit pas un mot, il ne fait pas une action, qui ne peigne aux spectateurs le caractère d'un méchant, et ne fasse éclater celui du véritable homme de bien que je lui oppose.

(Préface, ed. Rat, p. 682)

Nevertheless, despite this and similar denegations, the confusion occurs, occurs with a vengeance and a fury that betray more than just bad faith. The real nature of the confusion seems, and of course this is not novel, to be less a matter of intention − less, that is, the scandal of the author's avowed purpose in composing his play − than a scandal of interpretation, of subjectivity, of the subjectivity that inheres in all representation, and the representation that constitutes subjectivity.

This, of course, is what the more subtle censors of the play knew. It would be an act of extraordinary hubris on our part to think that Bourdaloue, for instance, was less perspicacious than we. It was simply that he saw the threat of the play as a real danger to an entire epistemological system, in which not only his religion but his being (as if one could separate the two) were invested. And in this he and his allies were, after all, right. They did see what Molière and the others didn't: that when a work questions the foundations of knowledge, those signifying systems that define certain supposedly "natural" institutions − the monarchy, the church, the family − and shows their predicates to be vulnerable, the entire edifice of the social life they subtend is shaken to the point that its eventual collapse becomes inevitable.

Tartuffe's scandal, therefore, is the scandal of literature, of representation. What the uproar over the play reveals is perhaps the first modern (even though unthought-of as such) battle waged between a totalitarian impulse towards domination and mastery − towards the reification of the Law of the Father that at the beginning of Louis's personal reign was too shakily in place not to resort to overt displays of its own insecurity – and a signifying system, a semiosis, that by its very nature cannot be contained in an univocal way. In this, then, Molière's play is symptomatic of a much greater threat, of a far more compelling scandal than the ostensible attack on religion. Religion is only a symptom, a particularly acute and sensitive symptom, of one of the ideological apparatuses the play invades. It would, however, be a mistake only to look at the individual symptom and ignore that symptom's insertion in the greater whole. The scandal of *Tartuffe* is its attack on the totalizing ideology that underlies the world of the "ancien régime," an attack waged by the indeterminacy of its own psycho-semiotic structures.

In order to understand the complex nature of the play's scandal, of the scandal of literature, we would do well to turn to the text and see how it inscribes within itself, and comments upon, its own scandalous plot. The word "scandal" appears twice in the play, twice in one of the most important scenes (IV, i) and both times in the mouth of Tartuffe. In response to Cléante's plea that he re-establish peace between Orgon and his son, Tartuffe responds:

> Après son action, qui n'eut jamais d'égale,
> Le commerce entre nous porterait du scandale ...
> > (IV, i, 1209–1210)

and

> Mais après le scandale et l'affront d'aujourd'hui,
> Le Ciel n'ordonne pas que je vive avec lui.
> > (IV, i, 1231–1232)

For Tartuffe, Damis's abortive attempt to reveal to his father Tartuffe's lust, the sexuality that threatens the stability of Orgon's marriage and that usurps his own sexual position as master of his wife and head of his household, is the scandal in the play. The outburst has, as we know, a contrary effect: Orgon, taken in by Tartuffe, banishes Damis from his presence, from his house (we shall return to this important act later on). The scandal of the play is the revelation from Tartuffe's own mouth – although he uses it as a deflection – of his attack on Orgon as husband, and his manipulation of him as father. The scandal which Tartuffe's self-defense underlines is, therefore, not just a supposed attack on piety (although it is that too) but his undermining of the family, that unit upon which all social, political and religious cohesion is based.

Le Tartuffe is central to Molière's production, not only in time but more importantly in the way it concentrates all the concerns of both the farces and the "serious" comedies on the dilemma of the family. Of all Molière's plays, and one might look even more far afield into the familial world of Cornelian or Racinian tragedy, we have no more complete an example of family (grandmother, mother, father, sister/daughter, brother/son, uncle) on the seventeenth-century stage. The play begins and ends with all the members of the Orgon household family either on stage or invoked on stage. The comedy thus repeats, in its structural integrity and in its narrative circularity, the very closure of the family as a fixed immutable unit that the machinations of hypocrisy would attack and subvert.

As the curtain rises this attack is already underway. What the crisis of Mme Pernelle's visit and her verbal onslaught serve to reveal is that an invasion of the family, its decomposition, has begun and that the very center of the familial fortress, the place of the father, is vacant. Although the banter between Mme Pernelle, a figure of both comic and terrifying proportions, and the members of her son's household constantly undercuts the initial impact of this absence, an absence that is articulated either as an abdication or an usurpation, this ambivalent state of familial affairs has far-reaching consequences for the social order as a whole.

Borrowing the term *oïkodespotès* from J. Habermas[4] who uses it to describe familial-economic organization in Greek society, I would suggest that the word fits admirably into our own purposes as a way of introducing the socio-sexual dimension of the role of the Father in Molière's comedy. It combines both the etymological connotations of house, home (and by extension husbandry, "household-economy") with the term for controller, ruler. This latter term echoes with the proleptic resonance of "despot." It is precisely the absence of both these things that Mme Pernelle laments. What she finds most distressing in Orgon's household is the lack of any economy; all of her criticism points to disorder ("la cour du roi Pétaud"), excess, and spending, be it the excess of language (Vous êtes, ma mie, une fille suivante / Un peu trop forte en gueule"), the lack of being properly "rangé" ("Vous êtes un sot en trois lettres, mon fils ... Vous preniez tout l'air d'un méchant garnement, / Et ne lui donneriez jamais que du tourment") or simply financial irresponsibility ("Vous êtes dépensière; et cet état me blesse, / Que vous alliez vêtue ainsi qu'une princesse."). What Mme Pernelle notices, and is frightened by, is that this family is no longer the bourgeois unit she desires. Orgon's family has fallen out of order and into a chaos that frightens and threatens her. It has left the realm of hoarding, enclosure and economy for the more threatening world of "dépense." Confronted with this disorder, a disorder where she no longer has a place, which excludes her, it is not surprising that she, alone among the different members of the family, shares her son's infatuation with Tartuffe. Rather than an usurpation of her son, she (mistakenly) sees Tartuffe as an extension of him, as his surrogate who will aid in the restoration of order in the tumult that surrounds her. In a sense, therefore, but in a very overdetermined sense, Mme Pernelle is placed in the position of appealing to the mistaken unity of Orgon/ Tartuffe, which she sees as the Father, that is, the ruler of the house (the *oïkodespotès*). The desire to be tyrannized, to be subjected to the "despot" in order to find one's place and have one's being ratified, is only the first of a series of sexual/political poles that the comedy of *Tartuffe* sets in motion as the play begins. Mme Pernelle ardently desires her own subjection to the Law of the Father and his representative as the only salvation both for the family and for herself.

In a perverse reversal, which nevertheless retains its comic thrust, the members of the household also see Tartuffe as a despot. The words used to describe his invasion of the family are clearly charged with political overtones bringing into the center of the domestic realm those searing debates about just and unjust monarchy that so actively engaged political thinkers and writers during the premiership of Richelieu and the troubles of the Fronde.[5] "Un pouvoir tyrannique," "contrôler tout," "s'impatronniser," and "faire le maître" point to him as having taken the place of the rightful head of the household. In this sense we are, or rather the text is, drawing a fine line of distinction in the world of patriarchy between the rights and rewards of a legal, benevolent monarchical/familial power, and the perversion of that power, its usurpation and corruption as "tyranny."

Clearly, then, the play begins as a debate, a debate between the "Mother" who represents a bourgeois order of economy and the concomitant desire for containment (one might even say confinement), setting off one of the poles, the masochistic, around which the whirlwind of scandal will revolve; and the other, the order of the family as "dépense," but *dépense* that is coded as freedom (perhaps the intrusion, the comic intrusion into this bourgeois household of nobiliary pretensions?). And, at the beginning, as we've seen, the center of the family is already absent. Both physically and metaphysically, the role and place of the Father, the pivotal structure around which the family and thus the State are organized, is empty.

It is this absence of the father and the usurpation of his place that sets the play in motion, aspirating into its center, in ever more complex levels of sexual and political disarray, those signifying systems the family both anchors and naturalizes. At the same time the disarray in this family signals a general threat to society. We must not forget that in the tightly structured world of patriarchal monarchy, one can never attack the father without in some way committing a crime of "lèse-majesté." Every father in his household is the mirror of the King, the "father of the Nation," in his kingdom.

The *Tartuffe*, then, as comedy, situates itself within the same anxiety as the major tragedies of the period, the anxiety of patricide, the desire/fear of the father, of the Father as object both of love and of aggression, and the greater fear, the unthinkable of seventeenth-century French political musings, of a society unhinged from the father's Law, a society which abandons the father and kills its King. It would seem hasty, therefore, to define comedy, in its opposition to tragedy, as "the triumph of the son over the father":[6] that opposition may work (or be made to work) only in some abstract psychoanalytic framework which ignores the mutual imbrication of ideology and the unconscious and where, more to the point, in that psycho-ideology, the son is always also the father and vice-versa.

The political role of the father in this play is inseparable from his sexual role, and both are necessary for the grounding of his relation to his world, and to that world's ability to define itself. It will not surprise us, therefore, to learn that the political disarray into which Orgon's family has been thrown immediately takes on sexual overtones – is immediately sexualized – by the comic rhetoric of Dorine:

> Mais il est devenu comme un homme hébété
> Depuis que de Tartuffe on le voit entêté;
> Il l'appelle son frère, et l'aime dans son âme
> Cent fois plus qu'il ne fait mère, fils, fille, et femme.
> C'est de tous ses secrets l'unique confident,
> Et de ses actions le directeur prudent;
> Il le choie, il l'embrasse, et pour une maîtresse
> On ne saurait, je pense, avoir plus de tendresse;
> ...
> Enfin il en est fou; c'est son tout, son héros ...
>
> (I, ii, 183–190; 195)

Although Dorine's explanation of the new state of affairs of the Orgon household is meant to appear funny, the connotations underlying her speech betray a sexual malaise that the comedy can only hesitantly keep at bay. All the words that Dorine uses to describe the indescribable, to indicate what has suddenly gone wrong with Orgon, point to a sexual attraction that cannot be normalized. What we learn about the relation between the two men is that, from Orgon's side at least, it is a desire for totalization. Tartuffe has taken the place of all his other affections. Orgon treats him with more respect, attention and fondness than if he were a "mistress," and finally, for Orgon, Tartuffe is his "tout" (everything, but more resonantly, his "all," his plenitude).

The relation between Tartuffe and Orgon has been analyzed and commented upon by all those critics who have attempted to explain the play; L. Gossman comes closest to unraveling the complexity and the danger of this liaison by pointing to its dialectical nature:

> Orgon ... must believe in his idol himself; he too must feel himself seduced, captivated, carried away, not indeed by any deliberate effort on the part of Tartuffe, but by the very nature of Tartuffe's superior being. At the same time, however, since he wants to have this idol for himself, to enjoy through him the absolute superiority that he recognized in him, he must attach him to himself, win him over, make him into an inalienable part of himself. He must in short seduce Tartuffe.[7]

While Gossman's own discussion is based on a finely tuned analysis of the subject–object dialectic that Tartuffe and Orgon refigure, a dialectic that, as we see in the above quotation, his own vocabulary sexualizes, his analysis does not explore the theoretical implications of its own insights. It will appear obvious that the dialectic that is established between the two men enters into the dynamics of mastery and submission, as that dynamic functions as a sexual, that is a homoerotic, attraction. I would not want to reduce the complexity of this textual nexus to a banal discussion of what was obviously unthinkable for the characters and audience of the play: Orgon is not (just), as a character, a representation of repressed homosexuality (to Cléante's question what can he possibly see in Tartuffe, the only answer Orgon can come up with, is the erratic, ejaculative "C'est un homme ... qui, ... ha! un homme ... un homme enfin"). Rather, it seems to me that in the constellation of sexual and political forces the play, as representation of patriarchal society, sets in motion, we must see this homoerotic element as meshing into a larger circle of ideological forces: forces of representation, forces of normalization and of verisimilitude, that constitute the essential parameters of power, and therefore meaning, in the comedy.

Obviously, the very definition of ideology implies its invisibility: ideology is what cannot be directly seen or perceived by the members of any given society, but which nevertheless controls and directs what they apprehend as the limits and possibilities of their own subjective insertion into the "real" that surrounds and illudes them. It should come as no surprise, therefore, were I to suggest that the unraveling of the text's inner network reveals the blind spot of its ideological investments. I would like to suggest that at the very center of the complex textual network there exists a "master code" that permits the functioning of all the signifying systems in the play, that includes in itself the indeterminability of both the sexual and the political investments of the comedy, that accounts largely for the comedy itself of the play, and finally that engages the characters in the ambiguous dialectics of seeming and being, of truth and hypocrisy, that the theater (as a particularly overdetermined instance of representation) both affirms and denies in its own dialectical seduction of the spectators by the spectacle. The single most insistent linguistic sign in the comedy of *Tartuffe* is the polysemous indeterminacy of the verb "voir" with all the echoes, literal and metaphoric, attached to it. Lest this affirmation seem hasty, I would like to remind us that Molière himself, in the several prefaces and "placets au roi" that he placed before the published version of *Tartuffe*, engages our interpretation in a network of visual metaphors by his own rhetorical figures:

Voici une comédie dont on a fait beaucoup de bruit ... Les marquis, les précieuses, les cocus et les médecins ont souffert doucement qu'on les ait représentés, et ils ont fait semblant de se divertir, avec tout le monde, des peintures que l'on a faites d'eux ... (*Préface*, p. 681)

Le devoir de la comédie étant de corriger les hommes en les divertissant, j'ai cru que, dans l'emploi où je me trouve, je n'avais rien de mieux à faire que d'attaquer par des peintures ridicules les vices de mon siècle ...
(*Premier placet*, p. 686)

From the beginning, then, Molière describes his play as a "painting" in the metaphorical sense that word carries as a (visual) form of representation. At the same time, in these same defenses of his text, the play is of course called a "poem":

il ne faut qu'ôter le voile de l'équivoque, et regarder ce qu'est la comédie en soi, pour voir si elle est condamnable. On connaîtra, sans doute, que n'étant autre chose qu'un poème ingénieux, qui, par des leçons agréables, reprend les défauts des hommes ... (*Préface*, p. 683)

There is a slippage in Molière's own rhetoric between words and paintings, between the lexical and the visual, whose difference is erased in their communality as representation. This effacement is interesting, if only when we remember to what degree the study of "optics" invaded seventeenth-century thought, philosophy and representation.[8] The most celebrated example is, of course, the *Discours de la Méthode*, which was originally a preface to Descartes's own work on optics. It is precisely this slippage between the lexical and the visual that coheres in *Tartuffe* around the paradigmatic chain of the verb "voir," which in its several and ambivalent meanings engages the very heart of the debate raging around the *Tartuffe* as a form of representation: it is this ambivalence that engages the seduction of theater, in its collapsing "truth and illusion" into representation that allows for the impossible battle of interpretation that the *Tartuffe* spawned and which has not ceased to the present day.

The verb "voir," because of its constant oscillation between literal and metaphorical connotations, because of the easy slippage between "seeing" and "knowing," is essential for understanding the way diverse textual networks of the comedy slide into each other creating an homogeneous representation of the "real" of the text. The dynamics of vision, where vision is evoked as an appeal to some available "truth," engages the heart of the play's dilemma between being and seeming that is central to the controversy over religious piety and hypocrisy. It is also imperative for understanding the relation between sexuality and subjectivity as they are revealed and determined by the characters' relation to the scopic drive as it meanders through and across the text, joining and separating the main characters first in a dialectics of voyeurism and exhibitionism, then in this dialectics' imbrication in a thematics of narcissism. Finally, the verb serves as a pivot in the comedy of the play, uniting the spectators to the characters, thus engaging the very dynamics of theater as they are emmeshed in the ideology of patriarchy. In a world of appearances, in a world that exists in order to know and constantly reaffirm the "truth" − that is, in a world that needs constantly to be able to confirm its own sexual and political a-prioris, that needs to dissect reality down to its most indivisible particles, down to the most unassailable grounds, in order thereupon to anchor the subject of this world − seeing is invoked in all its supposed transparency, in all its supposed ability to discern reality from mere appearance. In this supposed visual anchoring of the world, the characters of the *Tartuffe* are set adrift, unhinged by the very ambivalence of the word, of the act, that they invoke for their own salvation,

As Jacqueline Rose reminds us in *Sexuality in the Field of Vision*, from the very beginnings of Freud's explorations of the unconscious, of his discovery of the role that sexuality, both repressed and conscious, plays in determining the way the human being comes to situate him/herself in the symbolic gendering of the body, visual representation plays a key role:

Freud often related the question of sexuality to that of visual representation ... He would take as his model little scenarios, or the staging of events, which demonstrated the complexity of an essentially visual space, moments in which perception founders ... or in which the pleasure in looking tips over into the register of excess ... The sexuality lies less in the content of what is seen than in the subjectivity of the viewer, in the relationship between what is looked at and the developing sexual knowledge of the child. The relationship between viewer and scene is always one of fracture, partial identification, pleasure and distrust. As if Freud found the aptest analogy for the problem of our identity as human subjects in failures of vision or in the violence which can be done to an image as it offers itself to view.[9]

Vision is always excessive, always a too-much of pleasure that threatens the subject with dispersion, fragmentation. It is both constitutive of the suture of the imaginary and symbolic registers that situate the subject along the axes of gendering and disruptive of any stable fixing of this gendering. It is always what attempts to "elude" castration and what finally lures the subject into the Law of sexual difference.[10] Paradoxically, the force of the visual, the desire of the scopic drive, is part of the very forging of sexual identity which nevertheless remains insecure, unstable, exposed to the excessive thrust of the drive.

The odd couple that Tartuffe and Orgon present to the incomprehension of their entourage can be read as but two poles of the visual dialectic. On the one hand Orgon seems most radically marked as a desire to see, as a *Schaulust*, with all the connotations that term has as a particularly coded "masculine," drive: it is a desire to possess, to know, to penetrate; a desire to cut off, divide and make order. It is also (and this will not surprise us), on a metaphysical level, the desire to find an integrity of being, an apprehension of the self as entire that is, in diverse ways, essential to all of Molière's (male) protagonists. It is the desire for integrity that situates Molière's protagonists firmly within a patriarchal economy based precisely on the dichotomization of a "full," "self-sufficient" masculinity, always threatened by the menace of castration, and the "lacking" (because already castrated), excessive economy imputed to "femininity."[11]

In this economy, Tartuffe, in relation to Orgon, exists not so much to see as to be seen, and more to the point, to see himself being seen. He is pure projection, constantly offering himself to the vision of the other(s), either actually, or metaphorically in his rhetoric (and it is here that the slippage between seeing and saying, between the visual and the lexical, that we have already noticed in the *préfaces* returns in the dynamics of the comedy. I will return to this presently.) He is, in his constant self-positioning, in the way that he is always aware of how he is being seen, in the way he sees himself seeing himself, a perfect example of the "feminine" as J. Lacan would define it.[12]

This feminine, based as it is on the illusion of vision, on the vision of an illusion, is incorporated by Lacan into what he calls (following J. Rivière) the dialectics of the "masquerade." This masquerade is the feminine holding up to the masculine what it wants to see, the masculine participating in this same masquerade by pretending to give the feminine what it wants to have. Together they form the illusory vision of sexual complementarity.[13] In this masquerade of sexual illusions the feminine serves as a form of *trompe-l'œil* for the masculine.

None of the members of Orgon's household can understand, any more than we, the hold Tartuffe has over their father. From the valiant bourgeois he was during the troubles of the Fronde, doing his duty, defending his king, he has undergone a radical change that has left him "hébété." His stubborn refusal to see what all the members of his household see is, for them, inexplicable. They can only articulate his new state as a bewitchment, a spell. His relation to Tartuffe is described as a "caprice," an "enchantement," a "charme," all words that point to something that escapes the reality of their world, that conjures up a vocabulary of magic, of sorcery, in its attempt at explaining the inexplicable. At the same time these words come from and share the traditional petrarchan vocabulary of *innamoramento*, thus carrying with them the shudder of a love that is not natural, that has strayed from its proper object and come, inverted, into the space of domestic intimacy. How can we understand Orgon's passionate attachment to Tartuffe, his "blindness" ("votre aveuglement fait que je vous admire ...") except in the terms in which it is presented to us, except as a visual dysfunction? Orgon, we are told, is "ébloui par un faux éclat," seduced by "cent dehors fardés."

Orgon is the prisoner of a vision, of an image, but at the same time he is primarily trapped within this vision as it focuses on his own desire. In his conversation with Cléante (I, v), Orgon narrates to him his first encounter with Tartuffe, a narration that is entirely inscribed within a visual framework:

Ha! si vous aviez vu comme j'en fis rencontre,

. . .

Chaque jour à l'église il venait, d'un air doux,
Tout vis-à-vis de moi se mettre à deux genoux.
Il attirait les yeux de l'assemblée entière
Par l'ardeur dont au Ciel il poussait sa prière;
Il faisait des soupirs, de grands élancements,
Et baisait humblement la terre à tous moments.

(I, v, 281, 283–288)

The most remarkable revelation in this narration of his originary *innamoramento* is its obsessive, repetitive nature − it is an image that occurred "chaque jour" − so that in a sense, each sighting is a re-sighting, a recapture of the gaze that is not allowed to wander but always comes back to its own point of departure, and that point inscribes itself in this dialectic as a desire for mirroring, a desire in which what the subject is "looking for" is somehow its own projection reflected in the returned glance of the object. What seduces Orgon is the reflection of himself which Tartuffe presents to him by creating himself as his mirror − "Tout vis-à-vis de moi se mettre à deux genoux." In another context, N. Gross tells us why this positioning, in a church, is particularly remarkable: "Tartuffe seems to face Orgon, while his gestures of mortification and worship seem addressed to Orgon, drawing attention to both of them and distracting from the service at the altar."[14] In fact, Tartuffe, by making a spectacle of himself, that is by positioning himself as Orgon's reflection, his mirror, positions this reflection as a vision of unity, of integrity, as the lure of the subject who is complete. He does become Orgon's god. He becomes his double/other, the image of completeness, of wholeness, that ensnares and traps Orgon, a creature of desire and therefore of lack (that this lack be interpreted in spiritual terms, or not, is not the point). Tartuffe entraps his prey, in such a way as to pleasure him: Orgon claims that in his subjugation to Tartuffe ("qui suit ses leçons") he both becomes another and "savors" a profound tranquility ("goûte une paix profonde"). It is this unfathomable repose that most notably marks the aphanisis of the wounded subject we must suppose Orgon to be, his volatilization into a nirvana-esque (re-)union with his own desire. Paradoxically, this "quietude" may be compared in religious terms to a "ravissement," to a dispossession of the self and to its integration in an image in which it exults. In this way, we may compare the ecstatic reaction of Orgon to the famous "infant" described by Lacan jubilating at his captured image in the mirror:

Il y suffit de comprendre le stade du miroir comme une identification au sens plein que l'analyse donne à ce terme: à savoir la transformation produite chez le sujet quand il assume une image ...

L'assomption jubilatoire de son image spéculaire par l'être encore plongé dans l'impuissance motrice ... nous paraîtra dès lors manifester en une situation exemplaire la matrice symbolique où le "je" se précipite en une forme primordiale ...[15]

What, of course, is significant in this jubilation, in this capture of an image of wholeness, is that it precipitates an illusory apprehension of subjectivity as integrity. For any reader of Molière it will come as no surprise that Orgon is just one in a declension of "partial" characters who are problematic precisely because they desire integrity, as does perhaps the whole of the Molierian corpus, while that integrity constantly eludes them. It would not be too much of an exaggeration to suggest that this is perhaps the underlying dynamic of all of Molière's great creations, all those plays that supposedly represent the Classical ideal. Think of Arnolphe, Argan, Dom Juan, Alceste, all men, all undone by a flaw that sunders them, renders them "childlike" and therefore comic. This flaw is exaggerated by the very laughter they spawn, which is the laughter of the other to whose place they aspire, though it is forever denied them. We must, therefore see this jubilation as complicitous with the defeat of the integral subject they would be, because it is both jubilatory and mortiferous. The reflection of the mirror stage condemns the subject, the core of whose "ego" is herein constituted, to its own alienation as a necessarily fractured subjectivity. Before Lacan, Freud had warned us of both the jubilatory and the nefarious attraction of doubling. On the one hand the double can represent an enhancing of the ego. On the other, it also signals the ego's destruction:

This invention of doubling as a preservation against extinction has its counterpart in the language of dreams ... Such ideas, however, have sprung from the soil of unbounded self-love, from the primary narcissism which holds sway in the mind of the child as in that of primitive man, and when this stage has been left behind the double takes on a different aspect. From having been an assurance of immortality, he becomes the ghastly harbinger of death.[16]

Tartuffe serves as Orgon's mirror, serves as his double, his completion. He lures him into the seduction of the imaginary, and there traps him, clasps him to himself in an erotic embrace, which like all eroticism has a double valency: both and at the same time exalting and deathly. It is in this visual embrace that Orgon's subjectivity is produced, whole, illusory, as subjugation. Orgon is subjugated to the illusion of Tartuffe as masquerade. There is a mise-en-abyme of subjectivity that only starts here. But it is one way for us to understand the desperate (funny?) attachment Orgon demonstrates towards Tartuffe, to understand the pathos in his cry, "Non, vous demeurerez: il y va de ma vie," when Tartuffe pretends he will leave the household. For in this "cri de cœur" we hear the fear and anxiety of a subject who knows that without his mirror he no longer exists, no longer knows the sweetness of "une paix profonde" that he can only find, not with his family, not with his wife, but with his "semblable," his "frère."

Only when we understand the totalizing, death-dealing capture of Orgon by Tartuffe can we begin to understand the enormous threat Tartuffe, as masquerade, as hypocrite, and as supreme narcissist, presents for the safety and stability of Orgon's, and the King's, family. Narcissism, from its very inception as myth, is intimately related to, cannot be separated from, death,[17] and that death is itself carried along, supported, by the fascination of the visual/image.[18]

Orgon believes what he sees: "Je suis votre valet, et crois les apparences," he tells his wife. Orgon's blustering betrays one of the valences of narcissism – the childish belief in the power of one's own ego to dominate the world, to create reality ("Mais je veux que cela soit une vérité," he tells his daughter, "Et c'est assez pour vous que je l'aie arrêté") that in its violent, imperialistic form meshes perfectly with the greater, more perverse narcissism of Tartuffe. Tartuffe's narcissism, his ability to project an image of himself that is totally enclosed on itself, an image that exists without a discernible desire that would betray its lack, its point of fracture, is best realized in his production of himself as a work of art, as an artifice, and finally, as far as Orgon is concerned, as a perfect "trompe-l'œil," in the sense that J. Baudrillard has given that term:

On sent que ces objets se rapprochent du trou noir d'où vient la réalité, le monde réel, le temps ordinaire. Cet effet de décentrement en avant, cette avancée d'un miroir d'objets à la rencontre d'un sujet, c'est, sous l'espèce d'objets anodins, l'apparition du double qui crée cet effet de séduction, de saisissement caractéristique du trompe-l'œil: vertige tactile qui retrace le vœu fou du sujet d'étreindre sa propre image, et par là même de s'évanouir. Car la réalité n'est saisissante que lorsque notre identité s'y perd, ou lorsqu'elle ressurgit comme notre propre mort hallucinée.[19]

Tartuffe's entire being exists as a work for the eyes. For him, to be is to be seen. He exists only insofar as he can enter into and colonize the visual field of the other, draw that other into his artifice, and there kill him.

Certainly his entrance on to the stage, an entrance that has been, as Molière reminds us ("J'ai employé pour cela deux actes entiers à préparer la venue de mon scélérat," *Préface*, p. 682), minutely prepared, is only the most obvious indication that Tartuffe exists to satisfy the appetite of the eye. Molière inscribes one of his very few didascalia – "Tartuffe, apercevant Dorine" – to tell us how Tartuffe is to make his entrance. Tartuffe enters the world of the play not only with all eyes fixed upon him, but knowing that those eyes are there, knowing that they are waiting for him, knowing that he is there to satisfy the appetite of those eyes. Tartuffe enters the universe of the play, and the world of the playgoers, seeing himself being seen. He is there to draw the eye's attention to himself, and by so doing, to trick it, to betray it: he offers himself as an image that passes itself off as real, as substantial, but which in reality is only a mirror, the eye caught in the game of seeming/being. Tartuffe's role, his enormous narcissistic production of himself, is precisely to situate himself in the field of vision of that (those) eye(s) and to hide/reveal by that visual seduction the artificiality (that is, the essence, as "art" – artifact – production) of the "world."

I have been attempting to describe the dialectics of mastery and subjugation that links Orgon to Tartuffe as a form of homosexuality subtended by the dynamics of seeing/being seen that is polarized in the couple they form. I would like to carry this dynamic one step further. I have intimated that Tartuffe is narcissistic in a way that would, in the ideology of patriarchy that informs this comedy, associate him with a perversely passive femininity. Even in his first "tête-à-tête" with Elmire – even, that is, when he is alone for the first time with the object of his desire – Tartuffe articulates his satisfaction through a strangely visual construction:

> J'en suis ravi de même, et sans doute il m'est doux,
> Madame, de me voir seul à seul avec vous.
> (III, iii, 899–900)

The self-enclosed reflexivity of the construction "me voir" points, it seems to me, to the essential feature of Tartuffe's self-perception, as a closed off, self-contained wholeness. It is this state that appears as a non-desirous being that works to entrap Orgon. This self-enclosure, which we have already noted in the didascalia, the way he enfolds the visual world on himself, creating himself, one could say, as the "visible spot (*tache*)" that ensnares the eye, reflects a narcissistic hold on the world that Freud associates primarily with "beautiful women, noble felines, and great criminals."[20] This type of character has, we are told, "great attraction for those who have renounced part of their own narcissism and are in search of object-love" ("Narcissism," p. 89). Tartuffe's presentation of himself, his production of himself as image/lure, is therefore particularly attractive for Orgon. First because of the way this illusion of self-enclosure seduces him, but more importantly when we look behind the image to see (as A. Green reminds us), beyond the appearance, the invisible object whose lure exerts such seduction on the beholder.[21]

I would like to suggest that behind the appearance of Tartuffe, behind Tartuffe as image, hides a more dangerous, more threatening fantasy, the fantasy of union. This fantasy is hinted at not only in Orgon's own words, "paix profonde," but also in Dorine's derision, "son tout," "son héros." This "hero" is, of course a mistress, and hides, I would suggest, the "image" of the One, towards which all narcissism tends[22] as the pre-Oedipal unity of the child and mother. I am hinting at Tartuffe's seduction of Orgon being essentially the play of a certain desire for the Mother. (Let us remember that the words that describe Tartuffe, "gros," "gras," "le teint vermeil," as well as the scene in which these words occur – a scene that associates Tartuffe with nourishment, the pleasure of ingestion – lurk in the memory of the text as one more possible association to the maternal as both attractive and repulsive.) What this particular illusion of unity reminds us of is, paradoxically, the floating image of a stage of pre-sexuality, of an amorphous composite body that exists before the scission, before the imposition of the Law of the Father, and the child's entrance into sexual difference and into language that traduces that difference. Orgon is seduced by Tartuffe as image – and this, I suggest, is the real danger of Tartuffe: the danger of the "imaginary" instance that coexists in a tenuous dialectic with the institution of the symbolic as the Law of the Father, and that represents for that law a destabilizing drive.[23]

The character who is meant to represent Tartuffe's moral opposite, Cléante, is also, in terms of the visual imagery that dominates the rhetoric of the play, the most interesting for his completely opposite visual valency in the economy of the text. Whereas Tartuffe, as hypocrite, is characterized by his imaging of himself, his production of himself as artifact that forces its recognition in the play's field of vision, Cléante is characterized, ethically, by his invisibility. He is, he tells us, in his use of words, transparent:

Et je vous ai trouvé.
Pour vous en dire net ma pensée en deux mots.

Je vous le dis encore, et parle avec franchise.

Cléante is clear and frank. In this he seems to be different from the other characters, who all exist in a universe of unclear signs, or at least in a world in which they are suspicious of their ability to interpret signs correctly. They would seem to represent a lingering malaise that signals us that for them, for the world of the play, for the world of Molière, the revolution in epistemology that (according to Foucault) was occurring at this time, carrying the world out of the order of resemblances and into the order of transparency, has not as yet taken place.[24] Or rather, it is taking place for some but not for others. For the other characters who are constantly interpreting Tartuffe's actions, who suspect him of being a hypocrite, there still remains, attached to the relation of words and things, an obscurity, an apotropaic talismanic quality that pushes them to interpretation without that interpretation being articulable as anything other than a "suspicion," a wary mistrust in which the possibility of their own error, their own inability to interpret correctly, floats just below the surface of their discourse.

Cléante, on the other hand, does not seem to have these problems, these doubts ("Je sais, pour toute ma science / Du faux avec le vrai faire la différence"). His identifying mark in the comedy is precisely a stance in the world that does not need interpretation. He is what he says. This, however, is neither as easy nor as unproblematic as it first appears. On the contrary, in a sense Cléante, the "honnête homme" of the play, is in perhaps the most ideologically overdetermined subject-position. If by "Classicism" we mean that epistemic moment when the difference between words and things is reduced to the merest hair's breadth, where words are the transparent signifier of reality, Cléante's definition of himself as "transparent" makes of him Classicism incarnate. With the transparency of Classicism coded as progress, we must ask ourselves what does it mean, in an Absolutist state, for a subject to be invisible to himself, to others, to power?

"Honnêteté" is what exists in society by not being seen. It is the position of the subject who is so entirely subjugated to the gaze of the Other (Monarch) that he has become one with this gaze. He has internalized it to such a degree as to become one with it. An "honnête homme ne se pique de rien" means that in the world of "honnêteté" one is "honnête" in one's inability to react in any way that would make one visible, call attention to one's presence, that would separate one from the total, symmetrical reflection of the Sovereign's gaze, or if we wish, of the gaze of society (an accepted set of social/value judgments) and be particularized. To the degree that Cléante is "frank" ("net") he is precisely not visible, cannot and will not exist as an "attrape-l'œil," as a spot that can stop, fix, the gaze of the world. It seems, therefore, that when a critic like G. Defaux states that Cléante is the center of the play, that Cléante is Molière's representative, he is correct, but perhaps not for those reasons he offers, for Defaux does not seem aware of the terrible price of invisibility, its terrible collusion with a power it apes, and that has already vampirized it (Cléante), and its (his) position in the world.[25]

The dynamics of the play, as we have been discussing them up to this point, all swirl around the visual, around the production and seduction of images and subject-positions. Tartuffe, as I have suggested, is the most coded visual presence in the play: his hypocrisy is dangerous precisely because it is essentially a false image, but one so intimately camouflaged that it confuses the essence of "true" meaning with only a superficial appearance of devotion. It is precisely this confusion, this invasion of "the true" − of, that is, an entire system by which a culture renders its productions verisimilous, "natural" − that is effaced by its colonization by the imaginary, by the seduction of the image.[26] In a further twist of our own interpretation, it now appears that what is really at stake in *Tartuffe*, what is the cause of its "scandal," is that the Law of the Father upon which the entire ideology of patriarchy is grounded, the symbolic order based on castration and difference, is being invaded and undermined by the Imaginary. Released from its subordination to order by Tartuffe's seduction of the Father, the Imaginary now threatens to overwhelm the entire domain of patriarchal authority.

If Tartuffe were only a "visual" image he would be much less effectively threatening. From the visual field Tartuffe parasitizes the symbolic itself by his mastery of devotional rhetoric (and from this rhetoric the entire semiotic order of Christianity). Not only does Tartuffe exist as a visual reflection for Orgon: more importantly, his narcissistically invested homilies and recriminations serve as a linguistic mirror that reflects back a troubling, troubled subjectivity to those who share the metaphysical premises of a language grounded in a severely dichotomous opposition between good and evil, sacrifice and redemption, heaven and hell. It is a discourse whose predicates suppose and uphold a universe of Law, of order, of God.

The slippage we have noted in Molière's own rhetoric between visual and lexical representations is encoded in the text of the play, where Tartuffe uses words to reflect back to his interlocutors his and their own bad faith:

> Dès que j'en vis briller la splendeur plus qu'humaine,
> De mon intérieur vous fûtes souveraine;
> De vos regards divins l'ineffable douceur
> Força la résistance où s'obstinait mon cœur.
> Elle surmonta tout, jeûnes, prières, larmes,
> Et tourna tous mes vœux du côté de vos charmes.
> Mes yeux et mes soupirs vous l'ont dit mille fois,
> Et pour mieux m'expliquer j'emploie ici la voix.
>
> (III, iii, 973–980)

Clearly in his mouth words serve as both offensive and defensive weapons. The seduction takes place in the moment of slippage, in the abandonment where one rhetorical trope evolves into the other. It is at this moment of aphanisis of language, its apparent vaporization as vision, that Tartuffe seduces Orgon, and hopes to seduce Elmire.

It is in this dangerous passage from the visual to the lexical that Tartuffe is most pernicious. Tartuffe's use of language brings out the inherent ambivalence of words, their status of sign rather than reality. Language is not a crystalline mediation between words and things but a turbulent, beckoning, ever-changing reflection of the person to whom the speaker addresses himself. Tartuffe uses words in such a manipulative way as to make them into self-conscious reflections not of some exterior reality but of their own unreality, of their own status as "social productions." Tartuffe's rhetoric, as seduction, infuses words with desire, unhinging them from any anchoring in a "reality," and sets them adrift as pure illusion. The effect of this seduction by rhetoric is to point out not the "truth" of a world grounded in language, but its vanity, its hollowness: what this language points to is itself. This is not a small accomplishment, for in the fervent religious climate of the seventeenth century (but also in ours as well, where perhaps not religion, but certainly other equally invested ideological systems, continually try to disguise their own predicates), when the medium of the message is shown to be free-floating it undermines any attempt at fixing a meaning that would be immutable, absolute.

In Tartuffe's mouth words are dangerously seductive, for they never point to any reality that is not him. His speech is an artificial, narcissistic mirror that Tartuffe turns to the world to capture in his person/discourse not its presence, not its material weight, but its metaphysical assumptions, its "invisibility": that is, those beliefs – religious, metaphysical, philosophical – that structure the world, that legislate the parameters inside of which individuals are subjected to Lav.. By his manipulation of the words governing that legislation Tartuffe points to their artificiality, their status as "artifact," rather than to their status as fact, and thereby undoes not only the illusion of "truth," and of religion, but also that of the family and of the State. Once these institutions have been set adrift as in the mirror of words, the subject formed at their interstice, as well as the very possibility of subjectivity, is shown to be impossible.

The full implications of this threat to the patriarchal family are staged for us in the scene that pits Damis against Tartuffe and which ends with Orgon's committing the most "unnatural" act on the seventeenth-century stage. This scene is particularly perverse in its demonstration that there is no truth (for Orgon) other than the truth of Tartuffe's image (verbal and visual). What strikes us about the scene is the representation of contrition, Tartuffe's miming the pose of supplication – he is on his knees – and how this image is used to counter the veracity of his confession, a confession that, although using words to say the "truth," reflects to Orgon not guilt but spiritual superiority. The dovetailing of word and image authorizes Orgon to hear, to interpret, those words in a sense that is directly contrary to their literal meaning, but perfectly consonant with their cosmetic function. All these words do is to use a rhetoric of Christian contrition to seduce Orgon, who does not hear the "truth", but sees an image:[27]

ORGON   (A son fils)   Ingrat!
TARTUFFE   Laissez-le en paix. S'il faut, à deux genoux,
   Vous demander sa grâce ...
ORGON, à Tartuffe   Hélas, vous moquez-vous?
   (à son fils)
   Coquin! vois sa bonté.   (III, vi, 1114–1116)

The scene which starts out with the exultation of the son who has finally, he believes, the proof of Tartuffe's perfidy in hand ends not with the conversion of the father to truth, but with the banishment of Damis. Damis is chased, cursed, from his father's house:

> Vite, quittons la place.
> Je te prive, pendard, de ma succession,
> Et te donne de plus ma malédiction.
> (III, vi, 1138–1140)

In his stead, Tartuffe is enthroned as his replacement:

> Je ne veux point avoir d'autre héritier que vous,
> Et je vais de ce pas, en fort bonne manière,
> Vous faire de mon bien donation entière.
>
> (III, vii, 1177–1179)

This scene can only be read as the final triumph of Tartuffe over the Law of the Father, if we understand Damis's banishment as a metaphorical castration of the son. In the ideology of patriarchy this must be also and coterminously a castration of the Father. By depriving himself of his "legal" progeny (in social, economic, and political terms) he is effectively and retroactively denying his own position in the realm of patrilineal descent and undoing his role as familial centre. It is for this reason that the father's "cutting off" of his son is the most heavily invested act in the play. It is here that the greatest threat to the family occurs. It is no longer in the realm of the repressed, but passes into the domain of the real – with potentially fatal consequences.

This act, the direct consequence of Orgon's perverted seduction by Tartuffe, is an "unnatural" act in several resonant senses. First, as I have mentioned, the castration of the son is also a self-mutilation – the deprivation of one's future as a man in a male-ordered economy of descent. By "castrating" the son the father effectively destroys the ties, the ties of sublimation, that bind him both to his past (his father) and his future (his son) along a well-ordered progression of male prerogative, based precisely on the repression of castration and its sublimation in an universal obedience that binds all men together in a masculine essentiality under the Law.[28] When Orgon refuses this sublimation, he not only threatens his own subjugation to the genealogical order of descent that defines him, gives him a place and an identity: he also threatens the "order" as such. He is effectively denying family as a system of male privilege.

Even more, it is clear that this destitution is intimately connected with a homosexual desire to be united to Tartuffe through the latter's union with his own daughter. When we consider the conflicted, unconscious sexual attractions between parents and offspring, Orgon's imposition of Tartuffe on Mariane, his insistence on their marriage, can only be seen as a sexual ploy whereby Mariane is being used to mediate Orgon's own unavowable ambivalence. She serves as the mediating object not only of Tartuffe's lust, but of Orgon's, and even more perversely, of Orgon's lust for Tartuffe. It is only through her that Orgon can ever achieve the unthinkable, but no less desired, union with Tartuffe. Only by eliminating the son, the symbol of his own investment in heterosexual masculinity, and by substituting, through a marriage to his daughter, a new lover/ son, can Orgon, in one more avatar of exchange, be placed in his daughter's bed and there be united with the Father/son of his own desire. Thus by threatening the family at its very heart, by substituting for an economy of masculine descent and prerogative a descent through the female (the prospective marriage of Mariane to Tartuffe), by the intrusion of an homoerotic passion (produced, as we've seen, by the lure of the imaginary) into the world of heterosexual ordering (the symbolic ordering of sexuality) there results a strange crossing-over of familial/sexual lines that effectively condemns first the family, and then the State that it reflects, to its ruin.

By the end of Act III, therefore, the family seems to be mortally wounded. Sexually and politically it has been undone. It needs only the economic "coup de grâce" of Act IV to be effectively eliminated. It is at this juncture, when all seems lost, when Orgon seems to have abandoned all contact with (familial) reality, all contact with himself, that the family regroups around Elmire, that strangely ambivalent figure of femininity (mother/wife/mistress), to save itself from its own demise.

By all reckoning Act IV is one of the most "hilarious" in Molière's comic production. While up to this point it may appear that I have left aside, forgotten, that the *Tartuffe* is a comedy I have only been waiting to arrive at the high point of the comic to demonstrate what I stated at the beginning of this essay: that the visual is integral to the comic aspect of the play, that it is the pivotal link between the internal world of the spectacle and the exterior reality of the parterre, and that rather than undermining my own argument it – the comedy – is essential for understanding the imbrication of laughter and ideology in the formation of the Classical subject.

When things are at their most desperate Elmire steps in to take the matter in hand. Although presented as a rather shallow character, Elmire has insight enough to know that the only way to re-establish flagging familial order – an order in which, we note, she, like the other women, is but an object of exchange among men – is to engage Orgon where he is most vulnerable, most desirous, in his scoptophilia:

> J'admire, encore un coup, cette faiblesse étrange.
> Mais que me répondrait votre incrédulité
> Si je vous faisais voir qu'on vous dit vérité?
>
> (IV, iv, 1338–1340)

Quel homme! Au moins répondez-moi.
Je ne vous parle pas de nous ajouter foi;
Mais supposons ici que, d'un lieu qu'on peut prendre,
On vous fît clairement tout voir et tout entendre,
Que diriez-vous alors de votre homme de bien?

(IV, iv, 1343–1347)

The comedy of this scene that Elmire stages for the pleasure of her husband and ours is, I suggest, intimately connected to the scopic drive as it orchestrates what is, finally, a "dirty joke" in the sense Freud gives to this term:

Generally speaking, a tendentious joke calls for three people: in addition to the one who makes the joke there must be a second who is taken as the object of the hostile or sexual aggressiveness, and a third in whom the joke's aim of producing pleasure is fulfilled.[29]

I am less interested in the particulars of this scene than in its dynamics. What finally is funny? What makes us laugh? Clearly, it seems to me, the cause of our mirth is Elmire's discomfiture, her vulnerability to Tartuffe's lust from which she expected to be protected by her husband, while her expectations are deceived. Our laughter is produced precisely because Orgon does *not* burst forth from his hiding place to save his wife from the sexual advances of Tartuffe. We laugh because he constantly delays appearing, constantly waits for something else. His waiting, which increases Elmire's anxiety, makes us laugh. What exactly, we might ask, is he waiting *for*? What, in other words, does he want to see? The answer to this enigma, the punch line of the joke, is given us by him in response to his own mother's refusal to believe Tartuffe's duplicity (a reversal, a comic come-uppance that repeats Orgon's own "blindness" at the beginning of the play) in Act V. To her incredulity, to her refusal to believe, what now he knows to be true – knows it because he has "visual proof" – he sputters out the truth of his own desire, the cause of our laughter in Act IV:

ORGON Vous me feriez damner, ma mère. Je vous di
    Que j'a vu de mes yeux un crime si hardi.
MME PERNELLE Les langues ont toujours du venin à répandre,
    Et rien n'est ici-bas qui s'en puisse défendre.
ORGON C'est tenir un propos de sens bien dépourvu.
    Je l'ai vu, dis-je, vu, de mes propres yeux vu,
    Ce qu'on appelle vu ...
MME PERNELLE   Il est besoin
    Pour accuser les gens, d'avoir de justes causes;

Et vous deviez attendre à vous voir sûr des choses.
ORGON   Hé! diantre! le moyen de m'en assurer mieux?
Je devais donc, ma mère, attendre qu'à mes yeux
Il eût ... Vous me feriez dire quelque sottise.

                                    (V, iii, 1670–1676, 1684–1689)

In the ellipses of the three dots ("Would you have wanted me to wait until he had ... her in front of my very eyes?") is the punch line of our visual joke. The answer is, of course, "yes" (and "no"). What Orgon was waiting for, what kept him in his hiding place and kept us laughing, was, I would suggest, his desire to see the "primal scene" of adult sexuality. He wanted (we wanted) to "see" Tartuffe reveal his desire, unveil the "phallus" that had masqueraded as "indifference" (that is, not there, not visible, "no-thing") and by so doing recreate an Œdipal scenario that would "correctly" sort out the confused sexual roles, that would establish the primacy of the symbolic over the imaginary and re-insert, into confusion, order. In other words, we were all waiting to see Tartuffe rape Elmire.

What this scene also underlines for us is the sadistically aggressive side of the scopic drive that pleasures in the suffering sacrifice of Elmire, thus pointing to the collusion between the laughter evoked by Molière's comedy with an entire patriarchal order that is based on the sacrifice, destruction, of women.[30] This "destruction" is not, however, a simple exploitation. Elmire situates herself in this scene; she in fact orchestrates this scene, which places her in the center of everyone's gaze as a sexual object. It is as if the only choice left to women in an Absolutist, patriarchal monarchy was the pleasure in the masochistic sacrifice of their subjectivity. In order to exist, they must opt for the negative empowerment of their own alienation. Women must assume the alienating position of object (object of exchange) in the sexual attraction/rivalry of men. Elmire places herself squarely in the visual field of Orgon (and, by extension, of the spectators, whose own gaze is relayed by Orgon's) as the mediating object, the sexual object of exchange between the men. This object "exchanges" a male homoerotic binding for the sadistic consumption of the female, who exists in this scene as the symbol of sexual difference. She is the "difference" that assures men of their difference, as power, as superiority. In this scene of sado-masochistic aggression and laughter, Elmire assumes the non-identity that is hers in a patriarchal society, sacrifices her subjectivity in order to save that society from its own self-destruction in a homoerotic embrace that would effectively signal the disappearance of all those signifying systems based on the initial, essential imposition of sexual scission, of the entire semiotic order based on phallocentric symbolization which is generated around the fear/fantasy of castration.

The importance of Elmire's self-sacrifice cannot be underestimated for the dynamics of subjectivity that subtend the production of the comedy in the play. As I've suggested, what she stages for the pleasure/appetite of Orgon's eye is the origin of his "I," that is the origin of his subjectivity as that subjectivity comes into being through the imposition of difference, through the imposition on the imaginary of the Law of scission, which is, as Lacan has claimed, coterminously the entrance into language/sexuality. What the primal scene orchestrates, what it fantasizes, is the "origin of the individual who always sees him/herself figured in the scene," as the product of sexual difference.[31] We can thus also understand why structurally Orgon cannot come to his wife's rescue, for in this scene, caught up as he is in his/its fantasmatic power, he exists not as husband, but as child. He has effectively been placed in such a way that his *Schaulust*, that has held him in its sway, is here brought back to its/his originary moment, where it is directed at what it always wanted: to see sex, to see sexual splitting (as difference) and in that splitting to found Orgon's subjectivity as gendered. The trauma of the scene, as Freud reminds us in his analysis of the Wolfman, is precisely

the wish for the sexual satisfaction which he was at that time longing to obtain from his father. The strength of this wish made it possible to revive a long-forgotten trace in his memory of a scene which was able to show him what sexual satisfaction from his father was like; and the result was terror, horror of the fulfilment of the wish . . .[32]

Freud theorizes, in another essay, that the fear of this castration is inseparable from the "narcissistic interest" young boys have in their genital organ.[33] By following this hypothetical line of reasoning, we are thus able to see the coming together in this scene of all the visual/psychic elements that have structured the play all along – their coming together and their sorting out, through Orgon's "shock" (trauma) of seeing what all along has been denied him. This shock shatters the utopic plenitude of Orgon's vision of Tartuffe. In a sense it is the shock of visual excess that imposes on the subject held in the sway of the imaginary the cutting weight of the symbolic, of sexuality as difference. The vision is a sexual one in that it reveals the sex of the Father/Mother. By revealing (uncovering, showing) their truth, it does away with Tartuffe's "illusion," his masquerade, and its projection of non-difference. This flashing, blinding vision of sexuality re-situates Orgon into the order of masculine, sexual economy, returns him to the center of his *oikos* as "Father" (that is, no longer sexual mate of Tartuffe, but sexual rival), and reinstates the integrity of the family:

> Comme aux tentations s'abandonne votre âme!
> Vous épousiez ma fille, et convoitiez ma femme!
> J'ai douté fort longtemps que ce fût tout de bon,
> Et je croyais toujours qu'on changerait de ton;
> Mais c'est assez avant pousser le témoignage:
> Je m'y tiens, et n'en veux, pour moi, pas davantage.
>
> (IV, vii, 1545–1550)

Orgon's re-inscription in his "place" comes, alas, too late. He no longer is master of his household. In fact, there is no longer any household. Tartuffe is now in legal possession of Orgon's house, and in a scathing reversal orders Orgon and his family out:

> C'est à vous d'en sortir, vous qui parlez en maître:
> La maison m'appartient, je le ferai connaître.
>
> (IV, vii, 1557–1558)

So the comedy that began with the absence of an *oikodespotès* ends (almost) in the very real absence of *oikos*. The family, defined most radically by its situation as that unit that lives together under one roof, is now roofless, no longer "domesticated" but cast out on to the street, with (as we soon learn) its head under the threat of death. The family is symbolically, but also legally and very physically, at the point of its dispersion, its ruin, its extinction.

It is, of course, at this juncture, when all seems lost, when Tartuffe as pure lust has reduced the family to nothingness, that some exterior force must intervene to save the family – and thus the state – from its demise. When we understand the intimate connection that the sexual/political economy of the family has for the regime of Absolute monarchy, how it is the basic and most heavily invested of all those "apparatuses" by which the state defines itself, maintains itself and its subjects in the proper relation to their own sexuality, to that sexuality as "proper" and "natural," the ending of the play no longer seems quite so contrived, the *deus ex machina* no longer so unmotivated. Rather, this *deus ex machina*, which in this instance is a *rex-*(s)*ex-machina* is so totally imbricated in the ideology of family, patriarchy and sexuality that has been threatened by Tartuffe's image-ing of himself that it/he cannot enter on to the scene of comedy. He enters it as the "invisible" (the prince is not seen, he is represented), as the "real" veiled phallus – the sign of power/desire that functions as the Law of the symbolic who, through the very visual imagery that has dis-oriented the subject/father of the play, restores it/him to its and his rightful place.

The entire metaphoric structure of the last speech, the speech of truth and resolution, describes the Prince, his power, in visual terms. What distinguishes the Prince is that his vision, as opposed to the unreliable father's, is infallible:

> Nous vivons sous un prince ennemi de la fraude,
> Un prince dont les yeux se font jour dans les cœurs,
> Et que ne peut tromper tout l'art des imposteurs.
>
> (V, scène dernière, 1906–1908)

The prince sees through artifice. He alone sees what is true and is capable of separating out truth from falsehood. His vision is piercing, penetrating; it sees beyond appearance into the "soul" of his subjects, into their true nature: "D'abord, il a percé, par ses vives clartés / Des replis de son cœur toutes les lâchetés" It is also an irresistible force ("de pièges plus fins on le voit se défendre"). His vision is "straight" ("droite vue") and upholds a rigid understanding ("ferme raison") of the workings of human nature. What these obvious references bolster is the phallic presence of the prince, the prince as phallus, who, precisely, controls and directs the "excessive" drive of *Schaulust* into culturally acceptable channels of desire. In a strange, paradoxical way, this sovereign – who is described as an "Omniscient eye/I," as the invisible but all-present, all-knowing model who watches over all his subjects, who sees into their innermost recesses, who knows who's been bad or good:

> Et c'est le prix qu'il donne au zèle qu'autrefois
> On vous vit témoigner en appuyant ses droits,
> Pour montrer que son cœur sait, quand moins on y pense,
> D'une bonne action verser la récompense,
> Que jamais le mérite avec lui ne perd rien,
> Et que mieux que du mal il se souvient du bien
>
> (V, scène dernière, 1939–1944)

and who deals out fit punishments or rewards – is never there. He is not localizable except in a discourse of invisibility, a discourse of his vision/power that cannot be seen but is everywhere. In a sense, what this panoptic power of the prince represents is his power to be part of every one of his subjects.[34] They are part of his gaze (the best example, again is Cléante). This vision is an internalized sense of one's being watched, of living under an omnipotent eye. What this sense of being contained in the eye of some never-present beholder represents is the coming into being of a subjugation and subject-ivization that, although repressive, is felt as salutary: it saves the family (that is, us) from its own demise. It is only under the eye of this just Monarch/father, in his adoration by his subjects, in their subjugation to him, that the play can end. The anxiety caused by Tartuffe's near-destruction of the family, his playing too freely with all those systems that his manipulation of images shows to be too vulnerable to ground subjectivity in any way that is not already undermined, is itself overcome by and through the "incorporation" of the Absolutist gaze. At the end of the play the family, newly situated at the very center of its invisible Lord's field of vision, significantly reestablishes its pre-eminent situation at the center of the represented universe. Sure of its newly bolstered foundations, the family, as the mediating locus of an Absolutist imperative of the sexual and economic organization of society, can safely propel itself into a future of perpetual continuation, and this "comedy" that almost fell into the tragic can at last end, as all comedies do, with the promise of marriage.

6

RACINE'S CHILDREN

Est-ce qu'en holocauste aujourd'hui présenté,
Je dois, comme autrefois la fille de Jephté,
Du Seigneur par ma mort apaiser la colère?
(*Athalie*, IV, i, 1259–1261)[1]

"Sa haine va toujours plus loin que son amour."
(*Mithridate*, I, v, 354)

"La grande angoisse humaine est de tendre les bras vers un être
qui se révèle meurtrier."[2]
(Ch. Mauron)

Among the innovations he brought to the seventeenth-century theatre,
Racine was, we are told, the first to place a child on the stage.[3]
This novelty transforms the world of Classical dramaturgy into a
compelling scenario of horror and sacrifice; for this child, led out into
the public's embrace, is brought forth upon the scene of Classicism
as its victim. Racine puts children on his stage to immolate them,
or at least to keep the threat of immolation suspended over their
heads. The impact of this threatened slaying informs a complex
vortex of dramatic, social, and psycho-sexual tensions around which
swirls, in ever more opaque waves of poetic horror, the tragic
message of Racinian theater. For while this child is offered up as a
propitiatory victim to satisfy the anger/love of the gods, to slake
the unquenchable bloodlust of his own parents and family, the tragic
"frisson" of his impending immolation also functions as a lure
ensnaring and appeasing the desire for theater – for a theater of
cruelty and beauty, of terror and release – of the audience.

From *Andromaque*, the first radically new tragedy of his career,
to *Athalie*, his last, and including such plays as *Mithridate, Iphigénie*
and *Phèdre*, to a greater or lesser degree the intensity of tragic
emotion turns around the haunting scenario of the child that must be
killed. The obsessive nature of this dramatic fantasy of infanticide,

especially as it forms an inextricable knot with its obverse, patricide, has not gone unnoticed or unexplored by those writers who have renewed Racinian criticism in the last half of our century: Goldmann, Mauron, Barthes. For both Mauron and Barthes this fantasmatic knot is the central issue of Racinian dramaturgy.[4] For both, however, infanticide seems to play a lesser role compared to the more heavily invested scenarios of patricide (and matricide) – perhaps because this latter act, the perverse triumph of the powerless over the powerful, is heavily invested (as Barthes suggests) with political implications. Racine's theater is haunted by the same scenarios of patricide/regicide that we have already seen at work in Corneille and Molière. In the pages that follow I would like to focus my attention on what, I believe, has been more easily elided, because too uncomfortable, too unthinkable: the direct attack on children in Racine's theater and on its implications for seventeenth-century Absolutism and for twentieth-century terror. What does it mean for a society to stage for its own horror and fascination the immolation of its children, the sacrifice of its future, and, of course, the obliteration of its past?

As we move through the great tragedies, that "space" L. Bersani has called the "clean blankness of being,"[5] that vast field of possibility that was left to Astyanax at the end of *Andromaque*, gradually and inexorably, like a "peau de chagrin," shrinks, turns in on itself. Caught up in the ever more convoluted play of familial binding, it looses its purely immanent potential, to become, finally, bound in and to the representation of the last, the only, child of Racinian tragedy: Eliacin/Joas of *Athalie*. In a curious fashion this move from a child whose function in representation is purely fantasmatic – Astyanax is never seen on stage – to the final actual presence of the child (Eliacin) corresponds to an obverse dialectic on the part of the Racinian parent. As Mauron has shown, the father who is absent in the first series of tragedies returns in *Mithridate*, grows in stature and terror through *Phèdre* and ends in *Athalie* as pure immanence: the Father finally become one with God. Nevertheless, as the very titles of his tragedies attest – *Andromaque, Iphigénie, Phèdre, Athalie* – this paternal apotheosis is necessarily accomplished through and across a dialectics of sexuality, of a mythic struggle for dominance of the opposed forces of masculinity and femininity. In contrast to this receding image of the Father we have the ever more precise, more disquieting, representation of the Racinian mother. In this battle for supremacy, a struggle that ends (as we know) with the ultimate destruction of the powerful, threatening mother (Athalie) and with the triumph of the Father (let us not forget that the very last word Racine wrote for the theater was "père"), it is the women, not the men, who are the center of the Racinian world. Certainly, it is the passion of those heroines (Andromaque, Agrippine, Roxane, Phèdre, Athalie) and their ultimate defeat that is at the center of the most troubling of Racine's tragedies. It is this coupling of "femininity" with maternity, and this maternity's indentured service to patriarchy, that creates the tragic dimension of Racine's greatest heroines.

It is at this juncture of the mythic confrontation of the paternal and maternal in and across the passion of the Racinian heroine that the mediating role of the child comes to the fore. As the child becomes more and more "real" (that is "on stage"), the Father becomes more and more unreal, or at least more the pure fantasm of the Father who has always haunted Racinian tragedy as some distant, cruel, punishing other – the "dieu caché." It is, therefore, in this move towards a father who is pure sublimation, pure "absence," in this drive towards the transcendent order of the One, that Racinian tragedy would seem to play out the Absolutist imperative that we have seen essayed in the tragic parcours of Corneille and in the comic seriousness of Molière. It would appear – and this comes as no surprise – that the Law of the Father, inherited from his predecessors, but more importantly, from the invisible parameters of seventeenth-century Absolutism, from the fascination with the images and imaginary of the Sun-Father-King, also legislates, not unequivocally but with persistent force and resolve, the tragic universe of Racine's women and children.

What makes Racinian tragedy particularly compelling is perhaps the ease with which Racine functioned within the confines of Classicism's aesthetic parameters. Unlike Corneille, Racine seems to have used those unities of time, place and action to his advantage, seems to have been able with no trouble at all to fit his dramatic vision into the very straitened limits of neo-Classical conventions. The resulting plays inhabit a tragic locus novel in its intensity and narrowness of focus. It is within the constricted confines of this new tragic space that the two main vectors of Racine's dramatic plots – the emergence and apotheosis of the Father, the passion and destruction of the Mother – meet and cross in the sacrifice (real or threatened) of the child. This tightly organized, compressed tragic arena is always represented in Racine as the space of the family. Racinian tragedy is always a family affair.[6] In the world of Classical dramaturgy, this tightening represents one more suffocating twist of the tragic knot that condemns the subject of this tragedy to ever

more violent efforts to escape his/her fate, a fate that seems to close
ever more tightly around him/her, with harrowing consequences.

The narrowing of the tragic, familial locus allows us to speculate
on the very major differences between Racinian and Cornelian
dramaturgy and on the subjectivity this dramaturgy inscribes. As
I have suggested, Cornelian tragedy would seem to correspond to
that historical passage that M. Foucault has hypothesized as "le
moment du grand renfermement": that is, that moment when those
structures defining self and other gradually but inexorably shift
European civilization out of the order of the analogous and into the
world of Classical representation.[7] Corneille would represent this
moment of passage precisely by figuring it in the clearly delineated
sexual/political divisions that legislate his dramatic universe: the
importance of symmetry – sexual, political and aesthetic – is worked
out in his plays against the larger canvas of a social conflict that
pits the individual against the family/state. Nevertheless there is
still, in the Corneille of the great tragedies, a separation, if only the
separation of the mirror, between family and state: the one reflects
and stands in a homologous relation to the other. In Racine, however, we have moved to a world already on the other side of that
great divide, a world that is firmly entrenched in the *epistemè* of
Classical representation. What this means for Racinian tragedy is
manifold. On the one hand there is no longer any separation between
family and State; dramatically from the beginning (we shall return
to this in a moment), in *La Thébaïde*, the family *is* the State. There
is no longer any division possible between the political dimensions
of the tragic and the private/sexual world of the protagonists. The
"origin" of tragedy, the "origin" of family are one: the founding
moment of the State is a sexual/political moment, the coupling of
the throne and the bed:

> Malgré tout son orgueil, ce monarque si fier,
> A son trône, à son lit daigna l'associer ...
> > *(Bajazet*, II, i, 467–468)

> Peut-être on t'a conté la fameuse disgrâce
> De l'altière Vasthi, dont j'occupe la place.
> Lorsque le roi, contre elle enflammé de dépit,
> La chassa de son trône, ainsi que de son lit.
> > *(Esther*, I, i, 33–36)

On the other hand, what this also means is that once reduced to
its most intimate concentrated dynamic – what happens once the
great enclosure is accomplished, once there is no longer any outside

at all, once we are all trapped in the suffocating space of this Family/ State – is that the clear boundaries of sexual symmetry are blurred. As the exacerbation between characters and desires is turned inward, it becomes internalized as conflict and doubling, contradiction and bad faith. As R. Barthes has remarked, this new dynamic signals a profound change in seventeenth-century sexuality, for what happens in Racine, as opposed to Corneille, is that sexuality, as a supposed "natural," biological distinction, is confounded: "nature" is shown to be a play of forces, a play that determines, by situating the strong against the weak, the executioners from the victims, a redistribution of sexual roles.[8] Sexuality now becomes a production, the production of political forces rather than the unmediated fiat of biology. The essentialization of masculinity and femininity, so firmly articulated (even if to be undermined) in the Cornelian canon, is no longer operative in Racine.

In Racine's internalization of difference the remarkably stable "sexual essentiality" of Corneille's great plays is inverted, confounded and confused. While in Corneille difference (that is, inner conflict) is imposed from the outside – the hero's dilemma is conventionally an impossible option between his/her sexual desire and the correct political/social choice that is antithetical to it – that dilemma is external to those desires. It is in the opposition between the individual and the social that conflict is born in Corneille. A sense of self, of one's subjectivity, emerges as the suture of that conflict. The "moi" of the Cornelian hero/heroine (cf. Rodrigue and Chimène, Pauline and Polyeucte, Camille and Horace) issues triumphant precisely because it overcomes the conflict by repressing the personal and balming the wounds of desire's sacrifice by jubilating in its own aggrandized reflection in the mirror of the Polis.

In Racine, however – and this is perhaps a sign of his "modernity" – the difference is already a "difference within." The characters suffer first and foremost because they struggle with an internal division that they seem incapable of suturing, that refuses a compromise with the omnipresent social gaze which envelops them and increases their sense of always being somehow lacking, guilty. This interior difference, which we can schematize as a form of collective and individual paranoia, a sense of always being watched and of always watching oneself being watched, has a double function in the definition of Racinian subjectivity.[9] This split is cast outward into the world in all those "doubles" that populate the Racinian universe, and interiorized as (guilty) conscience. This internal conflict condemns Racinian protagonists to an abortive prolepsis: they always project into the future a harmonization in the (external) world of what cannot be soothed in their own being. Secondly, this split within compels them backwards into their past, towards their genealogy, where once again they cannot escape the duality that inheres in them, their being always a dual being, the product of sexual union. In this way, we will see that that union – that is, sexuality, the two that produce one, the one that is always two – is firmly and inevitably situated at the center of the tragic dilemma. For in the world of the Absolute it is this impossible, essential dichotomy that is untenable.

Significantly, Racine's step forward in tragic complexity is represented as a backward movement in representation. Racine retreats from the stage of history and returns to the more archaic cosmology of myth for his greatest creations – *Andromaque, Iphigénie, Phèdre*. All of these different scenarios are affiliated in their genealogy, as Philip Lewis has demonstrated, to the overriding myth of Œdipus, his family, his descendants, and with the consequences of his fate.[10] Even those historically based tragedies, *Britannicus* and *Mithridate*, or the Biblical tragedy of *Athalie* can be seen, conjuring up as they do forces of an "unconscious" familial-sexual terror, to supersede the merely picturesque qualities of the historical and to plunge back into the mysterious, sacred world of Œdipal fantasies. All the tragedies in the Racinian canon are linked to a common grounding in a mythic vision that is at once familial and terrifying. Could we offer as an hypothesis that the entire Racinian endeavor is merely to rescript, in an obsessive return of the past, the story of Œdipus as it intersects with Racine's own "personal myth(ology)"? It would, it seems to me, be more fruitful both to acknowledge the obvious hold on Racine of this conflict of subjectivity that the Œdipus myth represents – especially as it acts out the imbrication of desire and Law in and through the subject formed at its interstice – but even more important, to ask why and to what effect does this re-writing of Œdipus as the drama/tragedy of familial sexuality appear at this historic juncture? What is the importance of the re-representation of Œdipus on the stage of seventeenth-century Absolutism? How and why does the theater mediate the relation between cultural myths and individual identity?

It is at this junction that we can begin, in almost tautological fashion, to understand the intimate, inextricable relation that ties the birth of the individual subject, as a subject of a law that pre-exists him/her, to the mysteries of family in the elaboration of a social network that passes inexorably through the myth, real or imagined, of (human) sacrifice:

La vertu de cette thériaque qu'est le mythe provient donc d'une sorte d'unifi-cation, comme d'un entraînement, à partir justement des différences que chacun découvre dans sa relation au mythe, et qui, en définitivè, rejoignent ainsi une "voie commune." De sorte que partant d'une singularité sans avenir, ou même pouvant être néfaste, il entretient une fascination, des identifications, quant à un projet commun. L'individu, par ce biais, arrive à accepter, d'ailleurs, à son insu, les lois, sociales, morales surtout, pour lesquelles sa structure n'était point faite. Nous y verrions un effet "fétiche" du mythe par rapport aux pulsions du sujet.[11]

Using this definition of how myth operates as my starting point, I would argue that it is this "fetishistic" function of myth that Racine's tragedy stages for us, representing the impossible demands of Absolutist ideology for the order of the One in a subject who is always double, always subjected to difference, to sexual difference. Without wishing to be too reductive of the enormous complexity of Racinian tragedy, nor ignore the equally intricate involution of Racine's personal history in the social problems of his period, I think that we can, for hypothetical reasons, reduce the conflict of Racinian tragedy to the battle for integrity in a subject whose very existence is not integral, that is not one, but two. At the same time, and by the very same token, this duality, this duplicity which must be removed, repressed or extirpated, which forms the impediment propelling tragic action and informing the very being of the tragic hero, is at the very heart of myth as it constantly attempts to replay, to refashion the journey of the subject away from forces of duality and contra-diction towards an attempted (but always unsuccessful) compromise with societal laws.

It is perhaps here that Racinian tragedy as a form of representa-tion is most intimately reflective of its sociological context, of the context not so much of "French society" of the seventeenth century as of an Absolutist ideology: of the political ideology of Louis XIV's court despite the real and often complex divergences in that ideology's apparent workings. What is really at stake, I would argue, in the hermeneutics of the Racinian corpus is not so much determining the exact correspondences between his immediate social milieu and his texts as understanding the ways in which his plays express the desires of that or those milieu(s). In spite of the enormous differences in the details of their works, the representation of those desires situates Racine along the same vector as Corneille and Descartes, Colbert and Poussin, in elaborating a paradigm of the seventeenth-century *socius*. This *socius* corresponds to a certain political, economic and libidinal strategy, delineating, perhaps unbeknownst to itself, a being subject and subjected to the rule of the One, the law as it is handed down by a King who is also a Father (of his people); whose family, whose court becomes the mimetic model for the indivisible organization of society in the hierarchy of paternal descent.

The newly emerging subject of the seventeenth century can no more than we live his individuality, the impossible rupture between the interior and the exterior, between the emerging split of the private and public, without the myth of family and the family as myth. It is Racine's *mise-en-scène* of this chiasmus of the public and the private as tragedy that attempts to suture that rift. Despite all the socially specific elements that can and have been extrapolated from his plays, the mythological scenario precisely transcends a particular historical moment and plunges us back into a time that paradoxically existed before the "setting" of the Law, before our own subjugation. Racinian tragedy situates us over and over again at that moment when the Law as the law of difference and denial is about to be; at that trembling moment of violence and terror when the subject is subjugated to that which s/he desires and refuses, to that moment when we become "One" in the sacrifice of our ambivalence. This sacrifice is the epiphanous moment in which Racinian tragedy engages us, forcing us into the roles of both officiating priest and propitiatory victim as the immolation plays on and out our own subjectivity.

This dichotomization of subjectivity could be seen, on one level at least, as representing the battleground where an impossible desire for an integrity of being precisely forecloses its realization as anything other than a fantasy. The invisible Oedipal parameters informing subjectivity as an impossible plenitude of being fluctuate in Racine between two more archaic – one might call them pre-Oedipal – poles that are immediately gendered: on the one hand, the haunting guilt, an original debt to the father whose love can only be won by suffering and death (the sadistic spectacle of that suffering), and on the other, the alternative of a dispersion, either as the aphanisis of the subject in a suffocating embrace or in its violent sundering in a murderous attack of the mother (the masochistic, because passive, pole). In either case, what we have is an archaic fantasy of a destructive, devouring, merciless parent – a Father/Mother – in whose gaze stands, or rather trembles, the child.[12]

The irony of this compelling fantasy is that in order to attain that Father, to have him acknowledge the existence of his offspring, the child must first risk the passage through castration (sacrifice) and death. It is this desire, that inheres in all the protagonists of Racine's world and that pushes them, in their drive for totality, against themselves, that in a perverse fashion is exactly what, because they desire it, proves itself to be forever beyond their grasp, forever an ideal that drives them on, that sunders them in their very being, and that, despite their own subservience to that desire/God, can do nothing other than crush them.

Across the Racinian universe, a world that in its essentially "mythic" dimension defies change and constantly recasts as its outer limits the same desire for a compromise that is in its essence impossible, and whose impossibility forms its tragic center, we do move from the imminence of sacrifice to its transcendence, or rather its reversal. It is in this space of reversal, where the child's sacrifice becomes the slaying of the parent, Pyrrhus/Athalie (and for the time being I would like to insist upon the sexual indeterminacy of both that child and that parent) that we must dwell if we are to unravel the different strands of politics and sexuality, of family as the ur-model of politics, that constantly inheres in Racinian tragedy.

In his preface to *Athalie*, among the other picturesque details about the ancient Hebrews, their religion and the schism that forms the history of his new tragedy, Racine reminds us that the temple, the scene of his tragedy, was situated exactly on that spot, that "mountain," where Abraham took his son Isaac to be sacrificed to his God:

C'était une tradition assez constante que la montagne sur laquelle le temple fut bâti était la même montagne où Abraham avait autrefois offert en sacrifice son fils Isaac.   (*Préface*, ed. Rat, p. 651)

This same detail is repeated in the play itself:

> N'êtes-vous pas ici sur la montagne sainte
> Où le père des Juifs sur son fils innocent
> Leva sans murmurer un bras obéissant,
> Et mit sur un bûcher ce fruit de sa vieillesse,
> Laissant à Dieu le soin d'accomplir sa promesse,
> Et lui sacrifiant, avec ce fils aîné,
> Tout l'espoir de sa race en lui seul renfermé?
> (*Athalie*, IV, v, 1438–1444)

Racine's double insistence on recalling this other origin – monotheism's origin in the sacrifice of the son by the father – only reinforces the love/hate ambivalence that we know to be the lot of all human children caught up in the conflicted desires of the Oedipal scenario. The father/God of the old testament, who demands unreflective obedience to his Law and punishes all transgression with death, can be seen to correspond to the tyrannical, murderous, unreachable father of the primal horde, who castrates his sons.[13] In a curious fashion the myth of revenge, at least in those great religious myths that Racine also inscribes in his text, never actually represents the destruction of the father. That revenge is always occulted, always repressed but none the less present, as fantasy, and perhaps as theater. It is here, in Racine's re-inscription in his theater of the founding myths of western culture, in his imbrication of the trajectory of individual desire (the Œdipus complex) and social idealization, that we can begin to understand the role and the fascination of infanticide/parricide in Classicism's tragic universe. The Racinian stage functions as an altar upon which is played out, through the fantasies of a particular playwright, an entire society's own feelings of ambivalence towards those very structures, sexual and political, that define it to itself as culture.

When we look at seventeenth-century France, so invested as it now seems to us with the cult, the spectacular ceremonial, of Monarchy, with the adoration of the Monarch as the vehicle for social ideals, and if we understand the ideological investments of those images of the Monarch in Christianity (especially as it too, in that culture, was undergoing a resurgence in intensity, was re-experiencing with delectation the passion of Christ), we can begin to link the different strands that lead from the individual to the social as a passage (in a strongly patriarchal society) that necessarily must pass through what is most intensely disturbing, most searingly incomprehensible (cf. Pascal) in that cycle, its kingpin and its vanishing point: God's sacrifice of his only son.

Anchoring his explorations in the fundamental discoveries of Freud in both the clinical and metapsychological works, the French psychoanalyst Guy Rosolato has attempted to examine the irreducible importance of the role of child sacrifice in all three of the major western monotheisms. Starting with the ancient Hebrews, the (interrupted) sacrifice of his son Isaac by Abraham seals the alliance between God and his chosen people. In Christianity, this immolation is carried out in the putting to death of God himself, in the person of the Son, only to be recuperated in the myth of resurrection. Islam, too, resorts to the ritual sacrifice of the son (Ali) to mark a major moment in its foundation.[14] While in Greek religion infanticide appeared to be the least important of familial crimes, with the advent of the major monotheisms, all religions of the Father, infanticide becomes the central most heavily invested act, the incomprehensible, originary act of that religion's mediating relation between God and the world.[15]

Racine's children

In patriarchal societies, such as those in which monotheism as a religion of the father was born, and as it was being reaffirmed in seventeenth-century France, the unthinkable, the blind spot of ideology is any direct attack upon the father in any of his legal, theological or merely familial avatars.[16] This does not mean, however, that the intense feelings these social organizations carry with them simply do not exist. Rather, the more intense the attachments, the more intense the love that is demanded, the more intense the feelings of aggressivity and of guilt that must be repressed or sublimated into acceptable outlets. In a curiously paradoxical analysis Rosolato hypothesizes that what is actually at stake in all the myths of child sacrifice so essential to western religion is the actual murderous drives against − the attack on − the father.[17]

This psychoanalytic scenario attempts to explain, on the one hand, how fathers and children, within a hierarchically disposed system of male devolution, are locked into a struggle engaging our most powerful emotions and desires for power, for sovereignty. The son seeks to take the place of the Father, the father tries to retain his pre-eminence by eliminating the son. Nevertheless, what we must also realize is their mutual imbrication, in social terms, in a power structure that is there to receive them and their ambivalence in such a way that this ambivalence be socially mediated so as to protect society against its own dissolution. Racine's theater, especially in its occultation of the conflict between the father and his children in the passion of the heroine, can be seen as one form of mediation where the constant reciprocity of violence and desire is played out for the spectators as a projection of their own potentially dangerous ambivalence towards the parental structure into which they come and which they must, through a sacrifice of their own inherent duality, reproduce.

Racine's insistence on situating his plays − and here *Athalie* is only the most concentrated example − at the violent center of the sacred, at the locus where sacrifice and spectacle are conflated and form the single, densely contracted scene of tragedy, always responds to another scene, an even more primal scene of carnage, an originary memory for which the present sacrifice is the surrogate, the attempted propitiation.

In *Athalie* the originary scene is double. It is both the murder of the innocents, the children of Ochosias, and the "first" slaughter by Jéhu of Athalie's family, but most specifically of her mother:

151

> Hélas! l'état horrible où le ciel me l'offrit
> Revient à tout moment effrayer mon esprit.
> De princes égorgés la chambre était remplie;
> Un poignard à la main, l'implacable Athalie
> Au carnage animait ses barbares soldats,
> Et poursuivait le cours de ses assassinats.
> Joas, laissé pour mort, frappa soudain ma vue.
> Je me figure encor sa nourrice éperdue,
> Qui devant les bourreaux s'était jetée en vain
> Et, faible, le tenait renversé sur son sein.
> Je le pris tout sanglant.
>
> (I, ii, 241–251)

> C'était pendant l'horreur d'une profonde nuit;
> Ma mère Jézabel devant moi s'est montrée,
> Comme au jour de sa mort pompeusement parée,
> Ses malheurs n'avait point abattu sa fierté ...
> ...
> Et moi je lui tendais les mains pour l'embrasser;
> Mais je n'ai plus trouvé qu'un horrible mélange
> D'os et de chairs meurtris et traînés dans la fange,
> Des lambeaux pleins de sang, et des membres affreux
> Que des chiens dévorants se disputaient entre eux.
>
> (II, v, 490–493, 502–506)

To these imaginary scenarios at the end of Racine's theatrical career corresponds with haunting regularity the same dynamic encountered in the beginning: Astyanax must be killed in order to complete the picture, to suture the wound of the nightmarish scene of his own father's death and the destruction of Troy:

> Songe, songe, Céphise, à cette nuit cruelle
> Qui fut pour tout un peuple une nuit éternelle;
> Figure-toi Pyrrhus, les yeux étincelants,
> Entrant à la lueur de nos palais brûlants,
> Sur tous mes frères morts se faisant un passage,
> Et, de sang tout couvert, échauffant le carnage;
> Songe aux cris des vainqueurs, songe aux cris des mourants
> Dans la flamme étouffés, sous le fer expirants.
>
> (III, viii, 997–1004)

Although these scenarios are intriguing for many reasons (not least of which is, as Mauron has pointed out, their status as precipitating moment of a sado-masochistic dialectic), I would like to insist here on two subsidiary factors of that dialectic. In these scenes there is a reversibility between child and parent that, as we have proposed, is

152

integral to the role of the subject in patriarchy; and, secondly, the scenes of carnage and of death always figure, with a kind of fascinated delectation, death as dispersal, as dismemberment, as the violent return of the body to a multiplicity, to a state of both non- and pre-integrity. Nevertheless, the fantasy of that state is also inseparable from the end of the subject. Subjectivity in Racine floats upon the fantasies of its own impossibility: either that pre-Oedipal multiplicity that has been repressed, destroyed, in order precisely for the subject to be; or that subject as an already gendered, but therefore guilty, being, trapped in a familial dialectic that condemns the subject to its own end. The entire ontological problematic of Racinian dramaturgy is present in embryonic form in this fantasy of impossibility: the problem of the tragic protagonist is a question of being. How can one be "integral" (that is, absolute), how can one stand alone when one is constantly trapped in a movement of oscillation, trapped in a constant genealogical becoming, caught in a never-ending history of family, between a past and a future, with the present always slipping away? How, in other words, can one escape the meanderings of becoming for an impossible stasis of being that would not be death?

To the threat of an impending violence against the child respond the memories of past violence against the parent. It is this indeterminacy between a past and a future that situates the present of Racinian tragedy as the spectacle of conflated desires. Interestingly, when we consider with Serge Leclaire one of the most complicated of Freud's essays on subjectivity, sexuality, masochism and sadism, "A Child is Being Beaten," we come to realize the importance of the startling ambiguity that presides over Racinian violence:

La formulation indéterminée du fantasme "on tue un enfant" est parfaitement adéquate: seul le verbe indiquant l'action de tuer, de mettre à mort, est précisé, mais on ne sait pas qui tue, ni quel "enfant" est tué ... La série des figures susceptible d'occuper la place du "on" qui tue est indéfinie.[18]

In Leclaire's essay, what is intriguing in the fantasy of the child who is being sacrificed is the sexual indeterminacy of both victim and executioner. This is the same indeterminacy we encounter when we consider, in its entirety, the Racinian corpus. The victim can be a male child – Astyanax, Xipharès, Joas, Hippolyte – or female – Iphigénie, Eriphile, Phèdre – and the murderer can either be male – Pyrrhus, Mithridate, Agamemnon, Thésée – or female – Agrippine, Eriphile, Athalie, Phèdre. In a general sense, therefore, what we have behind, or rather just below, the surface of a universe of specified, individuated characters is a bi-sexual fantasy where what is most

153

important is the dialectics of power, of activity and passivity in a pre-sexed, confusingly terrifying world.

What I am suggesting is that on some "archaeological" level Racine's theater harkens back to a psychological state of pre-sexualized non-difference where the world is seen on its most elementarily terrifying level as a battle between an aggressively devouring parent – Father–Mother – and an equal, but in Racine ineffectual, loving parent who will come to the rescue of the vulnerable infant. Certainly, in *Athalie* (to use this play once again as a *terminus ad quem* of Racinian tragedy) there is more than one crossing of sexual boundaries in the depictions of both Athalie and Joad, that infernal ur-couple locked into the battle for sexual/political power. From the beginning Athalie is described as an "unnatural" woman; she is a foreigner, a murderer, an usurper and a deicide:

> Huit ans déjà passés, une impie étrangère
> Du sceptre de David usurpe tous les droits,
> Se baigne impunément dans le sang de nos rois,
> Des enfants de son fils détestable homicide,
> Et même contre Dieu lève son bras perfide.
> (I, i, 72–76)

To the above list of her crimes must be added the common denominator, the scandalous reason for her enterprise: she is a "mannish" woman, a woman who refuses the limits imposed on her sex, who transgresses the sexual boundaries and threatens all order:

> Un bruit confus s'élève, et du peuple surpris
> Détourne tout à coup les yeux et les esprits.
> Une femme ... Peut-on la nommer sans blasphème?
> Une femme ... C'était Athalie elle-même.
> ...
> Dans un des parvis, aux hommes réservé,
> Cette femme superbe entre, le front levé,
> Et se préparait même à passer les limites
> De l'enceinte sacrée ouverte aux seuls lévites.
> (II, ii, 393–396, 397–400)

Athalie, like Agrippine, represents on more than one level, not only a projection forward (in the sense of a pre-figuration of some modernity)[19] but, more frightening, a projection backward to an archaic figuration of the phallic mother, that combination of the sexes in which the valency of activity, power and threat is still radically attached to one single image of "the woman with a penis,"

154

that woman/mother who in psychoanalytic theory represents the devouring, destructive threat to the integrity of the child.[20]

On the other hand Joad, Athalie's rival and mate, who throughout the play, in his role of surrogate father and surrogate God, stands for all that is implacable, incorruptible, and integral in this world of decadence and disorder ("L'audace d'une femme, arrêtant ce concours, / En des jours ténébreux a changé ces beaux jours") comes to be seen not only as the father of his ward, but more strangely, if only by omission, as a maternal presence also. Josabet, the timorous, loving, but ineffectual mother, too nervous in the presence of the prize she has snatched from the jaws of death, too unsure of her own role, abandons all care of the child to Joad:

> Du jour que j'arrachai cet enfant à la mort,
> Je remis en vos mains tout le soin de son sort;
> Même, de mon amour craignant la violence,
> Autant que je le puis j'évite sa présence,
> De peur qu'en le voyant quelque trouble indiscret
> Ne fasse avec mes pleurs échapper mon secret.
>
> (I, ii, 189–194)

Josabet's inability to assume the maternal function out of some fear of destroying her ward thrusts Joad into the ambivalent role of father–mother. Only on an apparent level of dramatic necessity is the unicity of Joad's masculine identity ever so slightly fractured by this intrusion of a maternal function that makes of Joad both father and mother to the orphan; on a more profound "archaic" level, be it that of the psyche or of myth, this attribution only adds to Joad's role of representing some "primal" father, an image that corresponds, once again, to a fantasy of unlimited power, as a power that defies the sundering (and thus the limitation) of genderization, and allows him to correspond, in homologous fashion, to the hybridized terror that is Athalie.[21]

It is this hybridization of the archaic parental image, an image that is in essence "unnatural", that is reproduced in the double being of the child – Eliacin-Joas – and which leads us back to the most overinvested aporia in Racine, the aporia of the double, the monster. What most characterizes the monsters that populate the Racinian universe, be they "real" monsters (the Minotaur, or the "bull from the sea") or metaphorical monsters (Néron) is their essential heterogeneity. They are all double. The Minotaur, of course, is half human, half animal, the product of the lustful "unnatural" coupling of Pasiphaë and a bull. The monster that Neptune sends

155

to frighten Hippolyte's horses and bring on his death is described
in the following way:

> Cependant, sur le dos de la plaine liquide,
> S'élève à gros bouillons une montagne humide;
> L'onde approche, se brise, et vomit à nos yeux,
> Parmi des flots d'écume, un monstre furieux.
> Son front large est armé de cornes menaçantes:
> Tout son corps est couvert d'écailles jaunissantes;
> Indomptable taureau, dragon impétueux,
> Sa croupe se recourbe en replis tortueux.
>
> (*Phèdre*, V, vi, 1513–1520)

The bull from the sea is a monster most noticeably because it is
a heterogeneous being, a being composed of parts from different
origins – mammal, reptile, actual animals and imaginary bestiaries.
At the same time, of course, its entire being is infused, doubled, by
and with the idea of an excessive sexuality that cannot be "properly"
contained, that in its essence represents transgression – the metaphorical echoes of both "cornes" and "jaunissantes" recalling the
traditional symbols of cuckoldry, adultery, and (by extension, in
this play) incest.

The heterogeneity of the mythological bull from the sea is reproduced, in a different register, in that first real monster of Racinian
theater, Néron. In *Britannicus* the play invites us to witness "the
birth of a monster."[22] Racine also specifies that the tragedy takes
place not on the public scene of empire, but in the closed, intimate
space of family: "Néron est ici dans son particulier et dans sa
famille."[23] Yet the Preface only states those acts that Nero will
commit, thus proleptically defining his being by his yet-to-be-accom-
plished actions; he is a "nascent" monster (the coupling of these
two words is, it seems to me, heavy with meaning). In order to
know the "essence" of Néron's monstrosity we have to turn to the
play itself.

And who better than his mother should be able to tell us why
Néron is a monster?

> Il commence, il est vrai, par où finit Auguste;
> Mais crains que, l'avenir détruisant le passé,
> Il ne finisse ainsi qu'Auguste a commencé.
> Il se déguise en vain: je lis sur son visage
> Des fiers Domitius l'humeur triste et sauvage;
> Il mêle avec l'orgueil qu'il a pris dans leur sang
> La fierté des Nérons qu'il puisa dans mon flanc.
>
> (I, i, 32–38)

Agrippine situates Nero's monstrosity in his double origin. He is a "mixture" of the Domitii and the Julio-Claudians. Like the bull from the sea, he is a heterogenous combination of two blood lines, two families, two parents, two sexes, and as such he is condemned to a never-ending battle for sovereignty, for integrity, for the elimination of his "difference within." The difference is maddening because he can't be free of it, can't be free of Agrippine, any more than he can be free of the external political manipulations of the diverse clans, families that all come together in him.

In this Nero is just paradigmatic of those hybrid Racinian child-heroes who are monstrous precisely because they are not one but two. Phèdre, "fille de Minos et de Pasiphaë," is, of course, the most famous, the most pathetic. She, like Néron, bears the internal duality of the underworld and the light of day: granddaughter of the sun, her father, "juge aux enfers tous les pâles humains." She, too, is the product of a mixture of bloods, of historics, of old debts that become her internal division, the victim of a curse she inherits in her being, a being that is monstrous because it is not pure, not one but two.

René Girard has written seductively of the essential reciprocal relation between doubling and monstrosity:

Le principe fondamental, toujours méconnu, c'est que le double et le monstre ne font qu'un ... Il n'y a pas de monstre qui ne tende à se dédoubler, il n'y a pas de double qui ne recèle une monstruosité secrète.[24]

We are beginning to see the pattern of internal contradiction that emerges in Racine's theater and that focuses on the child. For in an obvious sense all Racine's characters are children and therefore all are monstrous. All bear the burden of a heterogeneous past that strives to free itself from its own heterogeneity, that strives for the realm of the absolute. It is this impossible denial, a denial that resurfaces in the violence of murder, of incest, of sexuality, that makes these children the victims of their secret monstrous origin, and coterminously makes this origin always the result of an even more primeval violence.

More to the point for our discussion, Girard has gone on to speculate on the intimate connection that exists between the reciprocity of doubling and monstrosity and the violence of those sexual ties that bind members of families together, and specifically the members of that family which has become for modern discourse (but for Racine as well) the "originary" family of Classical subjectivity, the descendants of Laius and Jocasta:

157

Tous les épisodes du mythe d Œdipc sont en fait les doublets les uns des autres. Une fois ce fait reconnu, on s'aperçoit que tous les personnages du mythe sont des monstres et qu'ils sont tous beaucoup plus semblables les uns aux autres que leur apparence extérieure ne le laisse supposer. Tous les personnages sont des doubles, tous donc sont aussi des monstres.[25]

It is thus necessary for us to understand the hold that violence, doubling and monstrosity has on the Racinian universe if we are to return to the origins of that world, situated, as we know, in the crisis left in the wake of Œdipus' transgression.

La Thébaïde is both the origin of Racinian tragedy and the tragedy of origins. With the tautological rhythm which seems to be the rhythm of mythic repetition, Racine's theater starts out with a tragedy that reproduces a myth of the impossibility of sovereignty, of the impossibility of subjectivity as integrity. The other, greater tragedies will only play out, in different, more profound registers, this same impossible desire. The repressed beginning of the myth of the "warring brothers" recedes into another myth, the drama of the crimes of Œdipus – which, in turn, is not originary to him. Œdipus is cursed because he is the son of Laius and thus inherits the sins of his father. Laius' transgression, like Œdipus', is a sexual perversion: invited by Pelops to a banquet, Laius there rapes his host's son Chrysipus, who out of desperation, hangs himself. The origin of familial guilt, of familial retribution, is never actually attributable to the person in question but loses itself in a former crime, committed in a more remote time, by an ancestor. That crime, in these histories of families, is always a sexual deviation, or more simply, is always a narration of sexuality that refuses the bonds of familial (that is, societal) confinement.

It would seem, therefore, that from the beginning we are engaged in a mystery, the mystery of impossible origins, of origins that must always remain hidden, repressed. This repression resurfaces in the descendants as an "original sin," a familial stain that condemns the members of the family to repeat and play out a tragedy to which they themselves are the principal actors but which, on a more profound level, acts itself out through and among them without their seeming to understand its hold on them, nor their role in it.

In the youthful Racine of *La Thébaïde* the monstrous is not as yet internalized. Rather than a split within, this first Racine, perhaps still under the influence of Corneille, chooses the most intimate and most intense of doublings to play out his tragedy. The "warring brothers" dichotomize in the exterior world the forces of love/hate, desire/aggression, that the later plays will transport inward, into the tormented duality of the great Racinian heroes. Nevertheless, we still have here the entire thematics of monstrosity, of the child as monster, that will come to dominate in the later tragedies. Here, the children are the monstrous offspring of sexual perversion:

> Mais ces monstres, hélas! ne t'épouvantent guères;
> La race de Laius les a rendus vulgaires;
> Tu peux voir sans frayeur les crimes de nos fils
> Après ceux que le père et la mère ont commis.
> Tu ne t'étonnes pas si mes fils sont perfides,
> S'ils sont tous deux méchants et s'ils sont parricides.
> Tu sais qu'ils sont sortis d'un sang incestueux,
> Et tu t'étonnerais s'ils étaient vertueux.
>
> (I, i, 27–34)

The violence that invades the world of *La Thébaïde,* and that is about to strike the children/victims, is but an "après-coup" of the violence of parental incest. As the originary moment of Racine's tragic universe, this incest figures as a psychic structure, as the return of an inchoate sexuality, of sexuality as it exists in its most anarchic avatar and threatens the entire social order. The relation between the individual as a subject of desire and his insertion into a community where he becomes (also) a subject of Law is therefore memorialized in the myth of Œdipus, in the tragedy of Œdipus' family, as the originary chaos in which both the individual subject and the community meet their (imagined) end.[26]

In a sense, Racine's first tragedy mirrors Corneille's *Horace* in its separation of the world into the symmetrical opposition of the two warring sides. As in *Horace,* each brother offers a political argument to explain a separation that is not viable. There is no real difference, only a congenital hatred elevated to/sublimated in a political difference. In reality the two brothers are one, mirror images of each other, and for that reason engaged in a fight to the death. Their hatred is their monstrosity, the reflection of their sameness which impedes either from being free, from establishing an independent identity:

> Je ne sais si mon cœur s'apaisera jamais:
> Ce n'est pas son orgueil, c'est lui seul que je hais.
>   . . .
> Nous étions ennemis dès la plus tendre enfance;
> Que dis-je! nous l'étions avant notre naissance.
> Triste et fatal effet d'un sang incestueux!

Pendant qu'un même sein nous renfermait tous deux,
Dans les flancs de ma mère une guerre intestine
De nos divisions lui marqua l'origine.
...

On dirait que le ciel, par un arrêt funeste,
Voulût de nos parents punir ainsi l'inceste:
Et que dans notre sang il voulût mettre au jour
Tout ce qu'ont de plus noir et la haine et l'amour.
(IV, i, 913–914, 917–22, 927–30)

It is precisely their identity that neither can tolerate, the fact that they are one in two. Jocaste least of all can understand what, since Freud's essay on the "Uncanny," has become apparent to us: the double, rather than being a reassuring reflection of the ego, represents the greatest threat to the integrity of that ego, the threat of its dispersion.[27] Instead of the image of love as union that Jocaste would have them reflect to each other –

Commencez donc, mes fils, cette union si chère,
Et que chacun de vous reconnaisse son frère:
Tous deux dans votre frère envisagez vos traits,
Mais pour en mieux juger, voyez-les de plus près;
Surtout que le sang parle et fasse son office.
(IV, iii, 979–983)

– when each looks at his (br)other he sees the image of his own negation, of his own death.[28]

If *La Thébaïde* were only a play of fraternal jealousy it would never reach the tragic dimension to which it tends, but would remain simply in the realm of melodrama. What stirs alive this first attempt at tragedy, despite its limitations, despite the fact that the young Racine is still obliged to figure difference as an external split, is that from the beginning Racine never allows the familial, the narration of private sexuality and conflict, to remain simply familial, but rather shows it to be inseparable from the political. From the first, the family whose primary function is to produce and to reproduce the subjects of the Polis is clearly situated as the most important "ideological apparatus" of the state. In this context, it becomes clear that the family is delineated as the central nexus of all the political (that is, sexual, economic and social) investments underpinning the ideology of Racinian theater. It is an ideology that this theater, in turn, ambivalently celebrates.

The private and the public are inextricably woven together in this drama, as in all Racine, around the problem of Sovereignty – the rule of the One. The battle that opposes the two brothers is a struggle for the right to occupy the throne, a throne that cannot tolerate the "partage des femmes" proposed by Jocaste, but insists upon the unicity of the law of masculine prerogative:

> Jamais dessus le trône on ne vit plus d'un maître;
> Il n'en peut tenir deux, quelque grand qu'il puisse être!
>
> (IV, iii, 1172–1173)

In its ideological substructure, the entire play opposes the world of women – the universe of Jocaste, of Antigone, a world of compromise understood as "dissolution" – to the world of men, the world of integrity, of the Father, that aims to be absolute. This drive towards sovereignty is the central dilemma in *La Thébaïde*, as it will be in *Iphigénie*, in *Mithridate* and (in a slightly different register) in *Phèdre* and *Athalie*.

It will seem that I am only stating the obvious in insisting once again that in a highly patriarchal society the relation between Sovereignty in both its political forms (monarchy) and in its metaphysical imperatives (the relation between God and the world) turns, as Freud suggests, equally on the elevation and sublimation of the figure of the father and his destruction.[29] No divine-right monarchy is possible without the integral backing of a theological view of the universe that unites God, Kingship and Paternity along the same metaphoric axis, establishing a universe in which the devolution of power from male to male is mediated through the sacrifice of Patriarchy's other, be it the representation of the other Woman, of the feminine that must be eliminated, or the image of the obverse of the Father's unlimited power, the child as helpless and vulnerable.

The problem that is foregrounded in *La Thébaïde* and that forecloses any possible resolution is the compromised status of the father. In *La Thébaïde*, the father is already absent (as he will be in the first four major tragedies), and yet paradoxically, everywhere present in the conflict he has created. The antagonism that sunders the world is caused by the father's sins, and yet, he being already dead, there is no one upon whom the blame might fall, no guilty one to punish, no one other than oneself who can be sacrificed to end the conflict. This ambivalence, the absence/presence of the dead father at the beginning of tragedy, would seem to indicate, on a more archaic level, the ambivalence all children feel towards that person who has, by separating them from the warm but potentially suffocating embrace of the mother, led them into the social world. The father who has sundered that primary mother–child unity plunges his

161

offspring into a world of loss, into the world of sexuality (as scission) and language – into, that is, social being. This wounding, their subjugation, is their only chance, albeit a compromised chance, of becoming a subject of law, a subject of culture. The violence of this intrusion can only be lived ambivalently, both as the hatred of jealousy, the hatred of forever having been left bereft of a state of narcissistic self-enclosure, parasitizing the maternal; and (once this sundering has been integrated as difference) as love for the subject that orchestrates, with both despotism and tenderness, this transition. It is this inherent ambivalence of the child's attitude to his father that, Freud postulated, is projected outward into the world, both in the creation of the image of a fearsome and loving god and in the separation that projects the same ambivalence, divided equally between God and the Devil.[30] In this way religion as a social phenomenon would capture, in its own imagery and dogma, both the love the subject felt towards his omnipotent parent(s) and his resentment and anger that were also directed towards them, relaying and canalizing in socially productive forms these primitive and potentially destructive psychic forces.

Oedipus leaves his indelible mark not only on his family but on the world. Racine's entire universe revolves around the ambivalence that inheres in the child's relation to a parent who has both wounded and liberated him/her, and the parent's equally ambiguous feelings of both fear and desire towards his/her offspring. It would be too disingenuous not to see the relation of fathers and children in patriarchy in any way other than as a complex network of interrelated dependencies, dependencies that in a universe dominated by an ideology of pure difference – of sovereignty – are continually in conflict with   are continually trying to ignore, to repress – this ambivalence. It is the force of this ambivalence that is used to free the subject from the guilt he feels towards his own (ideal) father by its being projected out into the world on to a negative other – person or group – who appears to crystallize in his own being what, in the politically dominant group, has been repressed as unacceptable.[31] Although on a simple level it would seem that in the battle for sovereignty that opposes the father to any ties binding him to a becoming, rather than to a being, his superior physical strength and apparent invulnerability give him the upper hand, this would be to forget the importance of societal structures that make paternity depend, tautologically, not only in the imposition upon the child of the "name of the father," but also on the child's recognition of this imposition.[32]

Locked into this impossible bind, all of Racine's characters know themselves to be guilty of harboring murderous (incestuous) desires against their parents/children. Although I have been dwelling on the child as victim in Racine, I do not mean to imply that these victims are necessarily innocent. Racine's parents, particularly his fathers, are correct in realizing that the very presence of children is a threat to their illusion of sovereignty, if only because the presence of the child is always a reminder of our own mortality, of the passage of time, and of our inevitable end. The children are guilty, if of nothing more, then also of nothing less, than simply waiting – waiting to take our place, our power, our being.[33]

This purely "metaphysical" guilt becomes in Racine a matter of universalized guilt, a matter of political and social concern. Roland Barthes has spoken about the "culpabilité absolue" of the Racinian hero.[34] This absolute guilt, when transferred to the public domain, precisely defines Absolutism's hold on its subjects as the internalization of inadequacy, of the knowledge that one is always lacking in relation to the object of one's (political, sexual) desire in the sense that that love is also always compromised. At the bottom of all extreme longing for, identification with, the other is also the desire to be, to incorporate – that is, to kill – that other.[35] In this logic it is true, as Freud told us, but also as St. Augustine told the seventeenth century, that the child is already a guilty being, a subject of sin.

Joas is guilty of desiring Athalie's death. We know this not only because Racine tells us in his preface what he will become on the stage of Biblical history, but because Athalie knows it. Her dream tells her (us) that Joas wants to kill her, wants to do to her what she has already tried to do to him. We know it, too, because Mathan in his sycophantic espousal of tyranny turns an old woman's fears into a political necessity:

MATHAN Mais lui-même, après tout, fût-ce son propre fils,
  Voudrait-il un moment laisser vivre un coupable?
ABNER De quel crime un enfant peut-il être capable?
MATHAN Le ciel nous le fait voir un poignard à la main:
  Le ciel est juste et sage, et ne fait rien en vain.
  Que cherchez-vous de plus?

(II, v, 554–559)

Mithridate, of all Racine's fathers, corresponds most closely to the image of the leader of the primal horde: he is a brutal, arbitrary tyrant who has not only done away with (at least) one of his wives,

163

but has already killed two of his sons. Confronted with such force, such brutality, his remaining two sons, Xipharès and Pharnace, who both lust after his bride-to-be, are also guilty of trespassing on their father's prerogative, made to bear the burden of their guilt. In a classic Œdipal scenario the violent Father defies his young sons, witholds from them the object of sexual satisfaction and plots their castration (death). In their reaction to this threat and frustration both, but in diametrically opposed ways, attempt to turn their guilt into action. Pharnace commits a political crime that takes his Œdipal guilt out of the realm of intimate sexual desire and places it squarely in the domain of political treachery. In an act of open rebellion against the brutality of Mithridate he allies himself with Rome against his father and all that his father represents. Xipharès, while remaining slavishly attached to his father and (more importantly) to the ideal he has of the Father, is, nonetheless, by his birth guilty of political and sexual lèse-majesté. His mother, who betrayed her husband to the Romans, has paid with her life for her crime. Xipharès, however, bears her guilt as his own, with an insistence that reveals more about his own repressed hatred of Mithridate, as a sexual rival for Monime, than about his mother's hopeless attempt at revenge. This guilt/debt inheres in Xipharès, condemning him in his own eyes to a position of eternal inadequacy in relation to Mithridate. The only compensation for the hatred/guilt he feels is his own (self) sacrifice:

> Ici tout vous retient, et moi, tout m'en écarte:
> Et, si ce grand dessein surpasse ma valeur,
> Du moins ce désespoir convient à mon malheur.
> Trop heureux d'avancer la fin de ma misère,
> J'irai … J'effacerai le crime de ma mère.
> Seigneur, vous m'en voyez rougir à vos genoux;
> J'ai honte de me voir si peu digne de vous:
> Tout mon sang doit laver une tache si noire.
> Mais je cherche un trépas utile à votre gloire.
> (III, i, 936–944)

The examples of guilty children are legion in Racine. Hippolyte contravenes his father's orders; Britannicus is guilty by birth and political manipulation. The point is that guilt − mutual, reciprocal guilt − is necessary to secure the smooth working of a sacrificial theater whose role it is both to assuage this guilt and turn it into a cohesive social force. Through the (projected) sacrifices of the child, Racinian tragedy hopes to play out its own ambivalent, guilty relation to the ideological imperatives that both call it into being and define this being as conflicted.

Xipharès wants to sacrifice himself to pay an unpayable debt, to assuage his own sexual guilt. In *Iphigénie* the sacrifice of his daughter also appears as a test of Agamemnon's sovereignty, his political sovereignty as supreme leader — King of kings — but also his domestic and sexual sovereignty, his ability to give or withhold the object of Achille's desire. It is the conflict between these two poles that is at the crux of his and the play's dilemma. Should Agamemnon, like Abraham but with considerably more soul searching, opt for blind obedience to the gods, an obedience which in the blood of his daughter will gloriously seal his political fate, because her sacrifice would demonstrate his total renouncement of common humanity and thus place him in a special, sacred relation to the gods and to power? Or should he remain in the realm of the human?

Clytemnestra's protective fury uncovers her husband's bad faith in a decision she knows will inevitably fall on the side of the political:

> Laissez à Ménélas racheter d'un tel prix
> Sa coupable moitié, dont il est trop épris.
> Mais vous, quelles fureurs vous rendent sa victime?
> Pourquoi vous imposer la peine de son crime?
> ...
> Mais non; l'amour d'un frère et son honneur blessé
> Sont les moindres des soins dont vous êtes pressé:
> Cette soif de régner, que rien ne peut éteindre,
> L'orgueil de voir vingt rois vous servir et vous craindre,
> Tous les droits de l'empire en vos mains confiés,
> Cruel! c'est à ces dieux que vous sacrifiez.
> (IV, iv, 1271–1274, 1287–1292)

Perhaps nowhere else in Racine's theater is the dichotomy of power and powerlessness, of arbitrary cruelty and innocence, rendered as explicit as it is in *Iphigénie*.[36] Part of the terror the play maintains (until the end, when it falls from tragedy into melodrama) is precisely the horror of the father's unleashing on his own daughter his desire for supreme power. It is only when we understand that the pathos of the situation is archetypal, that Iphigénie shares with her surrogate, Eriphile, the perfect requisites of the sacrificial victim, that we can understand this horror as integral to the "aesthetic" pleasure, the pleasure of tragedy, the play produces in us.

In order for a community to live in and with sacrifice, the victim of that sacrifice must be perceived paradoxically as being both of and not of the community. The victim appears always to be in a liminal position of defining, by his presence, the limits of community. It is through him that the borders between what is communal and what is not are constantly reaffirmed.[37] However, in order for the victim to be first perceived as victim certain conditions must be met: s/he must be understood to be in some way innocent, vulnerable, to be in a certain sense *heimlich* with all the ambivalent echoes Freud heard in that term.[38] The victim is generally chosen from among a marginalized group – children, foreigners, the physically impaired – who, of course, because of this marginality, are seen as hybrid, as monstrous.[39] Their marginality, always culturally defined, is particularly significant because it permits and occults the reciprocal relationship between the victim and the community, between king and slave, in the spectacle of sacrifice. By the same token this spectacle underscores another important, if hidden, aspect of the sacrificial roles: they are innately reversible. The ambivalence that is fixed on the victim is arbitrary: in a certain sense all members of the community, in one way or another, can become the victim. Perhaps nowhere is this reversibility more acute than in the person of the King himself: a sacred person closest to the divinity, part of the sacredness of that divinity, but also because of this special relation most vulnerable to being sacrificed to that god. This, of course, can be used to explain why instead of the death of the child the tragedy can end with the sacrifice of the Leader/King – Pyrrhus, Athalie, Mithridate – without effectively changing the role of the sacrifice.[40] Rather than attack the King, however, most advanced societies substitute a surrogate victim, whose helplessness and innocence seem in direct opposition to the power and privilege of the leader.[41]

Such is the fate of Astyanax, of Britannicus, of Iphigénie/Eriphile, of Hippolyte and of Joas. All are liminal, all are either actually or potentially "foreign" (in relation to the way the Father defines interior and exterior), all are in the community and yet not of it. Each, in other words, bears in him/herself an internal (cultural) split that exactly mirrors the ambivalence of the Father and his community but which is ciphered as negative when articulated in the son/daughter. In the most extreme cases the child's very existence is clearly stated to be a threat to that community:

> Et qui sait ce qu'un jour ce fils peut entreprendre?
> Peut-être dans nos ports nous le verrons descendre,
> Tel qu'on a vu son père embraser nos vaisseaux,
> Et, la flamme à la main, les suivre sur les eaux.
> Oserai-je, seigneur, dire ce que je pense?
> Vous-même de vos soins craignez la récompense,

Et que dans votre sein ce serpent élevé
Ne vous punisse un jour de l'avoir conservé.
(*Andromaque*, I, ii, 161–168)

While in *Andromaque* the danger represented by Astyanax is perceived by the Greeks to be a purely political threat (the revenge for the sack and destruction of Troy), by *Phèdre* this same danger has become so internalized in the Œdipal conflict that politics and sexuality seamlessly coalesce. All the characters are entrapped in a reciprocity of desire in which each, by mirroring the desire of the others, becomes for those others a monster:

OENONE Mais, ne me trompez point, vous est-il cher encore?
De quel œil voyez-vous ce prince audacieux?
PHÈDRE Je le vois comme un monstre effroyable à mes yeux.
(*Phèdre*, III, iii, 882–884)

(Thésée to Hippolyte)

Perfide! oses-tu bien te montrer devant moi?
Monstre, qu'a trop longtemps épargné le tonnerre,
Reste impur des brigands dont j'ai purgé la terre,
Après que le transport d'un amour plein d'horreur
Jusqu'au lit de ton père a porté la fureur
Tu m'oses présenter une tête ennemie!
(IV, ii, 1044–1049)

(Aricie to Thésée)

Prenez garde, seigneur: vos invincibles mains
Ont de monstres sans nombre affranchi les humains;
Mais tout n'est pas détruit, et vous en laissez vivre
Un ...
(V, iii, 1443–1446)

At the end of Racine's career, politics and sexuality only reiterate, in ever more tightly constructed scenarios, the essential violence inherent in the Œdipal structure that was already present in his first tragedy. Sexuality, as L. Bersani has written, in its most fundamental aspect is always incestuous, and thus always inimical to society at large, to the family as produced by that society, and finally to the very subject formed at their conjuncture.[42] This sexuality, which reflects the Father's own desire as the return of precisely that which he has had to suppress to become the Father, can only be branded as "monstrous": it is the return of what in oneself annihilates this self; it is the return of what is most monstrous to us all, the promise of our own dissolution, the return of death. The sexuality of the child, which we might say is always the reflection of the desire of the parents, of law, reflects back to the Father the necessity of its sacrifice as that which founds the community. This community is united precisely because individual desire has in some way – in many different ways – been channeled into collective enterprise, into societal living. What this means is that the sacrifice of individual desire is relayed into a communality of mutually held Ideals of which the Father is the vehicle. At the very beginnings of community, in the first collective gesture, lies the renouncement of a portion of individual pleasure, a sacrifice of one's own desire. Sexuality is corraled into Law and politics, as the distribution of power among contiguous individuals is born. At the same time this containment is never totally successful; the repressed returns in those figures of otherness that Patriarchy cannot entirely subdue – the haunting fear of female sexuality, the woman as passion, and the equally mistrusted image of the child, the potential rebel, who has not as yet been brought into line.

The mythic substructure of Racine's universe teaches us the importance of this initial sacrifice over and over again. In a very simple sense, politics – that is, life in society – arises when sexuality is subdued. In Racine's particular form of Patriarchal drama, however, the sexuality that is restrained is principally coded as excessive sexuality and it is attached to the image of the passionate woman. Athens has been established as an independent Polis because of Thésée's heroism: the definition of this heroism is double. We are told repeatedly that Thésée is a hero because he slays monsters and seduces women. These two aspects of his being are inseparable and are in a sense the same thing. The chiasmus implies that slaying monsters and seducing women – the enslavement of the monster that is female sexuality to Thésée's virility – makes Athens (that is, culture) safe for democracy. In this universe of Paternal presence, the signifier of all value is the order of the One which reduces the other, be it foreign brigands, monsters or women, to the containment of the law. It is to this fetish that all is and must be sacrificed. This order exists, of course, as a metaphysical projection that refuses, as it must, any compromise with what inheres in it as its negative other. Rather, in its quest for Sovereignty this other is cast out, becomes the negative limits of society, the limits that must be constantly sacrificed in a ceremony that reaffirms the father's rule and the community's investments in that rule.

As L. Goldmann has suggested, sovereignty in Racine is unable to tolerate any compromise.[43] Desire and its movement are Absolute. It would nevertheless be an error, I feel, to see this theater as an unequivocal celebration of that Absolutism. Although we know that on one level Racine's own career "dans le monde" was based almost exclusively on his desire to be recognized by the monarchy, was most satisfied the closer it/he came to his monarchic ideal,[44] his tragedies play out the ambivalence of this unifocal drive by uncovering precisely what in this monolithic structure is occulted.

The sacrifice that is central to Racine's entire opus turns on ridding the community of the monstrous within itself. Concomitantly this monstrous is represented by and in the child. To repeat what I have been trying to demonstrate in these pages, in a world of Sovereignty the child, because always double, always the product of two, represents what is most inimical in a world that desires itself absolute. And, of course, what is particularly tragic for this drive to absolutism is that we are all children. The duality of being, which is always a becoming, inheres in all of us, secretly undermining any idcology of the One. It is, therefore, a particularly aggressive counterattack by patriarchy on its descendants that Racine's theater plays out. At the same time, however, this acting out reveals the hidden ambivalence of all sacrifice, for by attacking its children Patriarchy in a very obvious (masochistic) sense is shown to be obliged to always turn in and to attack itself.

Of all the children who are actually sacrificed in Racine – Iphigénie/Eriphile, Hippolyte and Phèdre – the last two, in the dyad they form, are the most riveting. The uncanny resemblance of the two, their almost complete rhetorical identity, has been pointed out by almost every critic who has read Racine's most evocative tragedy.[45] I would like to insist on this similarity, which is once again important to me because of its archaic echoes, echoes which are lost once we attempt to analyze the tragic in terms of character. The dyad Phèdre–Hippolyte responds to that other pervasive dyad we have mentioned, the coupling of the Primal Father and Phallic mother. As I stated in the beginning of this chapter, the sexual difference in Racine is not so much a biological difference as a political one: who has power, who hasn't. To the haunting figure of the devouring murderous parent – the Fathers/Mothers of Racine's theater, the Agrippines, Mithridates, Calchas, Thésées and Athalies – respond those (bisexual) child-couples, Britannicus/Junie, Monime/Xipharès, Bajazet/Atalide and (most disturbingly) Phèdre/Hippolyte. (In an even stranger twist we may see the couple Titus/Bérénice combine, in ever-so-subtle ways, not only the child-coupling but the parental as well.)

169

Although it may first strike us as odd, if not perverse, to see Phèdre and Hippolyte as but two differently gendered variations of the same, that is a bi-sexual, figuration, a two-headed "monster" of recalcitrant sexuality, because of the very obvious differences in the plot of the tragedy these differences should not blind us to the structural similarities that ally them to each other as victims of the familial order that destroys them. Each is condemned to the role of the victim by the internal, inalienable difference that they bear as children of a tainted lineage. Phèdre's predisposition to victimization is, as we have already seen, double: daughter of Pasiphaë and Minos, she is an unstable combination of the irreconcilable difference of the sun and the earth, and she bears, as we know, all the weight of the familial curse, the curse of excessive, transgressive sexuality. To this must be added her role as "foreigner": she exists as an intruder in the world of Athens. Hippolyte, likewise, is the tainted product of the cross between "nature and culture," between the world of the Father, the world of politics, and the savage universe of Antiope, his Amazon mother. From Antiope, we are told, comes his aversion to sexuality. But with such an antecedent this aversion can only be interpreted as the refusal of the sexuality of the Father, the refusal to assume a sexuality that is already inscribed in a patriarchal political network. It is for this reason that in a sense Hippolyte is figured as always being on the point of leaving the scene of tragedy and yet forever remaining. The reasons for his remaining are not as strange as they might at first appear. Actually, given his conflicted ascendancy, Hippolyte has nowhere to go. He is constantly saying he wants to leave to become like his father, to do what his father has done. Yet his bi-valent nature never permits him to enter totally into that world. Hippolyte always remains on the far side of the sexuality that defines Thésée's dominion over the world, always also within a sexuality that is other. When Hippolyte falls in love with Aricie this love only relays what is his bi-sexual nature; that is, he falls in love *outside* of paternal sexuality. His passion is "transgressive" because the only object it can find is out of bounds, is outside of his father's law.

Furthermore, his very birth defines him for Athens as not entirely *heimlich*: he too is tainted with foreignness. This "uncanny" aspect of Hippolyte's genealogy is echoed by the hesitancy that surrounds the devolution of the crown, of political sovereignty, when Thésée is believed dead. A debate ensues around the choice of the proper heir. His status as "foreign" is underlined (as will be Phèdre's in relation to Aricie's pretentions to the throne) by the fact that there are those who would exclude him from inheriting the crown:

(Panope to Phèdre)

Pour le choix d'un maître Athènes se partage:
Au prince votre fils l'un donne son suffrage,
Madame; et de l'état, l'autre oubliant les lois,
Au fils de l'étrangère ose donner sa voix.

(I, iv, 326–329)

Both Phèdre and Hippolyte are, therefore, in a liminal position: in and through both passes the border defining *heimlich* from *unheimlich*, culture from nature, self from other. More important still, in *Phèdre* all these differences are subsumed in one more metaphysical divide, the difference between contained and unfettered sexuality, between (that is) the Law of the Father and its obverse. All the internal differences that point to Phèdre's and Hippolyte's predestination as victim, point to them as predestined sexual victim of Patriarchal law. Each, in contrary ways, represents an excess: Phèdre the excess of passion, of lust, and Hippolyte (until he meets Aricie) an "unnatural" abstinence. This absence of sexuality is not just a sign of timidity, however: politically, it is the negation of virility as civilizing process. Hippolyte has not followed his father; no monster has been slain by him, no woman subdued:

Et moi, fils inconnu d'un si glorieux père,
Je suis même encor loin des traces de ma mère!
Souffrez que mon courage ose enfin s'occuper:
Souffrez, si quelque monstre a pu vous échapper,
Que j'apporte à vos pieds sa dépouille honorable.

(III, v, 945–949)

When Hippolyte does enter into the world of sexuality, he, like Phèdre, transgresses the law of the Father. His love for Aricie directly contravenes his father's interdiction of a sexual life, of the possibility of children, for Aricie. This interdiction is not merely spiteful. It is a political act assuring that the security of Athens remains in the family of Thésée rather than reverting to the anarchy of the Pallantides.

Both Phèdre and Hippolyte represent, therefore, two valencies of sexuality that are directly inimical to the life of the (patriarchal family) polis. Combined they form a hybrid sexual being, a monster that must be eradicated despite, and perhaps because of, the pity they inspire in the audience. Thésée, as the representative of Patriarchy, must intervene, must call down the gods' wrath and destroy his

171

family, lest that family, as unbridled sexuality, destroy civilization. Nevertheless, Thésée's revenge, the destruction of his son is tragic, is felt by us as tragic, because it is also a sign of the inability of Patriarchy to survive without castration – without that is, its self-mutilation. The destruction of the son is always also the end of the father. This is what every sacrifice of the child tells us. The father is aggressed through the sacrifice of the image and promise of his own continuity.[46]

Racine's tragedy, projecting this cultural aporia as theater, whirls around the ambivalence of the subject formed in the patriarchal family. Œdipus, the distant origin of this tragedy, continues to haunt the Racinian corpus as this corpus plays out over and over again the blinding insight of self-knowledge: we are all children, all contaminated by that which inheres in us and makes us always double. This knowledge of duality in a universe subtended by an ideology of the Absolute plunges us inward into our selves where we live our difference as guilt, as the fear of being found out by the Father and found wanting. Perhaps, as Mauron suggests, Racine lived his dichotomy between Port-Royal and Versailles as the dichotomy of a child split between death and salvation in the loving embrace of the Monarch's gaze. Nevertheless, by "writing out" his conflicted personal history in a series of tragedies, he transforms what may or may not have been a subjective history into a cultural ritual. It is perhaps only fitting that the stage serves Racine as the altar upon which the myths that he has transformed into dramas are a constant, ritualized re-enactment of the sacrifice of the other that inheres in us all. The stage as spectacle, with the "sacred art" that is theater, allows the audience to be transformed at each representation into participatory members of a community that both loves its King and kills him, too. This is perhaps Racine's revenge. Not being able to destroy the Monarch that lives in him, he writes transcendent tragedies where the King is destroyed by the sacrifice of his posterity.

Œdipus did not know his father and yet killed him. It is this initial crime that all the other children of Racine's theater must repress. And they do so, Racine's theater does so, by attacking the child. They all want to be free of the Dead father who inheres in them all. However, by attacking the child this theater only repeats over and over again the impossibility of that freedom. Despite, or perhaps because of, Absolutism's drive to sovereignty, freedom remains beyond the grasp of the individual. Ambivalence cannot be eradicated.

Finally, we should not forget that before Œdipus murdered his father, that father tried to kill him. This initial attack by the father, his turning on his own child to save himself, to save his rule, is the fearsome fantasy of Racine's tragic heroes. They are all the children of Oedipus and bear his heavy debt and his blinding insight. And in so far as Racinian tragedy inaugurates the reign of the modern, the impossible era of the divided self, our participation in that theater, our pleasure and terror that the sacrifice and reinscription of ambivalence conjures up in us, suspending its awesome power of hatred and passion over our heads, proves that we continue to act out Absolutism's conflicted legacy. On the inner stage of our own desirous fantasies, we remain the victims of Racine: we are all his children.

7

"VISIONS ARE SELDOM ALL THEY SEEM": *LA PRINCESSE DE CLÈVES* AND THE END OF CLASSICAL ILLUSIONS

> Voir ouvre tout l'espace au désir, mais voir ne suffit pas au désir.
> (J. Starobinski, *L'Œil vivant*, p. 13)

> She had lived quietly with her old mother, of whom she was the sole support.
> (Freud, "A Case of Paranoia," *St. Ed.* 14, p. 263)

The *Princesse de Clèves* is, I would suggest, the most theoretical text of the French seventeenth century. I am here using "theoretical" advisedly, and with less coyness than may at first appear. Across its origin, "theory" leads us back to a vision, to a sighting of the world arranged for the eye, for the appetency of the eye, as a "scene", a "tableau." With its source in *thea*, the Greek root meaning "look", "see," it intersects with "theater" as that space which is presented to the eye, given to vision, as a production, as an arrangement that transcends the indifferent heterogeneity of the world in an image of (created) order, a *theatrum mundi*.[1] Nevertheless, the chiasmatic juncture, the imbroglio of theory and theater, their inseparable origin in/as a vision, reminds us that there is never any simple division possible between the "intellectual" scaffolding of a metaphysical vision and the merely physical ocularity, framing the way we see the world in its supposedly objective reality. Both exist in collusion, the inextricable conjunction of illusion with reality, being with seeming, exterior reality with interior reality. To complicate matters further, vision is carried along, supported, by the invisible parameters of ideology that inhere in all imaging, all imagining of the world. The world as a vision, perhaps, but always a mediated vision, a vision that is produced as much as it is productive.

This vision that separates also orders. It situates the spectating subject within the axes of the political and sexual distinctions that delimit the world as a site/sight of coherent, if limited, meaning. Our view of ourselves is to a great extent consonant with the image inside of which we are produced as sexed, that is divided, beings, who are thus placed into those greater social divisions, the camps of masculinity or femininity that form the central, non-displaceable foundations of all social economy. It is in this collusion of vision, in the theater/theory of the world, that the human subject (according to psychoanalytical discourse) is sexually situated, must situate him/herself both as an object of sight, as the "I am a painting" ("Je suis tableau") of Lacan, and as a subject of a vision.[2]

The elaboration of sexual difference is equally mired in the invisibility of ideology that represents itself, as Freud tells us, first and foremost as a "vision" — the shattering sight of the other's difference, the young boy's realization that the penis is not the universal appendage, that it can be, and "in fact" has been, removed: a vision that in its harrowing possibilities precipitates his leaving the Oedipus complex and his entrance into the realm of guilt, and thus conscience. For the young girl, on the other hand, this vision seems to be more ambiguously coded:

little girls ... notice the penis of a brother or playmate, strikingly visible and of large proportions, [and] at once recognise it as the superior counterpart of their own small and inconspicuous organ. A little girl behaves differently. She makes her judgement and her decision in a flash. She has seen it and knows that she is without it and wants to have it.[3]

It is from this vision (of lack), so the theory goes, that the young girl enters into the Oedipus complex and into a life of (the much-decried) "penis-envy." For the moment, this scenario is not invoked for its truth value, but for its status as representing the collusion of theory with theater, the theorization of a sexual scenario, the elaboration of a vision of the world as a theory of sexual gendering. In the Freudian scenario, it is from this sight that the young human elaborates his/her own theory of sexual difference, begins his/her personal narrative of origins, most pointedly of his or her own origins, as a sexually, and therefore politically and socially, situated subject. That this narration is never simple, never complete, never not continually re-originating in fits and starts, is amply attested to in those secondary elaborations, the perversions — fetishism, hysteria and paranoia, the most "intellectually" rigorous, the most "theoretical" of psychic phenomena. Of all the major perversions, paranoia is the most obviously associated with visual dysfunction, with persecutory hallucinations.[4] It is a dysfunction that tautologically returns us to a sexuality that refuses to situate itself "properly" on one side or the other of that ideologically overdetermined divide in which masculinity and femininity are seen as symmetrical, natural complements. The excess of paranoia, the paranoid vision, is precisely a sexuality that refuses these containments in the self, that projects them outward, recolonizing the world with what is threatening, what returns as desire within an internal sexual economy that cannot accept it. This projection nevertheless affirms that repressive economy, too, as what cannot be avoided, as what returns sexuality to its origin as a sighting, a vision in which the subject is both lost and found.

It is in these senses that the *Princesse de Clèves* will be invoked as a theoretical text, a text that theorizes Classicism's investments in its own images of itself; a text that is a theory, a theory of sexual passion, a passion that is mediated by a vision, the spectacular staging of an ideology of difference which becomes a theater of paranoia. In that theater, on that stage, the Classical subject plays out its last, and quite possibly its greatest, role.

When the novel appeared in 1678, the greatest moments of Classical dramaturgy were already behind it. *Phèdre*, perhaps the zenith of that dramaturgy, appeared on the Parisian stage at the beginning of 1677. Although Racine was still to write *Esther* and *Athalie* it could be reasonably argued that, with the possible exception of the latter of those two plays, the tragedies and comedies that were to form the canon of French neo-Classical theater had already been created. Nevertheless, the waning of one moment of Classical representation, the death of the theater, saw the birth of a new canonical tradition: the novel of psychological intrigue of which the *Princesse de Clèves* is the first, and one of the greatest, examples. It would be futile as well as impossible to speculate on any radical separation between these two modes of Classical representation: the theater and the novel. Rather we must see their interreaction as a chiasmus, the invasion of the world of prose fiction by a certain coded theatricality, and (ultimately) the theater's eventual prosification. That the novel, in both its structure and in its presentation of the female protagonist, has, since its publication, been likened to the theater will not come as a surprise to us.[5] Its narrative divisions have been seen to reproduce the acts of a Classical tragedy. The only comparison Valincour, the text's first commentator, found apt to describe the effects of reading the novel (tears) was with Racine's *Iphigénie*: "avez-vous pu vous empêcher de pleurer? Je n'en voudrais pas répondre, quoique vous vous soyez vantée de n'avoir pleuré qu'une fois à *Iphigénie*. Mais à propos de tragédie, ne trouvez-vous pas que cet endroit de notre histoire ferait un bel effet sur le théâtre?"

La Princesse de Clèves *and the end of Classical illusions*

Later, the theatrical metaphor surfaces once again in the comparison of Mlle de Chartres to Molière's Agnès:

> Un homme que vous estimez infiniment et qui est assurément un des plus agréables et des plus polis esprits de son siècle, la comparait l'autre jour, fort plaisamment, à l'Agnès de Molière. Et en vérité si vous y prenez garde, le caractère de cette princesse, la manière dont sa mère l'instruit en l'amenant à la cour, les sermons que lui fait M. de Clèves ... l'aveu qu'elle fait à son mari de l'amour qu'elle a pour un autre homme ... il semble que la Princesse de Clèves ne soit qu'un portrait plus sérieux de cette innocente de la comédie.[6]

Most modern commentators of the novel, at least since M. Butor's 1959 article,[7] have been drawn over and over again to the famous scene of "voyeurism" – the duke spying on the Princess looking at his portrait, with, for an added dimension, the duke himself being watched by a gentleman in the Prince de Clèves's service: the mise-en-abyme of the gaze.[8] The very modern insistence on "voyeurism," caught as it is in an oscillating dialectic with a much less discussed "exhibitionism," points once again (I would suggest) to another capture of the text's theatricality, its spec(tac)ularity, with (in this insistence) the dialectics of vision inscribed in a theater of sexual politics.

The comfortable divisions of traditional literary history would have us separate the world of the seventeenth century into two distinct periods of representation. The first would be an excessive, feminine Baroque. It delights in the play of mirrors, in mutability and metaphor. The world appears as a carnavalesque "dépense" in which subjectivity, rather than being punctiform, is disseminated across the surface of ever-changing visual phenomena. The second would be the contained, more rigidly structured universe of Classicism. From this world has been banished all excessive corporality, all unseemly, inappropriate reference to the *Kreatürlichkeit* of everyday life. Subjectivity is reduced to the concentric ray – the eye – of perspectival representation. Nevertheless, as *La Princesse de Clèves* demonstrates, it is this second division that is invaded by the particularly overinvested Baroque metaphor of "all the world's a stage" which seems to survive the sundering of literary history and appear, inverted, at the heart of one of Classicism's most valued icons. That this *topos* survives the change perhaps gives the lie to such facile divisions. It is certainly not the only typically "Baroque" element that informs this text. Nevertheless, it survives with a valency that radically alters the weight it may have had in a "Baroque" scenario and reflects a radical rearrangement of the world of and in representation.

In the *Princesse de Clèves*, as we know, there is no division possible between the external ("real") world and the court: the court is the world and the world the court, there is no outside, nothing exists that is not already included within the representational parameters of the text/court.[9] This indivision would seem to mark a step backwards in the elaboration of the split between the private and the public spheres that we have seen adumbrated in the different dramatic texts we have analyzed. The choice of the court – that is, of the imaginary scene of a certain utopic vision of monarchy – would tend to situate the *Princesse de Clèves* as (at least in part) a reactionary text. Like the *Astrée*, it would represent the fantasy of some nobiliary dream of a world that no longer exists. Both texts are the work of members of an aristocracy beset with financial difficulties and living amid enormous social and political upheaval, chief among which is the displacement of economic power on to a new class, a class which their works radically exclude. The text's insistence on its own closure, on the projection of the world as closed, could thus be interpreted as a defense against the demands of that other world, the burgeoning bourgeois society that is beginning to threaten a noble order, beginning to replace what was a complicated "feudal" distribution of power, of sexuality and of social networking with a new, only dimly perceived order in which the pieces of the societal jigsaw puzzle are being redistributed in a threateningly novel way.[10] The fact that Mme de Lafayette situated her novel at the court of Henri II has, therefore, other more insistent claims to our attention than just supplying the picturesque background for an intimate love story. For what this division of the text should alert us to is precisely the literariness and the literalness of the "picturesque-ness" of the historical narrative and the fact that we will have to look elsewhere in this choice: to look differently, to see what this choice, distant in time from the author's own life and interest, tells us about the conflict the courtly dream would hide.

The discomfort that critics have shown with the novel's division, between those descriptions that smack too much of "chronicles" and detract from the central narrative thread – the detailing of the princess's interiority, the origin and progression of her passion – could be reduced if we were to understand this division as figuring the confrontation of the aristocratic with the bourgeois structuring of families and therefore desire. The text is divided, as we know, between a narrative of the world of the court, an elaborate political kinship network, and the depiction of the passion – that is, the individuated portrait – of the Princess, her inner turmoil, her attraction and resistance to a man to whom she is not married. What is at stake in the text's division into these two different networkings of society and sexuality appears to me as the conflict inherent in the epistemic change between these two systems that, I would suggest, was occurring precisely at the end of the seventeenth century, but which the author projects back to the reign of Henri II. The Princess is caught at the interstice of these two systems, at a moment when one system is gradually but relentlessly replacing the other. In a sense the novel problematizes, as the Princess's passion, as her moral dilemma, the changing relation of women to two different forms of patriarchal containment.

The representation of the court is inextricably bound to a politics of spectacle and sexuality, to the imaginary scenario that empowers. For the very essence of a court, of a king, is "parade," an ornamentalism that enhances what is mundanely universal and, with all the attributes of artifice, with all the protocols of rank, of dress, of "dépense," with all the prodigality of financial and sexual largesse, raises it beyond the general and into the empyrean of the unique. In this form of sovereignty, it is nothing so much as the image that defines the sovereign — to himself as well as to his subjects — as (illusorily) Other.[11] On a first level, the importance for sovereignty of "spectacle," of a life that is theatricalized, where the Sovereign is coterminously both the privileged spectator and the most compelling spectacle of his realm, where the image, the imaginary of power, is relayed through a spectacular dissemination, will be reproduced in those few, but heavily invested, descriptive passages of the novel, those passages whose "fairy-tale" like quality precisely underlines the invasion of the representational universe by the theater, that is by the force and focus of the visual. This explains the importance of the several spectacular descriptions of the court, of the court as spectacle, that pepper the novel:

Le matin, le duc d'Albe, qui n'était jamais vêtu que fort simplement, mit un habit de drap d'or mêlé de couleur de feu, de jaune et de noir, tout couvert de pierreries, et il avait une couronne fermée sur la tête. Le prince d'Orange, habillé aussi magnifiquement avec ses livrées, et tous les Espagnols suivis des leurs, vinrent prendre le duc d'Albe à l'hôtel de Villeroi où il était logé ... Les reines et les princesses avaient toutes leurs filles magnifiquement habillées des mêmes couleurs qu'elles étaient vêtues: en sorte que l'on connaissait à qui étaient les filles par la couleur de leurs habits.

(pp. 353–54)

The court, by constantly making a spectacle out of itself, reflects the order of the king, imaging itself in his image, and in this spectacular reflexivity closes the world in on itself. The world/court of the *Princesse de Clèves* is a perfectly contained, glittering theater that produces and reproduces itself as a pageant, as an object offered to the eyes of those who, losing themselves in the seduction of its mirrors, can exist only as image. The court, as the reign of those who are subjected to the realm of appearances, satisfies its members by reflecting back to them their image reflected in the generalized illusion of their world.[12] In this sense, the court is, as we are constantly reminded, an illusion, the space of exhibition.

But in this sense, the representation of the court, as a reflection of the "world" (that is of the real), would prefigure what Lacan will come to theorize as "voyure": that structuring of the world where the desiring subject is instituted as subject precisely by being caught in the split, the visually encoded split, between the fact that s/he sees from only one place but is looked at from everywhere.[13] Lacan spins out an elaborate analysis of the schism between the eye and the look, between the organ and its function, that is particularly relevant for understanding the "spectacular" investment of the subject as a sexually encoded subject, as it is elaborated in and commented upon by the *Princesse de Clèves*.

In the court's spectacularity, everyone exists in a visual relation to everyone else. The world is presented as "omnivoyeur." However, this literalization of the topos "all the world's a stage" marks a movement forward in the internalization of the gaze whose evolution we have traced from the *Astrée* through the theater. For here, in the novel, what has disappeared is the unifocal, exterior gaze of Albertian perspective, the direct line of sight uniting Monarch and subject. It has been replaced by a world in which this gaze has been both disseminated (it exists in everyone, everywhere) and concentrated (the text becomes a treatise on the impossibility of seizing the look).[14] In a world where all is appearance, where all verbal communication is either foreclosed or highly suspect (I will return to this point later), the only truth that may be had is the truth of the glance, of the darting look that seizes a blush, a surprise, a facial movement that is not controlled quickly enough. But even this seizure is always subject to ambivalent interpretations. It is this omnipresent ambivalence of the eye that cannot be avoided, that judges, condemns and punishes: the world/court/text becomes a locus of paranoia.

By the text's making a spectacle out of itself, it presents its protagonists as images, as images in a world that can only be seized in an approximative gesture of vision, but where there is an inversion:

the subject of the look is both part of the spectacle and a spectator. S/he both attempts to paint the world − that is, make sense out of it, construct it as a coherent image − and by the very gesture of trying to seize it, reveals that that coherency is precisely what remains beyond his/her reach:

> dans le champ scopique, le regard est au-dehors, je suis regardé, c'est à dire je suis tableau.
> C'est là la fonction qui se trouve au plus intime de l'institution du sujet dans le visible. Ce qui me détermine foncièrement dans le visible, c'est le regard qui est au-dehors. C'est par le regard que j'entre dans la lumière, et c'est du regard que j'en reçois l'effet. D'où il ressort que le regard est l'instrument par où la lumière s'incarne, et par où ... je suis photo-graphié.[15]

Thus, the very structuring of the novel as a closed field of vision constructs the subjects of the novel/court as subjects sundered by that vision, divided between their image in the world and their vision of themselves. They can only live the world as an alienation, lost as they are in its specularity.

By the specific choice of the closing years of Henri II's reign, Lafayette further complicates the delineation of the subject, by tainting the spectacular theatricality of its presentation with the added aura of tragedy. This court is presented in its magnificence as at once the epitome of all those Renaissance dreams of civility that since the *Cortegiano* had populated the imagination of European aristocracy, and its nightmare, too. For everything and everybody who makes up the court of Henri II lives under the sign of death. The world/the court is, we know as we read, dancing on the edge of a precipice: "vous êtes sur le bord du précipice," p. 277; "Elle trouva ... qu'elle s'était creusé un abîme dont elle ne sortirait jamais," p. 337; "il ne trouvait de tous côtés que des précipices et des abîmes," p. 350. It is a precipice from which they will topple and be engulfed in darkness: the king will die, the kingdom will fall into the chaos of civil war. All this is known and yet not known. It is all hinted at in the familiarly negative way Lafayette begins her novel, with the famous opening sentence "La magnificence et la galanterie n'ont jamais paru en France avec tant d'éclat que dans les dernières années du règne de Henri second," a sentence whose negativity is echoed in the equally melancholic last line of the novel which litotically tells us of the Princess' own death: "et sa vie qui fut assez courte, laissa des exemples de vertu inimitables." The novel is entirely contained, like the court it reflects, within the circle of these two phrases, within its perfect enclosure, besieged by this absence that is there, waiting. In a sense the theater of the *Princesse de Clèves* is very much a "théâtre macabre," where the narrative oscillates between the melancholia of absence and the fleeting spectacle of (a doomed) passion.

What strikes us as we move off the scene of drama and on to the stage of the court, into this closed narration of sexuality and power, is that the "nascent" nuclear family, that has played so central a role in both the tragedies and comedies of Corneille, Molière, Racine, is here much less clearly delineated. We have returned, by this leap back in history, to a more "feudal" concept of extended, kinship groups, which are families more in the sense of "maisonnée" than in the sense of a closed domestic unit. Political power depends on the manipulation by the different clans of individual desire. These kinship groups, of which the Guises and the Montmorencies are the two most active units, are basically heterogeneous associations of blood relations, domestics, dependants and other hangers-on who are joined together in systems of mutual aid, in networks of overlapping dependency, and who scheme together for common political pursuits. All these diverse "families" are situated in the same space – the court – and thus they are all subsumed by the larger "family," the "maisonnée du roi," of which they form the interlocking, constantly evolving, but basically static parts.[16] This extended household is presided over by the King and his powerful mistress, the Duchesse de Valentinois, who appear as the paradigm for the sexual division of that world into male and female camps. In this sense, if we wished, we could see the structuration of the world, its "feudal" nature, its depiction of an extended family, as participating in the same epistemological system as that represented by the *Astrée*. There, too, we have a large extended family, all the young lovers who drift into the Forez, presided over by the "sexless" parental couple of Adamas and Amasis. In a kinship society, the family is disseminated across the social landscape. The laws of sexual interdiction, the protocols governing that exchange of those women whom a man can or cannot marry, are social rather than passional. They are group-directed rather than inner-directed, constantly aimed outwards to situational needs rather than inward to the satisfaction of personal desire. In the court, therefore, desire is figured by its exchange, its circulation, outside of marriage, especially in those liaisons that so effectively traduce sexuality into power and vice-versa. What this structure implies is that in order for power/sexuality to circulate in the "world", that is for the court to be the court, characterized most notably by "une sorte d'agitation sans désordre, qui la rendait très agréable, mais aussi très dangereuse pour une jeune personne" (p. 253), there has to be the acceptance, of all and by all, that the object of desire is forever elusive, always lost: it is structurally impossible for it to be one's marriage partner.

When society moves from kinship families to the modern "capitalist" structuring in the tight concentration of the bourgeois family, the internalization of these disseminated social interdictions will form what we have come to call the "Œdipal scenario."[17] In this sense the historical narrative that serves as the scene upon which the passion of the Princess will be played out is important in that it represents an old, perhaps dying, order of the structuring of desire with which the focused individuated desire of the Princess will come into conflict. This is not to say of course, that one is necessarily better, more "liberating," than the other; for, as we will soon find out, the Princess rejects them both.

Although we could go on and find many other parallels between the *Astrée* and the *Princesse de Clèves*, this latter text is nevertheless more novel than I have been suggesting. This novelty is apparent not least of all in focusing our attention on what remained impossible for the *Astrée*, the sexuality of the parents. The spectacular passion of Henri II for Diane de Poitiers, a passion that is the model for all non-conjugal desire, is the generating nexus of all the passionate intrigues, all the political/sexual imbroglios, which occupy the entire theater of court life:

L'ambition et la galanterie étaient l'âme de cette cour, et occupaient également les hommes et les femmes. Il y avait tant d'intérêts et tant de cabales différentes, et les dames y avaient tant de part que l'amour était toujours mêlé aux affaires et les affaires à l'amour. Personne n'était tranquille, ni indifférent; on songeait à s'élever, à plaire, à servir ou à nuire ...

Although at first glance the description of the passionate whirlwind which engages all members of the court might make us think of a certain equality of men and women, their inmixture and confusion, in an imbroglio that effaced sexual difference, we are never allowed to forget the second aspect of this extended "royal household": the extraordinarily rigid, textually underlined separation of the world into two camps, the male and the female. From the outset there is an insistent narrative pressure to present us with this division, with the world separated into a clearly defined heterosexual opposition:

Jamais cour n'a eu tant de belles personnes et d'hommes admirablement bien faits; et il semblait que la nature eût pris plaisir à placer ce qu'elle donne de plus beau dans les plus grandes princesses et dans les plus grands princes.

(p. 242)

From this first, essential division, which by a positioning of sexual difference establishes these sexual parameters as both normative and prescriptive (the reference to "la nature" as tautologically grounding sexuality in a reproductive symmetry), all the other structures – of power, of desire, of narrative – will flow. Sylvère Lotringer is undoubtedly right to start his analysis of the novel by stating that the court is the locus "from which all comes and to which all returns." I would only like to add that I think that it is the court as symbol and locus of an overinvested (hetero-)sexual division that determines the possibilities of narration, the narration of desire and its frustration as already encoded in a theory that the text will be obliged to both illustrate and refuse.

Once the novel has separated the court into the two halves that complement each other, that look at each other across the abyss of sexual difference, the narration can go on to authorize the introduction into this arena of the protagonists who will repeat this essential division, but as that theory's quintessential representatives. Nevertheless this division is neither as stable nor as "natural" as the text would have us believe. On the contrary, as J. Rose reminds us:

The lines of that division [i.e. sexual difference] are fragile in exact proportion to the rigid insistence with which ... culture lays them down; they constantly converge and threaten to coalesce.[18]

We must therefore be wary of the very ways the text fixes the parameters inside of which it forces us to read it. How are we to understand this insistence on sexual difference? It is an insistence that returns us to a vision of difference, to difference as a creation of a vision which, as I've intimated in my retelling of the Freudian scenario, already implies a re-vision, a sighting from the male gaze that can only repeat its own origin – the site of the penis/phallus, the having or not having that most narcissistically invested organ from "which the male looks."[19] This look confirms the subject subjected to castration, to the cutting up of the world into those who are lacking and those who are not: to, that is, a tautological vision/version of male empowerment and female subservience. How, therefore, are we to accept/read this already-there of sexual difference in a text penned by a woman and that has as its center a female character, except as a narrative irony, as the setting up of an entire socio-sexual system that is given to us as a vision so that it may be all the better confounded?

This confusion is introduced when the text's focus changes, when it leaves the site of the court, for the sight of the Princess "en famille." We are introduced to this family when Mme de Chartres comes to the court to do business. She has reared her daughter, as we all know, away from this world, and brought her up according to her own radical pedagogy. When the Princess is sufficiently marriageable, she returns to the court with her in tow in order to find a suitable match:

Cette héritière était alors un des grands partis qu'il y eût en France; et quoiqu'elle fût dans une extrême jeunesse, l'on avait déjà proposé plusieurs mariages. Mme de Chartres, qui était extrêmement glorieuse, ne trouvait presque rien digne de sa fille; la voyant dans sa seizième année, elle voulut la mener à la cour. (p. 248)

In the divided world of the court, a world which from the outside appears to be an exemplary patriarchal monarchy, power, in a perversely beguiling narrative, is wielded by women. The initial sexual/political divisions of the court are subdivided into separate satellite courts, each one ruled over by an empowered woman:

Les dames avaient des attachements particuliers pour la reine, pour la reine dauphine, pour la reine de Navarre, pour Madame, sœur du roi, ou pour la duchesse de Valentinois. Les inclinations, les raisons de bienséance ou le rapport d'humeur faisaient ces différents attachements. (p. 252)

As I have said, the court of the *Princesse de Clèves* immediately recalls a nobiliary kinship system in which rival clans each vie for power. Power is attained through the ever-widening formation of male alliances, alliances which in this radically heterosexual world necessarily must be mediated by the exchange of women. For this reason marriage, that ritualized exchange of women between groups of men, is the most invested "familial" scenario of the text. Marriage is but a coded word for an entire institutionalized network of social, sexual, economic and political stakes. In this one word, this one metaphor for an entire system of rivalry, exploitation and intrigue, politics is eroticized and love politicized. Just as the closure of the world of the court prevents there being any possible representation of an outside that is not death, so does this same closure in the legal binding of sexuality to economics prevent there being an uneroticized politics, or an unpoliticized passion.

The central question, be it among mere "individuals" (that is, members of the nobility or the royal family), is "How can the tribe to which I belong profit, be aggrandized by marriage?" What we have here, in a very elaborate but not too subtle form, is an aristocratic "traffic in women." The importance of this traffic is enormous, not only for private alliances but for national well-beings as well, and this helps to explain why the central events of the novel which call for the most elaborate, spectacular descriptive passages always turn around engagements and weddings: the engagement of Claude de France and the Duc de Lorraine, the marriage of Madame, sister of the King, and the Duc de Savoie, the betrothal and marriage of Madame Elizabeth to the King of Spain, Nemours's long-distance courtship of Elizabeth, and the initial plottings and disappointments of Madame de Chartres in her attempts at finding a good match for her daughter.

Thus, on the one hand, Mme de Chartres, when she appears in the novel, is just like all the older women in the court, all power brokers in a sexual economy of exchange. On the other, what makes her different is precisely the ambivalent bonding that she has established with her daughter. Much recent analysis of the novel has dwelt at great length on the different aspects, implications and possible interpretations of this mother–daughter relation, often seeing it as the major passional relationship in the text.[20] I will not therefore pass over what I see as a firmly established analysis of one of the essential knots of the novel. I would only like to point out some of the particulars of this relation that I find relevant for my own discussion.

Mme de Chartres and Mlle de Chartres enter the novel, enter into the dichotomized world of the court, as a monad. They are to be seen at first as existing in a specularly narcissistic embrace which seems to have remained impervious to the intrusion of the law of the father, the law of castration, of difference. We can see their inseparability as forming a type of female homosexual bonding that resists the splitting, the separation that impels the subject into sexual difference (as lack) and into language. In a certain sense this couple, a self-enclosed parent–child totality come from another world, come from *beyond* the world, enters the court as (in the words of E. Lemoine Luccioni) "le vieux rêve féminin de la plénitude, de complétude: elle est homme puisqu'elle a le phallus (l'enfant) et elle est femme puisqu'elle est mère."[21] Mother and daughter exist as a form of self-enclosure that in terms of a male sexual economy, based precisely on the concept of desire as lack, would foreclose the possibility of object libido to either one of them. According to most (patriarchal) psychoanalytical theory it is not through the relation to the mother that the daughter can successfully establish her own feminine identity.[22]

What this means is that in a normalizing patriarchal society founded on the acceptance of castration, the girl child is always in an ambivalent, conflicted space, especially in relation to her first love object which she "must" renounce, her mother. In order for a child of either sex to leave the embrace of the mother, the realm of a certain pre-Œdipal indeterminacy, a third term, must intervene, be it the father or his representative, the Law. It is the intervention of the paternal signifier as the law of difference and loss that sets both the boy and the girl child off on their separate paths. Each path, however, is a path in castration, but of a difference in that castration.[23] That this passage is never navigated smoothly is attested to in all the conflicted sexual manifestations of adult life, in the perversions, neuroses and psychoses. Nevertheless this passage must be navigated for better or worse by all human children in order for them to become subjects subjugated to social imperatives.

It is interesting, therefore, that the most glaring absence in this text is the father's. All the fathers in the novel are strategically missing: they are either dead when the novel opens or are eliminated as it progresses. At first, we are simply informed that Mlle de Chartres's father "died young." The most powerful female figure in the novel, Diane de Poitiers, played an ambivalent role in her own father's demise. A few days after she has obtained his release *in extremis* from the death penalty ("je ne sais par quels moyens," Mme de Chartres naively tells her daughter after having said that Diane was extremely beautiful and had already caught the eye of the late king), he dies of fright. The textual ellipsis that joins daughter to father in this case is particularly revealing: "il mourut peu de jours après. Sa fille parut à la cour comme la maîtresse du roi" (p. 265). The father dies, the daughter appears. It would seem that the text predicates the empowerment of the daughter on the death of the father. The most spectacular textual patricide, Henri II's, is also elliptically linked to sexual empowerment:

La reine manda au roi qu'elle le conjurait de ne plus courir; qu'il avait si bien fait qu'il devait être content et qu'elle le suppliait de revenir auprès d'elle. Il répondit que c'était pour l'amour d'elle qu'il allait courir encore et entra dans la barrière. Elle lui renvoya M. de Savoie pour le prier une seconde fois de revenir; mais tout fut inutile. Il courut; les lances se brisèrent, et un éclat de celle du comte de Montgomery lui donna dans l'œil et y demeura. (p. 356)

Henri's death does away with the king, the titular "père du peuple," and ushers in a major change in the sexual/political organization of the court. Diane de Poitiers, who has reigned rather despotically over the court ("Depuis douze ans que ce prince règne, elle est maîtresse absolue de toutes choses; elle dispose des charges et des affaires," p. 268) is brought down by his death; power passes into the hands of her rival Catherine de Médicis, widow and mother.

The place of the real father in the courtly scenario is vacant. In his stead we have a succession of phallic women whose task it is to transmit the Law of the father in the absence of any man capable of assuming that function. This is not, however, as drastic a shifting of sexual roles as it at first appears. In the development of patriarchy, the role of the "dead" father, the impossible ideal of the father, is much more important than the presence of any individual father.[24] Where we find the persistent presence of this dead father is precisely in his dissemination as the Law, which in both the kinship structures of the court and the nuclear structure of the family whose merits Mme de Chartres tries to inculcate in her daugther are symbolized in marriage. Marriage, as we've already said, is that institution that most acutely articulates the Law, the distribution of sex and power, their mediation by and through the exchange of women. It is in the entire predicative structures of marriage that the father exists in this text, never available except, of course, as an ideal imposed on women, the ideal of virtue, of honor, of duty.

Let us look at the famous passage that describes Mme de Clèves's pedagogical imperative:

La plupart des mères s'imaginent qu'il suffit de ne parler jamais de galanterie devant les jeunes personnes pour les en éloigner. Mme de Chartres avait une opinion opposée; elle faisait souvent à sa fille des peintures de l'amour; elle lui montrait ce qu'il a d'agréable pour la persuader plus aisément sur ce qu'elle lui en apprenait de dangereux; elle lui contait le peu de sincérité des hommes, leurs tromperies et leur infidélité, les malheurs domestiques où plongent les engagements; et elle lui faisait voir, d'un autre côté, quelle tranquillité suivait la vie d'une honnête femme, et combien la vertu donnait d'éclat et d'élévation à une personne qui avait de la beauté et de la naissance; mais elle lui faisait voir aussi combien il était difficile de conserver cette vertu, que par une extrême défiance de soi-même et par un grand soin de s'attacher à ce qui seul peut faire le bonheur d'une femme, qui est d'aimer son mari et d'en être aimée. (p. 248)

What is strange about Mme de Chartres's lesson? It strikes me that her catechism is destined to failure from the very fact that its aim is at cross purposes with its rhetoric. What she is basically trying to do is to "show" her daughter the Law of the court, (notice the prevalence of those verbs, "voir", "montrer," those nouns "des peintures de l'amour," "l'éclat") while trying at the same time to inculcate in her the more "bourgeois" values of a private life. She is showing her the dangers of sexuality that is lived outside of the couple while the entire courtly model of love excludes sexuality (as passion) from marriage. Marriage is precisely what sends passion outside. In a certain, very obvious sense, Mme de Chartres is trying to play here a double role, perhaps an hysterical role: she is a father/ mother. She repeats the Law of the symbolic in terms that necessarily return the subject, object of that law, to the dominance of the imaginary, in such a way that the Law, which is always the imposition and acceptance of castration, is never articulable by her in a way that would prove effective. Although Mme de Chartres images the law of separation, thus attempting to take the father's place, she will be unsuccessful in imposing any such separation because of her own unresolved Œdipal attachment to her daughter. We might speculate that by living outside of the court, outside, that is, of a firmly articulated heterosexual universe totally dependent on the Law, they have never been able to accomplish a separation that would enable the daughter to desire outside of the mother's embrace. Rather their entire relation is based on non-separation, on the denial of castration, on the refusal of the phallus as alterity. In a sense Mme de Chartres's own relation to her daughter seems to be a form of fetishism; the daughter/child papers over the castration of the mother, a castration that Mme de Chartres is no more able to accept than to impose on her own daughter. The daughter serves as the phallus of her mother, the mother as the object of desire for the child. They live as a female unit, each reflecting back to the other an image of narcissistic self-enclosure that is rooted in the pre-Œdipal monad of child/mother. Because it never engages any desire on the part of the Princess, the marriage that the mother eventually contracts for the daughter fits within the parameters of the enclosed female unit as a non-threatening suture. The marriage just re-encloses the mother–daughter dyad upon itself.

Certainly M. de Clèves is incapable of effecting any scission between mother and daughter. Not only do we know that Mlle de Chartres feels no desire for him before the marriage ("Mlle de Chartres répondit qu'elle lui remarquait les mêmes bonnes qualités; qu'elle l'épouserait même avec moins de répugnance qu'un autre, mais qu'elle n'avait aucune inclination particulière pour sa personne," (p. 258) but that even after, her sexuality remains untouched by him. ("M. de Clèves ne trouva pas que Mlle de Chartres eût changé de sentiment en changeant de nom. La qualité de mari lui donna de plus grands privilèges; mais elle ne lui donna pas une autre place

189

dans le cœur de sa femme," (p. 260.) At the same time we are told that Mme de Clèves is aware of her daughter's lack of attraction to Clèves, but that she does nothing to stop a marriage that could not but lead her into precisely the position against which she has argued:

Mme de Chartres admirait la sincérité de sa fille, et elle l'admirait avec raison, car jamais personne n'en a eu une si grande et si naturelle; mais elle n'admirait pas moins que son cœur ne fût point touché ... Cela fut cause qu'elle prit de grands soins de l'attacher à son mari ...   (p. 259)

Rather than a radical difference, there is a collusion between Mme de Chartres and M. de Clèves, a relaying of roles that has been noticed by many readers of this novel.[25] M. de Clèves merely replaces Mme de Chartres once she has disappeared from the world of the text. He takes on the same role in relation to his wife that Mme de Chartres played. Essentially that role is to protect her against difference, against any desire:

quoique la tendresse et la reconnaissance y eussent la plus grande part, le besoin qu'elle sentait qu'elle avait de sa mère, pour se défendre contre M. de Nemours, ne laissait pas d'y en avoir beaucoup. Elle se trouvait malheureuse d'être abandonnée à elle-même, dans un temps où elle était si peu maîtresse de ses sentiments ... elle ne voulait point qu'il [her husband] la quittât, et il lui semblait qu'à force de s'attacher à lui, il la défendrait contre M. de Nemours.   (p. 279)

The twice-reiterated "défendre contre M. de Nemours," used once for the mother, once for the husband, reveals, besides a communality of psychic function, the intensity of a previously unknown, un-suspected desire that is felt as a threat, an aggressive attack against which she needs to be protected. It also and coterminously appears as the external object, the object of difference that for the first time separates the daughter from the mother, and then, in her desperate attempt to flee from its threat, joins the wife to the husband.

The narcissistically enclosed mother–daughter bonding serves as the matrix from which the text will generate a corresponding network representing and condemning the Princess's passion for Nemours. Since this dyad continually harks back to a pre-Œdipal structuring of passion, a passion irremediably linked to an imaginary instance, it will not surprise us that its representation, the text's self-represen-tation of passion, will be expressed most insistently in the visionary aspects of that passion, as a passion for images rather than as a desire for discourse.

On a more general level the enclosed relation of mother and daughter also helps to explain the enormous, totalizing role of female bonding in the novel. What may appear less evident at first, however, is the way these women, by manipulating sexual/political power in a game where the stakes are immeasurably important, are simply figures in an economy where they are predestined to debasement. When we look closely at the circulation of sexuality, power and money in this novel, we realize that this enormous "maison du roi," this brilliant, ambitious court, this court closed in on itself, is, for all intents and purposes, precisely that, a closed house: "une maison close." All the older women, each the head of her own bevy of younger girls, is very much in the position of those "mères maquerelles" who barter the sexual desirability of their wards. In a global network of exchange those "filles à marier" are exchanged in a system that, by creating newer, more expansive alliances, aggrandizes the social/political interests of their protectoresses.

Furthermore, when we understand this underlying dynamic, this prostitution of princesses, and when we re-situate it in the context of the court as spectacle, we understand that in a very real way this "maison close," in which we are told that the King first and foremost "aimait le commerce des femmes, même de celles dont il n'était pas amoureux (p. 242), where the polysemic insistence of "commerce" reveals what is never allowed to be textually articulated, signals to us that the surface brillance is merely a euphemism, an illusion. The court of Henri II is not only a "maison close", but more importantly (when we remember the intimate connection linking sexuality to a vision, where sexuality is always a sighting, a sighting that is also always an illusion), we understand that this court, which is presented as the locus of literary perfection, as the end of an entire tradition of courtly literature, is more properly "une maison d'illusion," a dizzying sexual/political house of mirrors where "ce qui paraît n'est presque jamais la vérité" (p. 265). Only a small step takes us from the world of the *Princesse de Clèves* to Genêt's *Balcon*.

It is into this world of illusion, into the "maison close" of the court, that Mlle de Chartres comes, or rather is brought by her mother. Significantly, she enters on to the "scène du monde" as a vision:

Il parut alors une beauté à la cour, qui attira les yeux de tout le monde, et l'on doit croire que c'était une beauté parfaite, puisqu'elle donna de l'admiration dans un lieu où l'on était si accoutumé à voir de belles personnes.

(p. 247)

This "perfectly" beautiful vision is spellbinding:

> Lorsqu'elle arriva, le vidame alla au-devant d'elle; il fut surpris de la grande beauté de Mlle de Chartres, et il en fut surpris avec raison. La blancheur de son teint et ses cheveux blonds lui donnaient un éclat que l'on n'a jamais vu qu'à elle; tous ses traits étaient réguliers, et son visage et sa personne étaient pleins de grâce et de charmes. (p. 248)

It is obvious from the two brief passages quoted above that Mlle de Chartres is first and foremost proffered as a lure for the eyes: that is, she is "shown" to the court (and to the reader) as a beautiful, appealing surface. Conventionally the presentation of the Princess is explained by suggesting that the text begins its exploration of her subjectivity by first describing her from the outside; then, as her passion grows, the text turns inward, creating interiority, depth of character. It seems, however, more interesting to say that at first she appears as the foil of a certain gaze. She is offered to our sight as its object, an object that captures the *Schaulust* of the gazes that are there waiting for it. She is seen as a surface, a reflecting mirror, an image of beauty, the most beautiful woman. But what does it mean when a text appeals to an immediacy of vision, a glimpse of perfect female beauty? In his article "Difference," Stephen Heath addresses precisely this question and suggests that

> where a discourse appeals directly to an image, to an immediacy of seeing, as a point of its argument or demonstration one can be sure that all difference is being elided, that the unity of some accepted vision is being reproduced.[26]

What is being reproduced in the appeal of/to the image is an ideology of sexual difference where the woman is looked at, upon, and seen to figure for the male viewer that difference that corroborates his own sexuality as superiority. Mlle de Chartres, as the narration first presents her, would seem to be the castrated object — the woman as other. Yet that difference-as-lack is also "sutured" over in the image by the textual insistence on her beauty. This "blinding beauty" functions fetishistically for the male viewer: it is both the sign of castration, the woman as other, and the refusal of that castration, its sublimation into metaphor as an object of devotion, of worship, a cultural icon of an ideal — beauty. The price paid by patriarchal culture for this reassurance of and against castration is the "beauty" of the woman/image, a beauty which, however, when it is perfect ("une beauté parfaite"), as in the case of Mlle de Chartres, does nothing so much as contradictorily present "a seamless image to the world so that the man, in the confrontation with difference, can avoid any apprehension of lack."[27]

The image that is Mlle de Chartres is, however, more complex, more troubling. What finally do we see, what do the men who look at her see? They see, it seems to me, nothing. She is described as "blond," "fair-skinned," with "perfect features" — hardly a physical presence, never a weighty reality. Although we may agree with R. Barthes that only the ugly is scriptable because it is always particular, that beauty is impossible to describe in any way that is not simply a reference to another cultural icon, to another object in the aesthetic canon, nevertheless the description of Mlle de Chartres, or rather the lack of that description, seems particularly overcoded in this narrative of a certain "feminine mystique."[28] Finally, she is, at least in her description if not in her image, a perfect blank in the text, in our vision: an "éclat."

This is not the first time the word "éclat" has appeared in the text. We have already seen it in the very first sentence of the novel ("La magnificence et la galanterie n'ont jamais paru en France avec tant d'éclat ..."), and it reappears strategically throughout the novel ("On proposa tout ce qui se pouvait faire de plus grand pour des ballets et des comédies, mais le roi trouva ces divertissements trop particuliers, et il en voulut d'un plus grand éclat. Il résolut de faire un tournoi ... (p.304). The importance of the visual image, its ambivalent status — the presence/absence of sexual difference — is strategically overdetermined by the slippage of meanings hidden and revealed by the word "éclat." For an "éclat," which is what we are told Mlle de Chartres is, circulates in the text, joining together in its semantic overdeterminacy the networks of sexuality, textuality and death in a single blinding image.

"Eclat," the dictionary informs us, is at the same time "a fragment of a whole," that is a synecdoche for a unity, an integrity of being that is lost. Thus we might say that it is, when used to describe the Princess, but another metaphor for the castration it would disguise, repress: it is a "brilliant flash of light" whose clarity blinds, a vision that is blinding in the sense that it shows us what can never be seen, turning us back once again with the cultural associations to the "blinding/blindness" of Œdipus,[29] to the image of beauty as simply the suture of a horrifying lack. It is, in a further, metaphoric extension of this definition, "magnificence, brillance" in a social sense, relaying us once again back to the opulence, the civility, the imaginary of the court. Finally, pointedly, it is in this novel a "splinter," a sharp, cutting object, the vehicle by which death enters into the world of the court, called from the circumference and thrown into its very center. An "éclat" is thrust into the eye of the king, the privileged spectator of all this brilliance, and kills him ("Il courut; les lances se brisèrent, et un éclat de celle du comte de Mongomery lui donna dans l'œil et y demeura," p. 356). In a very significant sense then, when Mlle de Chartres enters on to the stage of the court she appears to the eyes of those who covet her in an exceedingly conflicted textual position. She is both the apogee of courtly desire, and precisely what that desire obfuscates, the fascination with, the attraction of the impossible, of death.

From her first apparition in the novel, Mlle de Chartres generates an entire network of visual images, a network which actively engages the sexuality of the text, by which I mean the way the scopic drive in its passive and active aspects is made to delineate and reflect the division of the world/court into masculine and feminine essentialities and the consequences of that division for the subject formed in their intersection. On the one hand, we notice that as her passion for Nemours develops, the density of visual images, the use of the verbs "voir," "regarder," "montrer," becomes greater and greater. On the other hand, we might just as well turn this around to state that as the density of visual illusions increases so does the passion. This would lead us to the hypothesis that in the world of the court, in a world of spectacle, love is always a visual "passion," always the entrapment of the desiring subject in the illusion of the visual field, always a "trompe-l'œil."

In his *Three Essays on the Theory of Sexuality*, Freud proposes that "In the perversions which are directed towards looking and being looked at, we come across a very remarkable characteristic ... the sexual aim occurs in two forms, an active and a passive." [30] It is the ambivalence of the scopic drive, its inherent reversibility, that this text plays upon, creating a dizzying confusion of sexuality in the reader/voyeur whose own sense of sexual parameters is subtly thrown into disarray. [31] In traditional western narratives, the female is the object of the male gaze/quest. She is reduced to the passive side of the scopic drive. She is, as I have already mentioned, the object of a voyeuristic insistence: the gaze of the male looks, encompasses, possesses, penetrates. When a woman looks in western narratives she looks, as M. A. Doane writes, "intransitively," "she looks beautiful." [32] In this sense, at least in the first part of her novel, Lafayette's Princess simply comes into the space, the focalized narrative space, that western phallocentrism had assigned her. She is the feminine in the sense that she offers herself to the gaze of the other, and sees herself, seeing herself. [33] She is the blind spot of vision. The focal point of everyone's gaze, the vanishing point of desire. To look at her is to be transfixed, "surpris," "étonné." Thus her first encounter with M. de Clèves:

Comme elle y était, le prince de Clèves y arriva. Il fut tellement surpris de sa beauté qu'il ne put cacher sa surprise; et Mlle de Chartres ne put s'empêcher de rougir en voyant l'étonnement qu'elle lui avait donné. ... M. de Clèves la regardait avec admiration ... Il voyait bien par son air, et par tout ce qui était à sa suite, qu'elle devait être d'une grande qualité. ... mais, ne lui voyant point de mère et l'Italien qui ne la connaissait point l'appelant madame, il ne savait que penser, et il la regardait toujours avec étonnement.   (p. 249)

As this passage makes abundantly clear, Mlle de Chartres is lexically situated as the center of a series of visual references ("voir," "regarder," etc.), references that only continue to proliferate as her narrative of passion becomes more pronounced. What is interesting in this "imaging" of the Princess is that it serves the function of "highlighting" what becomes her distinguishing feature in the novel, her extraordinary beauty, her superiority over the other females in the text, her difference − which, of course, will become coded in her own rhetoric of self-imaging as her "uniqueness." Her introduction in the novel and in the court is marked by her sign of "less": she is less like any other woman because she is ignorant of desire, has no "knowledge" of desire;

Mlle de Chartres ne savait que répondre, et ces distinctions étaient au-dessus de ses connaissances. M. de Clèves ne voyait que trop combien elle était éloignée d'avoir pour lui des sentiments qui le pouvaient satisfaire, puisqu'il lui paraissait qu'elle ne les entendait pas.   (p. 259)

But this less is really a "more," an excess of morality ("vertu") that is so obviously lacking in all the other women of the court. Mlle de Chartres comes into the court as an ambivalent cipher, both a minus and a plus. She attracts many men but none dare to approach her; she is the woman all desire and none can have:

Mme de Chartres joignait à la sagesse de sa fille une conduite si exacte pour toutes les bienséances qu'elle achevait de la faire paraître une personne où l'on ne pouvait atteindre.   (p. 260)

The princess is "morally" different not only from all the women of the court, but from all other women. She is, we are told, "unique," alone of all her sex. In a strange reversal, she is both the generalized portrait of woman and the exception, a different difference:

Il (Nemours) trouva de la gloire à s'être fait aimer d'une femme si différente de toutes celles de son sexe.   (p. 337)

Ah! monsieur, reprit-elle, il n'y a pas dans le monde une autre aventure pareille à la mienne, il n'y a point une autre femme capable de la même chose. (p. 349)

J'ai eu tort de croire qu'il y eût un homme capable de cacher ce qui flatte sa gloire. C'est pourtant pour cet homme, que j'ai cru si différent du reste des hommes, que je me trouve comme les autres femmes, étant si éloignée de leur ressembler. (p. 352)

The text's insistence on the Princess's uniqueness is intriguing in that it creates her as a self-enclosed narcissism, a rhetoric of her difference that becomes the mirror of her own superiority. This narcissistic self-imaging produces, however, an oscillating indeterminacy. Her capture as beauty creates, in a blinding flash, a transcendental vision of "Woman" ("La femme"). She becomes in her total "éclat," that is, her blinding difference, Classicism's impossible icon for "Woman." Yet, since her difference is constantly a difference in kind — that is, she is but a synecdoche for all women, a part for the whole — the same description negates the very possibility of her subjectivity as integrity, as a totality. Thus the text oscillates between the projection, in a vision, of "Woman" as a totality one and entire, the lure of the male gaze, and the shattering of that totality by the same vision as "éclat," the impossibility of that image. The text would seem, in its intricate construction, in its constant shuttling back and forth between different visions, to be tracing the very dynamics of feminine sexuality as indeterminate, always divided, partitive, that will be theorized by Freud's French followers almost three hundred years later.[34]

The Princess's constant insistence on her uniqueness, on her difference from all other women, also betrays an investment in a narcissistic economy that repeats in one more metaphoric register the text's investment in images, in the specularity of being that reflects the court. It is because she is so perfectly beautiful, the exquisite exemplum of what "nature" has produced as most unique, that she can only find her complement in her mirror image: the Duc de Nemours, her counterpart in sexual difference, in perfection ("Mais ce prince était un chef-d'œuvre de la nature; ce qu'il avait de moins admirable, c'était d'être l'homme du monde le mieux fait et le plus beau," p. 243). Just as she draws all eyes to her, he too, when he appears, is the focus of everyone's attention ("on ne pouvait regarder que lui dans tous les lieux où il paraissait," p. 244). It is, of course, particularly intriguing that their meeting and their attraction is staged in spectacularly visual terms, terms in which for the first time the

Princess is shifted out of her position as pure spectacle and becomes also a spectator. Desire, when it finally manifests itself in Mme de Clèves, is a desire to see:

Mme la dauphine le lui avait dépeint d'une sorte et lui en avait parlé tant de fois qu'elle lui avait donné de la curiosité, et même de l'impatience de le voir.

Elle passa tout le jour des fiançailles chez elle à se parer, pour se trouver le soir au bal et au festin royal qui se faisait au Louvre. Lorsqu'elle arriva, l'on admira sa beauté et sa parure; le bal commença et, comme elle dansait avec M. de Guise, il se fit un assez grand bruit vers la porte de la salle, comme de quelqu'un qui entrait et à qui on faisait place. Mme de Clèves acheva de danser et, pendant qu'elle cherchait des yeux quelqu'un qu'elle avait dessein de prendre, le roi lui cria de prendre celui qui arrivait. Elle se tourna et vit un homme qu'elle crut d'abord ne pouvoir être que M. de Nemours, qui passait par-dessus quelques sièges pour arriver où l'on dansait. Ce prince était fait d'une sorte qu'il était difficile de n'être pas surprise de le voir quand on ne l'avait jamais vu, surtout ce soir-là où le soin qu'il avait pris de se parer augmentait encore l'air brillant qui était dans sa personne; mais il était difficile aussi de voir Mme de Clèves pour la première fois sans avoir un grand étonnement.

M. de Nemours fut tellement surpris de sa beauté que, lorsqu'il fut proche d'elle, et qu'elle lui fit la révérence, il ne put s'empêcher de donner des marques de son admiration. Quand ils commencèrent à danser, il s'éleva dans la salle un murmure de louanges.   (p. 262)

As I have already mentioned in the first chapter of this book, this scene is particularly overdetermined, because although it diegetically introduces the two protagonists, it also sets them off in a dance/ vision in which their difference and complementarity continually swirl before the enchanted eyes of the court, blending them together and separating them out from each other. More importantly, their dance structures them and their love as exempla of the entire sexual and political ideology of the court. Both are the unique, most perfect examples of sexual division, sexual difference. They fall in love with each other as mirror reflections of each other. They exist as a narcissistic chiasmus, trapped each in the image of the other:

Les jours suivants, elle le vit chez la reine dauphine, elle le vit jouer à la paume avec le roi, elle le vit courre la bague ... mais elle le vit toujours surpasser de si loin tous les autres ... qu'il fit, en peu de temps, une grande impression dans son cœur.

Il est vrai aussi que ... M. de Nemours sentait pour elle une inclination violente ... de sorte que, se voyant souvent, et se voyant l'un et l'autre ce qu'il y avait de plus parfait à la cour, il était difficile qu'ils ne se plussent infiniment.   (p. 263)

Nemours and Clèves as lovers are presented as mirror images of each other in sexual reversal. At the same time they reflect back to the court as "natural" its ideological investment in a narrow normative heterosexuality. The two protagonists are divided in the scission of reflection, and yet, as images, they are interchangeable for each other. In a sense, perhaps the only thing that distinguishes Nemours from the Princess is their ambivalent containment in the images they project of themselves, in the ambivalence of the one word "(se) parer" most often used to describe their visual presence in the world, a word that functions ambivalently in the text, collapsing sexual difference in itself and constantly re-separating it out:

Elle passa tout le jour des fiançailles chez elle à se parer ... Ce prince était fait d'une sorte qu'il était difficile de n'être pas surprise de le voir quand on ne l'avait jamais vu, surtout ce soir-là où le soin qu'il avait pris de se parer augmentait encore l'air brillant ...   (pp. 262–263)

il n'y a point de femme que le soin de sa parure n'empêche de songer à son amant; qu'elles en sont entièrement occupées; que ce soin de se parer est pour tout le monde.   (p. 271)

M. de Nemours y vint peu de temps après, habillé magnifiquement et comme un homme qui ne se sentait pas de l'accident.   (p. 307)

Il était paré pour l'assemblée du soir ...   (p. 344)

In the "bal masqué" that is the world of the court, where everyone is a spectacle for everyone else, where there is no adequately knowable fit of "être" and "paraître," Nemours and the Princess take up their sexual roles in front of one another in and through the image they project, an image that is a "sexual fix," a pure "parade." In a sense we might say that what is being exhibited in this "parade" is precisely the way sexuality, in a world invested in the illusion of heterosexual complementarity, is produced always as a lure, always as a masquerade. In this masquerade, what is disguised in the artifice of supplemental dress that allows Mme de Clèves to "appear" as an image of beauty is the fact that this image hides what the system refuses to contemplate, the structuring of femininity in another register, another suture of psychic life. As we've seen, feminine subjectivity is perceived as divided, doubled, non-integral, lacking the "phallus." This lack is made up for by woman's masquerade as a vision, a "beauty," an integrity, that traps the male in its illusion: what he desires in her is the image of his own reflection, the woman not as different but as same, as integral. The sign of this entrapment is his desire, made visible in spite of, or rather because of, himself:

198

"il ne put s'empêcher de donner des marques de son admiration." As for Nemours, "having" the penis, organ that represents the absent phallus, he adorns it/himself, puts it on "parade" in all the supplementary ornaments that displace his phallic presence, and struts it before the eyes of the court, becoming in this sense the universal object of desire ("il avait un enjouement qui plaisait également aux hommes et aux femmes." pp. 244–245) There is not a lady at the court who would not like to "attach" it/him to herself:

Il n'y avait aucune dame de la cour dont la gloire n'eût été flattée de le voir attaché à elle; peu de celles à qui il s'était attaché, se pouvaient vanter de lui avoir résisté, et même plusieurs à qui il n'avait point témoigné de passion, n'avaient pas laissé d'en avoir pour lui. (p. 244)

Their whirling dance before the thrilled eyes of the court is the dance of the masks, the masks of femininity and of masculinity, of the illusion of having and being, that they hold up to each other and the world as the illusion of a sexual symmetry: man and woman each the (illusory) complement of the other, the "natural" fix of sexuality that announces that for every "he" there is a "she" – without, of course, taking into account that sexuality (as S. Heath reminds us)

is not given in nature but produced; the individual subject is not constructed from sexuality, sexuality is constructed in the history of the subject …[35]

Finally we might speculate that what Lafayette gives us, "avant la lettre," is a Lacanian reading of sexuality as a game of "trompe-l'œil," a trompe-l'œil which because of its very nature precludes any happy ending, any possibility of a joining of these two beings in a "sexual relation." What the whole text is illustrating is precisely that the predicate of a transparent heterosexuality, which would oppose masculinity and femininity in a simple complementarity, is from the very nature of sexuality as a different subjective division in the symbolic register, precluded.

Thus the vision of Madame de Clèves and M. de Nemours serves as "trompe-l'œil" for the court and for themselves. What we have are two marionettes, disguised in some pre-existing ideal of womanliness and manliness. Perhaps it would be more appropriate to see Clèves and Nemours as the court's paramount pageant, which, in a sense, would, in this world of illusion mean its extreme transvestites, if we use this term in the way J. Baudrillard suggests:

Pour qu'il y ait sexe, il faut que les signes redoublent l'être biologique. Ici les signes se séparent, il n'y a donc plus de sexe à proprement parler,

199

et ce dont les travestis sont amoureux, c'est de ce jeu de signes, ce qui les passionne, c'est de séduire les signes eux-mêmes. Tout chez eux est maquillage, théâtre, séduction.[36]

The two most intensely invested scenes of passion that stand out in the text in oxymoronic reversal underline the enormous seduction of the visual, the protagonists' passion for images, and the dialectical impossibility of those images ever coinciding in a mutually consistent embrace. To the famous night-time vigil at Coulommiers, when the duke gazes ecstatically at the Princess paying rapt attention to his portrait included in the tableau of the siege of Metz, corresponds the Princess's glancing discovery of the duke's surreptious rape of her portrait from its box in her apartments. In both these instances, but especially in their chiasmus, resides, it seems to me, the lesson of the sexuality of the text, or rather of its impossibility.

In both instances what we must insist upon is the dominance of the image of the loved object over the object. What is the cause of a certain textual jouissance is never the object but the subject's loss in the contemplation of a representation — an image — of that object. In M. de Nemours's case, however, the situation is further complicated by the fact that for him, as well as for the entire masculine economy of representation, Mme de Clèves is never anything but a representation: she is always (already) a portrait, and her representation as portrait merely accentuates this alienation to another degree:

La reine dauphine faisait faire des portraits en petit de toutes les belles personnes de la Cour ... Le jour qu'on achevait celui de Mme de Clèves, Mme la Dauphine vint passer l'après-dînée chez elle. M. de Nemours ne manqua pas de s'y trouver; il ne laissait échapper aucune occasion de voir Mme de Clèves sans laisser paraître néanmoins qu'il les cherchât. Elle était si belle, ce jour-là, qu'il en serait devenu amoureux quand il ne l'aurait pas été. Il n'osait pourtant avoir les yeux attachés sur elle pendant qu'on la peignait, et il craignait de laisser trop voir le plaisir qu'il avait à la regarder.

(p. 301)

Not content with the surreptitious pleasure her view gives him, Nemours desires the more permanent pleasure of possession. He wants to possess the Princess, and to do this he must carry off her image:

Il y avait longtemps que M. de Nemours souhaitait d'avoir le portrait de Mme de Clèves. ...

Mme de Clèves aperçut par un des rideaux, qui n'était qu'à demi fermé, M. de Nemours, le dos contre la table, qui était au pied du lit, et elle vit que, sans tourner la tête, il prenait adroitement quelque chose sur cette table. Elle n'eut pas de peine à deviner que c'était son portrait, et elle en fut si troublée que Mme la Dauphine remarqua qu'elle ne l'écoutait pas et lui demanda tout haut ce qu'elle regardait. M. de Nemours se tourna à ces paroles; il rencontra les yeux de Mme de Clèves, qui étaient encore attachés sur lui ... (p. 302)

All the pleasure of this text passes through the eyes and it is in this sense always a solitary pleasure: "M. de Nemours alla se renfermer chez lui, ne pouvant soutenir en public la joie d'avoir un portrait de Mme de Clèves. Il sentait tout ce que la passion peut faire sentir de plus agréable ..." The only juncture possible is the joining of eyes. But that meeting is always surreptitious, always suspect, always the coming together of an aggression and its defense. In a sense the theft of the portrait reminds us of the extremely tendentious relation (or lack of it) between the sexes, especially when we recall a strikingly similar theft related by Freud.

In "A Case of Paranoia ..." Freud's patient, whose family situation reminds us of the Princess's ("She lived alone with her old mother of whom she was the sole support ..."), develops the paranoid fantasy that an image of herself in a compromised situation has been captured (by photography) and put into circulation. In the *Princesse de Clèves*, where the circulation of images (and of gossip) constantly threatens everyone with a disclosure and an uncovering that for most would be tantamount to (social) death, we can understand that the Princess's predicament, her inability to act because to act one way or the other would also reveal something that must be kept hidden, leads her down a path of suspicion and resentment that is very similar to a paranoid relation to her world. Dispossessed of her image by its capture in Nemours's aggressive, possessive gaze, Mme de Clèves's reaction to his intrusive stare is panic, flight, suspicion. The rape of her image, its use for Nemours's pleasure, is marked by a heightened sense of exposure, a sense of being vulnerable to a look, that although perhaps an expression of her own desire to be looked at returns to haunt her as an omniscient persecutor:[37] "Je serai bientôt regardée de tout le monde comme une personne qui a une folle et violente passion" (p. 352). The greater her passion for Nemours becomes, the more vulnerable she feels her self to be, the more she sees herself to be exposed to a generalized gaze of abasement.

In Freud's case, of course, he had to explain what seemed to him an anomaly: he had based all his initial work on paranoia on the intuition that at its origin was a suppressed homosexual desire.[38]

Since he was unable to find any homosexual component in what at first appeared to be a clearly heterosexual dynamics, this young woman's case eluded his theory. It was only after a second visit with the patient that a homosexual component emerged: an elder woman who worked with the patient, a substitute for her mother, was seen as the fantasized aggressor. What are we to think of Mme de Clèves? Her own "homosexual" attachment to her mother has been noted, but then again, Mme de Chartres is dead. Perhaps Mme de Clèves's own sense of persecution, of being hounded and spied upon, can be essentially traced back to the mother's representative, her husband, M. de Clèves. Textually it is M. de Clèves whose own inquisitive desire to find out the cause of his wife's desire, a more than persistent insistence that she loves Nemours (that he loves Nemours) causes her more and more anxiety as she feels his gaze envelop her, entrap her and make her reveal what she has sworn not to. In a sense, therefore, the greater her passion becomes the more she becomes the object of both these men's gazes − the one accusatory, the other desirous, both aggressive. Yet, perhaps, again, this aggression is merely Mme de Clèves's own desire to see the other which, meeting the resistance of her own moral code, the code of her mother, simply projects her own aggression outward on to the eyes of the court? The more this paranoid view of the court, and of her own vulnerability inside that court, increases, the more she must impose on herself the punishment, the self-sacrifice of depriving herself of her pleasure in seeing Nemours: "Faites que je ne voie personne," she beseeches her husband. "Au nom de Dieu, continua-t-elle, trouvez bon que sur le prétexte de quelque maladie, je ne voie personne" (pp. 339−40). Her only hope of recouping an image that she now feels is no longer in her control but has entered into the circulation of the court is to withdraw from that court's view, to go away from its omnipresent gaze to her "private" space, at Coulommiers. But it is of course here, at the center of her intimacy, that Nemours's insistent persecution of her reaches its apogee.

What is striking about the scene of Nemours's spying on Mme de Clèves is of course its voyeurism, but also its exhibitionism.[39] It is a scene of sexual passion that is played out in "trompe-l'œil," where what seems most salient is once again the criss-crossing of looks that can never meet except in the domain of the imaginary. Mme de Clèves is coyly presented to us as a re-vision. First we are told of the effect his seeing her has on Nemours:

> Il se rangea derrière une des fenêtres, qui servaient de porte, pour voir ce que faisait Mme de Clèves. Il vit qu'elle était seule; mais il la vit d'une si admirable beauté qu'à peine fut-il maître du transport que lui donna cette vue. (p. 366)

We are first told that M. de Nemours sees her and this vision "transports" him. Only after noting the effect the vision of such beauty has on him are we allowed to look over his shoulder and gaze on the scene. This is what we see:

> Il faisait chaud, et elle n'avait rien, sur sa tête et sur sa gorge, que ses cheveux confusément rattachés. Elle était sur un lit de repos, avec une table devant elle, où il y avait plusieurs corbeilles pleines de rubans; elle en choisit quelques-uns, et M. de Nemours remarqua que c'étaient des mêmes couleurs qu'il avait portées au tournoi. Il vit qu'elle en faisait des nœuds à une canne des Indes, fort extraordinaire, qu'il avait portée quelque temps et qu'il avait donnée à sa sœur ... Après qu'elle eut achevé son ouvrage avec une grâce et une douceur que répandaient sur son visage les sentiments qu'elle avait dans le cœur, elle prit un flambeau et s'en alla, proche d'une grande table, vis à vis du tableau du siège de Metz, où était le portrait de M. de Nemours; elle s'assit et se mit à regarder ce portrait avec une attention et une rêverie que la passion seule peut donner. (pp. 366–367)

Both of the protagonists are lost, undone by an image. Their passion, which here reaches its peak (the scene has obvious orgasmic overtones for both of them: both are described in conventionally post-coital terms, she "flushed" with pleasure, he "tellement hors de lui-même ... immobile") as each gives in to the image of the other, also reveals itself to be impossible: it is always a passion for the image of the other, for the other as image, which in the economy of this text returns us to the narcissistic hold of the imaginary register. There is no reciprocity of passion possible except as representation, that is alienation, in the masturbatory fantasy of seeing oneself being loved, not from where one is, but in some other place that is always beyond one's grasp, always other: "Jamais tu ne me regardes là où je te vois. Inversement, ce que je regarde n'est jamais ce que je veux voir."[40] In a way, perhaps unknown to itself, the *Princesse de Clèves* undoes its own investment in a patriarchal heterosexuality by showing us how the lure of complementarity is never realizable, by offering as its impossibility the vision of its own frustration.

This frustration is further underlined by the text's active and insistent exclusion of the symbolic level of discourse. The text's constant insistence on the visual is balanced by its narrative foreclosure of the verbal. Given the tightly contained, suspicious, "paranoid" atmosphere in which they exist, the characters are never allowed to articulate their feelings to each other, to any other. The very fact of courtly existence can be summarized by the "On vous observe" which, although spoken by Catherine de Médicis to the Vidame de Chartres, is nevertheless applicable to everyone. In the oppressive power structure of the court, where everyone exists in the gaze of everyone else, where that gaze can possess anyone else, the only private space possible is the space of absence, of silence. The importance of silence, of secrecy, for this text is enormous. What strikes me as particularly enigmatic, however, is not so much the entire network of secrecy and gossip, but rather the way in which the text functions so that the predominance of a certain imaginary, the network of images and vision, is always maintained over the symbolic register of language (all the while aware, of course, that the text is language, but a language that is constantly pointing away from itself as language, and disappearing into the ephemerality of vision).

We must remember that the duke and the Princess never actually engage each other in conversation until the very end of the novel:

L'on ne peut exprimer ce que sentirent M. de Nemours et Mme de Clèves de se trouver seuls et en état de se parler pour la première fois. Ils demeurèrent quelque temps sans rien dire ... (pp. 382)

Each time the possibility or the desire to address the other comes up it is short-circuited, ruled out by social pressure (one is never sure of not being overheard, and thus entering into the system of verbal exchange, gossip) or dismissed as being unable to surmount internal obstacles:

Tout ce qu'il eût pu souhaiter, eût été une conversation avec elle; mais il trouvait qu'il la devait craindre plutôt que de la désirer. (p. 352)

L'envie de parler à Mme de Clèves lui venait toujours dans l'esprit. Il songea à en trouver les moyens. Il pensa lui écrire; mais enfin il trouva qu'après la faute qu'il avait faite, et de l'humeur dont elle était, le mieux qu'il pût faire était de lui témoigner un profond respect par son affliction et par son silence ... (p. 353)

Il n'osa lui parler, quoique l'embarras de cette cérémonie lui en donnât plusieurs moyens: mais il lui fit voir tant de tristesse ... (p. 354)

In a perverse move, M. de Nemours is allowed to exist only as an image, as an imaginary construct of the male. His difference is, however, maintained safely contained in that image: he is never allowed access to the symbolic level of language, never allowed to articulate his desire. Thus he is denied by the text, the court, the Princess, the possibility of situating himself in the phallic role of having the "word," of manipulating and controlling the Law. He is always maintained, by the Princess's refusal ever to allow him the occasion to address her, to speak his desire, in the role of a tantalizing, but finally empty image. Mme de Clèves exists as both the cause of his desire and the impossibility of that desire's articulation. In a sense, Mme de Clèves imprisons him in the domain of the imaginary. She serves as an apotropaic warning to him that she will not be forced into accepting the manipulation of signs, of accepting the law of castration and its positioning of her into a certain ideal of woman unless she reveal what castration also and ultimately signals: the object of desire as the desire for death. Her forced entry into the symbolic register of discourse would, of course, precipitate the production of that discourse/subjectivity as death.

The few times in the novel that the characters use language, either in conversations or in the manipulation of written discourse, the outcome of that manipulation is fatal. In the revelatory conversation between Mme de Chartres and her daughter, Mme de Chartres articulates her daughter's desire, which is the latter's separation from and thus betrayal of her, at the price of her own life. The central episode of the misplaced letter, that indeterminate signifier that proves to be so dangerous, inducing the horrors of jealousy in Mme de Clèves, turning her from Nemours, exaggerating the animosity the queen feels towards the Dauphine, and most important, undoing the career at court of the Vidame de Chartres, is the most significant example of the mortiferous power of discourse. Although its reconstruction affords the Princess some of her happiest moments in Nemours's company, the consequences of the letter are fatal to all concerned. The famous, "invraisemblable" confession of Mme de Clèves to her husband, her breaking of her silence and all the codes of wifely behavior, serves him his death warrant. M. de Clèves will never recover from the blow this confession deals him, from the doubts that it spawns in his mind, from the consequences of his desire to know the object of his wife's attraction. What seems most implausible is not so much the confession (that simply serves to ratify what Mme de Clèves has said about herself all along, that she is the most unusual of women), but that it is finally a lethal act of aggression unleashed by Mme de Clèves against this persecutory husband. Also, of course, through her killing of him, she deals a rather solid blow to the Mother in him who refused to give up her hold on her.[41] Finally, the one and only conversation between the two lovers signals a death of another kind: the death of hope, of the possibility of a married future, the withdrawal of Mme de Clèves from Nemours's and the court's view.

The novel, as text, seems therefore to exist as an oscillatory phenomenon, in which the prevalence of a certain appeal to imaging, to the imaginary register, is constantly at cross purposes with, is constantly invading, the symbolic register of patriarchal law. If we transcode the difference between the imaginary and the symbolic as being, *grosso modo*, the difference between a certain attachment to the maternal register and the subjugation of that register to the law of the Father (a split that is never absolute, for these two registers do not exist independently of each other), we can begin to intuit another sexual dynamic that is at work in the novel, in the passion that the novel represents as the love of Nemours and Clèves.[42]

The prevalence of the imaginary register could be seen as an attempt of the text to situate its desire in the realm of a pre-Oedipal interchange with the maternal, rather than as existing under the aegis of the Symbolic, that is, within the dialectics of castration. In this way we come back to the self-contradictory gesture that is unavoidable in the way this imaginary is necessarily inscribed in the symbolic, a gesture that is perhaps the surest indication of a certain "textual femininity." The text is constructed, even if we just take as an example its famous Classical litotes, as a series of oscillatory moments, with (as A. Begin noted) the prevalence of negative sentence formations, formations that in essence offer something in order to immediately withdraw it.[43] What does it mean, for instance, when the novel begins with the (negative) statement "Splendor and gallantry had never reigned so brilliantly as at the court of Henri II," except exactly that it (they) never existed, and yet that they had. The entire text repeats this same (may we call it?) "hysterical" gesture – of advancing an idea, an image, a form of sexuality in order immediately to recall it, creating a text of radical indeterminacy:

Mme de Clèves avait d'abord été fâchée que M. de Nemours eût eu lieu de croire que c'était lui qui l'avait empêchée d'aller chez le maréchal de Saint-André; mais ensuite elle sentit quelque espèce de chagrin que sa mère lui en eût entièrement ôté l'opinion.   (p. 276)

For all the novel's supposed Classical clarity, for all, precisely, its "éclat," there seems to lurk at the heart of that brilliance an ambivalence of rhetoric, an aphanisis of language and thus of the subject-product of that language, where the text undoes the very (sexually normative) parameters that confine its narration. The text is riddled with sentences like the one just quoted, becoming thus a riddle of its own, perhaps we might say the Sphinx before Oedipus, or at the conjunction of Oedipal desire and a different enigma of feminine sexuality. Although on the one hand it is obvious that this type of rhetorical formulation is precisely what has made critics wax poetic about the subtlety of insight, about the finesse of Lafayette's understanding of the workings of the "heart," her particularly feminine sensibility, what these constructions do, textually, is constantly to undermine any effective way in which the text, and thus the subject it represents, could be firmly situated as the product of those tight parameters of sexual difference it represents as "natural." Its very "hysteric structure" (its oscillation in the weighting of imaginary and symbolic),[44] a structure of an irresolvable *fort-da*, points to, I would argue, the feminine of the text, a feminine that exists as congruent to, inside of, the prevailing patriarchal discourse. It would be a femininity that J. Mitchell, in *Psychoanalysis and Feminism*, has defined as

in part a repressed condition that can only be secondarily acquired in distorted form. It is because it is repressed that femininity is so hard to comprehend both within and without psychoanalytic investigation – it returns in symptoms, such as hysteria. In the body of the hysteric ... lies the feminine protest against the law of the father. But what is repressed is both the representation of the desire and the prohibition against it: there is nothing 'pure' or 'original' about it.[45]

The "feminine protest" that Juliet Mitchell talks about can be seen as a form of counter-discourse, that is, as (if we wish) the hidden, yet integral, part of the dominant discourse of patriarchy that the novel apparently "naturalizes" and yet quietly undermines. The "hysteric" symptoms resurface both in textuality, as the negative, litotic style, in thematics, as the ambivalence of feeling, in characterization and, in sexuality, as the very different desiring positions of M. de Clèves, Mme de Clèves, and the Duc de Nemours. Finally all these oscillatory ambivalences are subsumed in the textual dynamics which, as I hope to have shown, weighs a certain visionary appeal over what we can consider – what has been considered – as Classicism's investment in a clearly phallocentric discourse of Law.

This oscillatory ambivalence of the text, its essentially irresolvable ambiguity, reaches its most incandescent moment, as it must, in the troubling ending. It is precisely at this point, the point where the text can no longer remain in the position of "both/and," where narratively the confrontation of the two protagonists can no longer be delayed, where the text must end, that all the strands that have heretofore pertained are brought to their closest possible conjunction only to be inverted and forever dispersed. Mme de Clèves finally accepts (and denies) responsibility for her husband's death:

Quand elle commença d'avoir la force de l'envisager et qu'elle vit quel mari elle avait perdu, qu'elle considéra qu'elle était la cause de sa mort, et que c'était par la passion qu'elle avait eue pour un autre qu'elle en était cause, l'horreur qu'elle eut pour elle-même et pour M. de Nemours ne se peut représenter. (pp. 376–377)

After this confession she agrees to listen to M. de Nemours, to engage him in conversation: it is to tell him that she does love him ("vous m'avez inspiré des sentiments qui m'étaient inconnus devant que de vous avoir vu," p. 384), but that she will never give in to that passion, will never be blinded by it ("les passions peuvent me conduire; mais elle ne sauraient m'aveugler," p. 387).

The very terms she uses in the conversation only repeat the entire confrontation between the weight of the imaginary, that is, her involution in a desiring structure that ties her relentlessly to the Mother, to a refusal of castration and circulation; and the symbolic, the radical desire that Nemours introduced into her life and that was marked by castration – by the death of both her mother and husband for which and in which she knows she was complicit. The battle for Mme de Clèves is therefore a battle that can never be resolved, for it is a struggle between two systems that refuse to mesh, to become "one," which in a patriarchal culture would always pivot into the Law of the Father.

As long as Nemours remained an "image," Mme de Clèves could in a certain sense remain in her narcissistic enclosure, reasonably safe from the dialectics of lack and its corollary, courtly exchange – the exchange, debasement, of women. However, once her own desire for Nemours becomes too insistent, too persistent, once it becomes aggressively predatory, it succeeds in introducing into a closed sexual economy of Mother-husband/daughter the trembling scission of difference. Both her mother and her husband protected her against Nemours and against herself. Their protection continues after their death. In fact, in a perverse reversal it is their death, internalized, that returns as "imagination" ("son austère vertu était si blessée de cette imagination," p. 380; "Il est vrai, répliqua-t-elle, que je sacrifie beaucoup à un devoir qui ne subsiste que dans mon imagination," p. 389), coupled now with those idealizations of paternal interdiction, "vertu" and "devoir." More than any others those terms represent the sublimation of the "ideal" of marriage that her mother preached, and that forever protect her against an economy of desire that would precipitate her fall out of the imaginary and into the banality of sexual exchange.

We have noticed that there was no "real" father capable of assuming the function of the Law's representative. Marriage, rather, was the textual dissemination of the Law of the Father. Curiously, once Mme de Clèves has successfully eliminated her own husband (that is, her own marriage), it is he ("cet object funeste") who, promoted in death to a status he never enjoyed in life, effectively spells the end of any hope of a "happy ending." "Il n'y a point d'obstacle, madame, reprit M. de Nemours. Vous seule vous opposez à mon bonheur; vous seule vous imposez une loi que la vertu et la raison ne vous sauraient imposer" (p. 389). M. de Nemours, in his pain and his incomprehension, but also in his masculine egoism, states a truism that is a plausible excuse for legitimizing their passion in the economy of the court. Mme de Clèves, in her defense against that loss she knows to be inevitable in that same economy, ("la certitude de n'être plus aimée de vous, comme je le suis" p. 387) can only block that economy by using its own arms against it, but in a self-consciously perverse way. It is by claiming to be unable to detach herself from the law of the father, her internalization of guilt, of death, as "devoir/vertu," that she successfully blocks Nemours's passion, and assures herself of retaining her position "beyond" castration. This internalization, and the text's fetishization of "vertu" with all those virile connotations the word still retained from its Latin and Italian etymology, in a sense reiterates her position of not only "being" the phallus, object of contemplation and desire for the man, but of "having" it also. Being and having, a circle complete in itself: thus the final image of Mme de Clèves returns to the image of narcissism as a non-lacking unity closed in on itself, the reconciliation of sexual difference in a composite being, a being that excludes lack, the haunting return at the end of the novel of the androgyn. A being lacking nothing, she is thus freed at last from the role either of the two phallocentric systems of family – the kinship structure of the court, or the intimate retreat of a nuclear marriage – affords her.

Mme de Clèves's incorporation of "vertu" is inseparable from the image, the imagination of her husband, dead, that she maintains within her newly invested personal economy. She now lives with his ghost:

Quand je pourrais m'accoutumer à cette sorte de malheur, pourrais-je m'accoutumer à celui de croire voir toujours M. de Clèves vous accuser de sa mort, me reprocher de vous avoir aimé, de vous avoir épousé ...

(p. 388)

It is a ghost of her own inner vision, of her life as vision. In order to keep her "fantôme de devoir" in front of her eyes she must forever accept the sacrifice of Nemours: "je me priverai de votre vue, quelque violence qu'il m'en coûte. Je vous conjure, par tout le pouvoir que j'ai sur vous, de ne chercher aucune occasion de me voir" (p. 389). It is only through this sacrifice that she incorporates and makes her own death, the death that had in this novel been waiting, that had been structured as the frame inside of which the life of the court, the passion of the court, played itself out. It is only once she has turned her vision from the attractions of the court to her inner life ("Cette vue si longue et si prochaine de la mort fit paraître à Mme de Clèves les choses de cette vie de cet œil si différent dont on les voit dans la santé," p. 393) that Mme de Clèves can definitively leave that life behind.

The intrusion of death into the center of the novel has been noted. Death makes spectacularly appropriate appearances: everyone in the novel finally dies – the women in the intercalated narratives, Mme de Chartres, M. de Clèves, the king, and closing the circle, or rather attaching the center to the circumference in a moebius knot, Mme de Clèves. By this incorporation and affirmation of death, the text precludes, in a final instance, the illusion of representation, the illusion of a happy ending that would figure the satisfaction of the passion of Nemours and Mme de Clèves. This story is not a fairy tale, despite its fairy-tale setting. What the very ambivalent ending of the novel tells us is that happy endings – the union of those two terms that would affirm a sexual/political view of the world that is based on patriarchal heterosexuality – are but another illusion patriarchy holds out to those it subjugates. It is a structuring of subjectivity that allows the feminine no other role than that of object of exchange where men and women are reduced to sexual and social predicates that deny them as they define them. When at last the Princess has the "choice," she realizes that her only chance of happiness is not some "prince charming" but a "beyond," another place that is not the world of the court. This other place, finally, is a place beyond representation. Is it, however, a movement forward or a movement back? Does she go back, go home to the world from which she came? Does she choose to reside in the "house of the mother," that convent, a world of women? Is her "beyond" the incorporation of Death as a different law of the Father? A return to all those dead fathers who also legislate the protocols of marriage and desire in the court/text? Or, yet again, is it a return to a state before sexuality, to the indifference of death, as the impossible merger of the two? I think that it is finally impossible to decide between these, or still other, alternatives. A great part of the text's fascination, its radical otherness, resides precisely in this affirmation of an impossible oscillation. We are left hanging, caught in an indeterminacy that refuses the cutting, final answer of theory. Once more the *Princesse de Clèves*, by frustrating any theory that would contain it, any theory that would send it back into those paradigms of patriarchal thought, contaminates by a form of proleptic indecision the theoretical model that I have been using, in part, to explain the text, a certain Freudian theatricalization of sexuality. Across the centuries the Princess seems to smile enigmatically at Freud, just as Dora did before she walked out of his life, of his theory, forever. The only thing we will ever know with any certainty is that at each end of a certain epistemic spectrum both the Viennese teenager and the *Princesse de Clèves*, to a world that would subjugate them, to a theory that would contain them, just said "No."

NOTES

Preface

1 T. Eagleton, *Criticism and Ideology* (London: Verso, 1976), p.101.
2 It is, of course, Michel Foucault whose suggestive *Les mots et les choses* (Paris: Gallimard, 1966) has had such a great influence on the analyses of these shifts in "epistemic systems." For a similar approach to the English stage of the late Renaissance, cf. C. Belsey, *The Subject of Tragedy* (London: Methuen, 1985).

Introduction

3 Cf. G. Balandier, *Pouvoirs sur scène* (Paris: Balland, 1980), p.16, where he states that the force of all charismatic political leaders comes from their ability to "commander le réel par l'imaginaire." Cf. also J.M. Apostolidès, *Le Roi machine* (Paris: Minuit, 1981) and L. Marin, *Le Portrait du roi* (Paris: Minuit, 1981) and *La Parole mangée* (Paris: Klincksieck, 1986).
4 Louis XIV, *Mémoires*, ed. J. Longnon (Paris: Tallandier, 1978), p.134. Hereafter referred to as *Mémoires* with page reference in text.
5 E. Enriquez, *De La Horde à l'état: essai de psychanalyse du lien social* (Paris: Gallimard, 1985), p.169, "le fonctionnement social est un fonctionnement passionnel (et non rationnel) ..."
6 *Group Psychology and the Analysis of the Ego* (N.Y.: Norton, 1959), p.12.
7 *Ibid.*, p.13.
8 Cf. for contemporary political theorists, Le Bret (quoted in E. Thuau, *Raison d'Etat et pensée politique à l'époque de Richelieu* (Paris: Colin, 1966), p.277: "Un bon roi doit être père très débonnaire, provide et sage, modérateur, gouverneur vigilant, bénin et gracieux aux bons, austère et terrible aux méchants." For modern theory, cf. Enriquez, *De La Horde à l'état*, p.334, "il est indispensable en même temps que ce parti ait à sa tête un chef manifestant suffisamment de charisme et capable à la fois d'incarner et de symboliser l'Etat et la Nation dans leur permanence afin que la plus grande partie du peuple puisse avoir le sentiment que le corps social trouve son unité et son identité dans un corps physique, dont il peut admirer la beauté, la prestance, la force ou la richesse."

212

9 Louis wrote after his northern campaign, "je menai, à mon retour, la Reine avec moi à dessein de la faire voir aux peuples des villes que je venais d'assujettir", *Mémoires*, p. 241.

10 Cf. Marin, *Portrait du roi*, passim.

11 *Pouvoirs sur scène*, p. 19.

12 A. Green, *Narcissisme de vie, narcissisme de mort* (Paris: Minuit, 1983), p. 55.

13 *Ibid.*, p. 51.

14 *La Fable mystique*, I (Paris: Gallimard, 1982), p. 32.

15 Cardinal de Richelieu, *Testament politique*, ed. L. André (Paris: Laffont, 1947), p. 128.

16 *Ibid.*, p. 113.

17 Green, *Narcissisme de vie*, p. 164 and L. Marin, *La Parole mangée*, p. 215; "Et l'on ne perdra jamais de vue que le désir de l'absolu du pouvoir n'est qu'une des espèces de la pulsion de mort."

18 Cf., for a general discussion of the subjugation of the body in the seventeenth century, F. Barker, *The Tremulous Private Body: Essays on Subjection* (London: Methuen, 1984).

19 G. Rosolato, "Narcissisme," in *Narcisses* (*Nouvelle Revue de Psychanalyse*, 1976), p. 10, "le plaisir narcissique comporte … l'autonomie d'un être qui trouve sa toute-puissance dans une auto-suffisance, bien souvent synonyme du pouvoir, soit en ne dépendant pas des autres, soit dans une forme active, en soumettant les autres à ses volontés …"

20 For an interesting recent overview, in English, of the history of Versailles's construction, cf. W. Walton, *Louis XIV's Versailles* (Chicago: The University of Chicago Press, 1986).

21 N. Keohane, *Philosophy and the State in France* (Princeton: Princeton University Press, 1980), p. 59.

22 *The King's Two Bodies: A Study in Medieval Political Theology* (Princeton: Princeton University Press, 1956).

23 *Politique tirée des propres paroles de l'Ecriture Sainte*, in *Œuvres complètes* (Paris: Garnier Frères, 1846), vol. III, p. 152.

24 *Histoire de la vie privée*, ed. P. Ariès and G. Duby (Paris: Seuil, 1985), vol. II, p. 290.

25 *Positions* (Paris: Editions Sociales, 1970), p. 101, and again p. 103, "ce n'est pas leurs conditions d'existence réelles, leur monde réel, que les 'hommes' se représentent, dans l'idéologie, mais c'est avant tout leur rapport à ces conditions d'existence qui leur y est représenté."

26 F. Jameson, *The Political Unconscious* (Ithaca: Cornell University Press, 1981), p. 7: "ideology is not something which informs or invests symbolic productions, rather the aesthetic art is itself ideological, and the production of aesthetic or narrative forms is to be seen as an ideological act in its own right, with the function of inventing imaginary or 'formal' solutions to irresolvable social contradictions."

27 P. Smith, *Discerning the Subject* (Minneapolis: Un. of Minn. Press, 1988), p. 68.

28 Althusser, *Positions*, pp. 118–119.
29 For a discussion of this debate cf. Smith, *Discerning the Subject*, pp. 3–24.
30 Absolutism would be, according to William Beik (*Absolutism and Society in Seventeenth-Century France*, Cambridge: Cambridge University Press, 1985, p. 3), "a stage in the evolution of French society from feudalism to capitalism. The absolute monarchy is usually placed at an advanced point on the road leading from a decentralized 'feudal' monarchy to a 'modern' state."
31 *Group Psychology*, p. 55: "His intellectual acts were strong and independent even in isolation, and his will needed no reinforcement from others. Consistency leads us to assume that his ego had few libidinal ties; he loved no one but himself, or other people only in so far as they served his needs. ... He, at the very beginning of the history of mankind, was the 'superman' whom Nietzsche only expected from the future."
32 Green, *Narcissisme de vie*, p. 105, "la mort est la condition nécessaire pour que l'agrandissement du disparu passe par les signes qui lui restituent moins une présence qu'ils ne lui garantissent pour toujours qu'il sera pérennisé en cette absence qui lui conférera une puissance éternelle."
33 Cf. Freud, *Group Psychology*, pp. 54–60.
34 J. Mitchell, *Psychoanalysis and Feminism: Freud, Reich, Laing and Woman* (NY: Vintage Books, 1975), p. 391.
35 Cf. P. Smith, *Discerning the Subject*, pp. 71–82.
36 Cf. Beik, *Absolutism and Society*, p. 3: "general agreement on the depth and seriousness of the social discontent which filled the period 1610–1661 with noble revolts, popular insurrections and sporadic civil wars ..." Cf. also the writings of of both Richelieu and Louis XIV as they describe the situation in France at the start of each of their tenures at the head of government:

Lorsque V. M. se résolut de me donner en même temps et l'entrée de ses Conseils et grande part en sa confiance pour la direction de ses affaires, je puis dire avec vérité que les Huguenots partageoient l'Etat avec Elle, que les grands se conduisoient comme s'ils n'eussent pas été ses sujets, et les plus puissants Gouverneurs des Provinces comme s'ils eussent été souverains en leurs charges ... Je puis dire encore que les alliances étrangères étoient méprisées, les Intérêts particuliers préférés aux publics, et, en un mot, la dignité de la Majesté Royale tellement ravalée et si différente de ce qu'elle devoit être ...
(*Testament politique*, ed. L. André, pp. 93–94)

Mais il faut se représenter l'état des choses: des agitations terribles par tout le royaume avant et après ma majorité; une guerre étrangère, où ces troubles domestiques avaient fait perdre à la France mille et mille avantages; un prince de mon sang et d'un très grand nom à la tête des ennemis; beaucoup de cabales dans l'Etat; les parlements encore en possession et en goût d'une autorité usurpée; dans ma cour, très peu de fidélité sans intérêt, et par là mes sujets en apparence les plus soumis, autant à charge et autant à redouter pour moi que les plus rebelles ...
(*Mémoires*, p. 33)

37 Cf. H. Trevor-Roper, R. Mousnier, etc. in *Crisis in Europe, 1560−1660*, ed. T. Aston (London: Routledge, 1965); A. D. Lublinskaya, *French Absolutism: The Critical Phase, 1620−29* (Cambridge: Cambridge University Press, 1968); and M. Foucault, *Les Mots et les choses*.

38 Cf. Mousnier, in *Crisis in Europe*, but also his *Les XVIe et XVIIe siècles* (Paris: PUF, 1967), Livre premier, "Les Nouvelles structures de l'Etat," pp. 110−162.

39 Keohane, *Philosophy and the State*, p. 17.

40 J. L. Flandrin, *Familles, parenté, maison, sexualité dans l'ancienne société* (Paris: Seuil, 1976) and *Le Sexe et l'Occident* (Paris: Seuil, 1981); P. Ariès, *L'Enfant et la vie familiale sous l'Ancien Régime* (Paris: Seuil, 1973); F. Shorter, *The Making of the Modern Family* (NY: Basic Books, 1975); P. Laslett, *The World We Have Lost* (London: Methuen, 1971).

41 "C'est que la nouvelle monarchie mercantiliste se souciait tout autant de moraliser ses sujets que de les mettre au travail. Sa lutte contre la sexualité illégitime fut partie intégrante de son entreprise générale de surveillance et de contrôle des individus." J. Solé, *L'Amour en occident à l'époque moderne* (Paris: Albin Michel, 1976), p. 100.

42 M. Foucault, *La Volonté de savoir* (Paris: Gallimard, 1976), p. 143.

43 *Familles*, p. 208.

44 *Ibid.*, p. 10: "le concept de famille était écartelé entre l'idée de corésidence et l'idée de parenté ... Le mot évoquait en effet beaucoup plus fréquemment un ensemble de parents qui ne résidaient pas ensemble, et il désignait couramment aussi un ensemble de corésidents qui n'étaient pas nécessairement liés par le sang ou le mariage"; and p. 15: "en France comme en Angleterre, ce qui unissait les membres du groupe domestique − parents et serviteurs − en une "famille" c'était une commune dépendance vis à vis du 'père de famille.'"

45 P. Ariès, *L'Enfant*, p. 306.

46 R. Mandrou, *La France au XVIIe et au XVIIIe siècles* (Paris: PUF, 1967), p. 217: "Ce que nous appelons la France classique, c'est un choix politique et une façon de concevoir le cadre et l'illustration de la monarchie. De même que la royauté a prétendu imposer l'absolutisme centralisateur à une société qui n'y était pas du tout préparée, de même qu'elle a prétendu rétablir l'unité religieuse, alors que le pluralisme de fait créé par l'installation du protestantisme rendait ce retour en arrière impossible, de même elle a voulu se donner un décor sans pareil, et instaurer un ordre dans le domaine des Beaux-Arts."

47 Cf. F. Siguret, *L'Œil surpris* (Tübingen: Biblio 17, 1985) for an overview of the importance of optics in the seventeenth century.

48 *La Pratique du théâtre*, quoted in Murray, *Theatrical Legitimation* (New York: OUP, 1987), p. 282.

49 M. de Certeau reminds us how, for another seventeenth-century phenomenon, mystic discourse/experience, vision takes on new importance. Cf. *La Fable mystique*, p. 120: "Dans cette histoire multiple d'un 'corps

sacramental' en quête de son 'corps ecclésial' – ou d'une tête visible à la recherche de ses 'membres' – un trait intéresse plus particulièrement l'apparition de 'la' mystique: la concentration progressive de ces débats autour du voir ... La vision se substitue lentement au toucher et à l'audition. Elle transforme la pratique même du savoir et des signes."

50 Murray, *Theatrical Legitimation*, p. 120; "The cardinal's dais, located in the middle of the Salle and centered by the proscenium arch, placed Richelieu in the only position of perfect perspective in the house. For the other spectators, the theatrical experience was directed away from the stage to the one point in the playhouse from which the perspective achieved its greatest effect. They could enjoy the vanishing point only by imagining how it must look from Richelieu's place. The theatrical function of Richelieu's vision was an essential element of the spectacles at the Palais Cardinal."

51 Cf. T. E. Stevenson, *The French Stage in the Seventeenth Century* (Manchester: Un. of Manchester Press, 1957), pp. 125–135. For a fuller survey of the state of both the "Théâtre du Marais," and the "Hôtel de Bourgogne," the reader should consult the classic volumes of S. Wilma Deierdauf-Holsboer: *Le Théâtre de Bourgogne* (2 vols., Paris: Nizet, 1968, 1970); *Le Théâtre du Marais* (2 vols., Paris: Nizet, 1954, 1958); and *L'Histoire de la mise-en-scène dans le théâtre français de 1600–1673* (Paris: Nizet, 1960).

52 For an illuminating discussion, cf. N. Bryson, *Vision and Painting* (New Haven: Yale University Press, 1986), pp. 105–115.

53 Cf. Louis Marin's analysis of subjectivity constructed by Rigaud's "Portrait de Louis XIV," in *La Parole mangée*: "Le corps glorieux du Roi et son portrait," pp. 195–225. It must be obvious that the analogy that I am making between pictural subjugation and a theatrical equivalent is tendentious. We are aware of the great tumult that attended theatrical performances in the Parisian theaters, of the intermingling of parterre and stage which would seem to argue, at first sight at least, for the "non-subjugation" of the spectators to the spectacle. Subjugation is not just the result of visual perspective, but of the intermingling of this perspective with the internal dynamics of plot, peripateia, etc, and the necessary identifications and pleasurings they entail. Nevertheless what I am aiming at is the general, overarching containment that the theater both submits to and helps institute as the century progresses and as "Classicism" becomes the ideological mode of cultural hegemony.

54 Cf. F. Barker, *The Tremulous Private Body*.

55 Green, *Un Œil en trop*, p. 35, and A. Ubersfeld, *Lire le théâtre* (Paris: Editions Sociales, 1978), p. 39; "il devient clair que l'activité théâtrale, dans la représentation, est par excellence, un lieu dialectique".

56 Cf. Freud, "Family Romances," Standard Edition, 9, pp. 237–241.

57 Mitchell, *Psychoanalysis and Feminism*, p. 373: "the systematic exchange of women is definitional of human society. This act of exogamy transforms "natural" families into a cultural kinship system."

58 *Ibid.*, p. 379.

59 *Ibid.*, p. 378.

60 E. Sagan, *At the Dawn of Tyranny* (N.Y.: Knopf, 1985), p. 236.

61 *Ibid.*, p. 232.

62 *Ibid.*, p. 275: "it has been observed that monarchy could not be stabilized until there was monogamy and primogeniture — until there was no question about who was the legitimate successor to the King. It is possible to have a king without a family, but it is impossible to have Kingship (a king followed by a king) without a royal family."

63 For an interesting development of the theory of plot, cf. Theresa de Lauretis' comments on Propp in her *Alice Doesn't: Feminism, Semiotics, Cinema* (Bloomington: Indiana University Press, 1984), p. 113: "he cautions plots do not directly "reflect" a given social order, but rather emerge out of the conflict, the contradictions, of different social orders as they succeed or replace one another. The difficult coexistence of different orders of historical reality in the long period of transition from one to the other is precisely what is manifested in the tensions of plots …"

64 Cf. A. Ubersfeld, *Lire le théâtre*, p. 265: "tout texte théâtral est la réponse à une demande du public, et c'est sur ce point que se fait le plus aisément l'articulation du discours théâtral avec l'histoire et l'idéologie." Also, for theatrical pleasure as essentially masochistic, cf. Freud, St. Ed. 7, p. 306; J. F. Lyotard, "Œdipe Juif," in *Dérive à partir de Freud et Marx* (Paris: 10/18, 1973). For the socially restrictive aspect of theater, cf. M. H. Huet, *Rehearsing the Revolution* (Berkeley: University of California Press, 1982), p. 35.

65 Green, *Un Œil en trop*, pp. 53–54: "Se demander si ce sont ces relations de parenté qui constituent le tragique ou si c'est le tragique qui éclaire ces relations de parenté n'a peut-être pas de sens, ainsi formulé. Disons plutôt qu'elles nous révèlent quelque chose d'essentiel sur la subjectivité qui est inséparable du tragique, par la mise au jour de la relation du sujet à ses géniteurs ou que l'étude de ces relations ne se conçoit pleinement que dans le cadre du tragique, pour dévoiler son rôle constituant de subjectivité."

66 For a more detailed discussion of this, cf. M. Greenberg, *Corneille, Classicism, and the Ruses of Symmetry* (Cambridge: Cambridge University Press, 1986), "Introduction."

67 "Le théâtre de la cruauté et la clôture de la representation," in *L'Ecriture et la différence* (Paris: Seuil, 1966), pp. 341–367.

68 Cf. Lacan's analysis of the "scopic drive" in *Seminaire*, 11, *Les Quatre Concepts fondamentaux de la psychanalyse* (Paris: Seuil, 1973), p. 74: "La pulsion scopique … est celle qui élude le plus complètement le terme de la castration."

69 *Discerning the Subject*, p. 107: "Whereas 'plaisir' relies upon the fixity of the 'subject' within the codes and conventions it inhabits, 'jouissance'

is specifically transgressive and it marks the crossing by the human agent of the symbolic codes which attempt to keep us in place as 'one' subject."

1 *L'Astrée* and androgyny

1 The *Princesse de Clèves* shares with other major Classical texts the "already-there" of an internalized Oedipal desire structured by and through the interdicting gesture of paternal authority. We only have to look at the role of "devoir" (the State/Family) in Corneille, at the internalization of guilt that tortures the heroes/heroines of Racine, at the conflicted, taunted, but nevertheless undaunted role of masculine authority in Molière, to realize how Classicism in its major representations reflects a Patriarchal society upheld by a metaphysics of interdiction, transgression and culpabilization. For a more detailed analysis of the mechanics of this complex problematic cf. my own *Corneille, Classicism and the Ruses of Symmetry*, especially the introduction. For an analysis of the closure of the Classical "world" ("le monde") cf. R. Barthe's essay on La Bruyère in *Essais Critiques* (Paris: Seuil, 1966), and P. Brooks, *The Novel of Worldliness* (Princeton: Princeton University Press, 1969).

2 J. Ehrmann, *Un Paradis déséspéré: l'amour et l'illusion dans l'Astrée* (Paris: PUF, 1963), and G. Genette, "Le Serpent dans la bergerie," in *Figures*, I (Paris: Seuil, 1966).

3 H. Coulet, *Le Roman jusqu'à la Révolution* (Paris: A. Colin, 1967), tells us (p. 144) that the *Astrée* is "le premier des romans modernes," and M. Lathuillère, in "Aspects précieux du style d'Honoré d'Urfé" (*Bulletin de la Diana*, 1970, pp. 101–117) claims that in its vocabulary and syntax, *L'Astrée* is already a "Classical" text. Both Genette and Ehrmann also situate the *Astrée* as the "originary" text of Classicism.

4 All references to the *Astrée* are to the H. Vaganay edition, Lyon, 1925–27.

5 M. Foucault, *Les Mots et les choses*.

6 For a detailed and finely argued discussion of "exemplarity," and exemplary narratives in the French and Italian Renaissance, cf. J. Lyons, *Exemplum: the Rhetoric of Example in Early Modern France and Italy* (Princeton: Princeton University Press, 1989).

7 For an exhaustive account of d'Urfé's life, family and career, his intellectual sources and influences, as well as for an interpretation of the novel as a reflection of the complex economic and social relations of the d'Urfé family, cf. M. Gaume, *Les Inspirations et les sources de l'œuvre d'Honoré d'Urfé* (St. Etienne: Centre d'Etudes Foréziennes, 1977).

8 For these distinctions, especially the question of the inscription of sexuality and the body, for its production and the political implications of this production, cf. S. Heath, "Difference," in *Screen*, Nov.–Dec. 1978.

9 It should be obvious to the reader that in these pages I must concentrate on the central conundrum of the text, the dialectics of love as it is presented in the major episodes of the two protagonists and in several of the best-known ancillary narratives. I am not attempting here a detailed explication of the "encyclopaedic" nature of the novel. I believe, however, that for the purposes of this study my concentration on the central dilemma of the novel clarifies the "textual" necessity for this encyclopaedic accretion. Interesting analyses of specific subgroups of the text are to be found, for instance, in M. Bertaud, *L'Astrée et Polexandre: Du roman pastoral au roman héroïque* (Geneva: Droz, 1986), K. Wine, *"L'Astrée's* Landscapes and the Poetics of Baroque Fiction," *Symposium*, 40, 1986; N. Chabert, "L'Amour du discours dans *L'Astrée*" in *Dix-Septième siècle*, 33, 1981; D. Judovitz, "The Graphic Text: The Nude in *L'Astrée*" in *Papers on French Seventeenth-Century Literature*, 15, 1988.

10 It is also, obviously, a sign of the tradition of "romance" narrations. For an interesting collection of essays on this tradition, cf. K. Brownlee and M.S. Brownlee eds., *Romance: Generic Transformations from Chrétien de Troyes to Cervantes* (Hanover: University Press of New England, 1985).

11 S. Freud, *Beyond the Pleasure Principle*, St. Ed. 18, pp. 14–23 and 34–43.

12 For one version of the "ideology" of the novel, a version that owes more to literary history than to a "political" analysis, cf. P. Koch, "L'ascèse du repos, ou l'intention idéologique de *l'Astrée*," *Revue d'Histoire Littéraire de la France*, mai–août 1977. For an historical/social history of this period, cf. R. Mousnier's *Les XVIᵉ et XVIIᵉ siècles*. F. Braudel's two major works, *The Mediterranean and the Mediterranean World in the Age of Philip II*, 2 vols. (Eng. trans. S. Reynolds, New York, Harper and Row, 1973) and *Civilization and Capitalism: Fifteenth to Eighteenth Century*, 3 vols. (Eng. translation by S. Reynolds, New York: Harper and Row, 1981), are invaluable to understanding both the permanent features and the social and economic changes of the world in which d'Urfé lived.

13 My reading here would seem to be in contradiction with L. Horovitz's interpretation in *Honoré d'Urfé* (Boston: Twayne, 1984) where she insists on the importance of parental interdiction in the *Astrée*. I, too, see this interdiction as pervasive, but it strikes me, nevertheless, that in the actual narration of individual stories the presence of the parental couple is, except in three episodes, lacking. It is this narrative absence that I find intriguing.

14 It is not merely a cloying coincidence that all the young lovers call Amasis and Adamas "ma mère" et "mon père," and are in turn called by them "mon fils," "ma fille."

15 That this "authority" is strictly rhetorical, that is, "fictive," becomes apparent as a novel spins its tale, as the political that has been submerged in the passional reasserts itself in the entire Polémas episode (his attempt to subvert the laws of the Forez, to usurp the throne and the "unnatural" situation of a female ruler) and the necessity for the women to call in their neighboring and amorous princes to defend them and their kingdom against Polémas' attack.

16 For the importance of vision in the novel, besides Ehrmann, *Un Paradis désespéré*, cf. M. Laugaa, "La peinture dans l'*Astrée*," *Bulletin de la Diana*, 1970, pp. 71—100.

17 *Vision and Painting* (New Haven: Yale Un. Press, 1984), p. 98.

18 Ehrmann, *Un Paradis désespéré*, p. 110: "l'individu vit en représentation."

19 Cf. N. Elias, *The Court Society* (New York: Knopf, 1980), and Ehrmann, *Un Paradis désespéré*, pp. 107—109.

20 *Symposium*, in *Dialogues* (trans. B. Jowett, New York: Random House, 1937), p. 316.

21 *Ibid.*, p. 317.

22 *Ibid.*, p. 316.

23 For an interesting recent analysis of transvestism cf. E. Lemoine-Luccioni, *La Robe* (Paris: Seuil, 1983), and J. Baudrillard, *De la séduction* (Paris: Galilée, 1978).

24 Cf. C. Lévi-Strauss, "Structure du mythe," in *Anthropologie Structurale* (Paris: Plon, 1958) and J. L. Nancy, *La Communauté désœuvrée* (Paris: Galilée, 1986).

2 The grateful dead: Corneille's tragedy and the subject of history

This chapter appeared in a slightly different form in the *Stanford French Review* (Summer 1987).

1 Cf. J. M. Apostolidès, "The Problem of History in Seventeenth-Century France," *Diacritics*, 12, 1982, pp. 58—68. Cf. also his recent *Le Prince sacrifié: théâtre et politique au temps de Louis XIV* (Paris: Minuit, 1985). The principal proponent of Corneille's theater as a representation of its immediate historical moment is, of course, G. Couton. Cf., for example, *Corneille et la Fronde* (Paris: Belles Lettres, 1955) or *La Vieillesse de Corneille* (Paris: Maloine, 1949). Besides the works of Couton, other major studies that deal with "history" and Corneille's dramatic universe are: S. Doubrovsky, *Corneille et la dialectique du héros* (Paris: Gallimard, 1963); P. Bénichou, *Morales du grand siècle* (Paris: Gallimard, 1948); B. Dort, *Pierre Corneille, dramaturge* (Paris: L'Arche, 1957); R. J. Nelson, *Corneille, His Heroes and Their Worlds* (Philadelphia: University of Pennsylvania Press, 1963).

2 This difference between the return of the same in myth and the possibility of linear history corresponds to the epistemic changes M. Foucault discusses in *Les Mots et les choses*.

3 Cf. the recent work of Orest Ranum, *Artisans of Glory: Writers and Historical Thought in Seventeenth-Century France* (Chapel Hill: University of North Carolina Press, 1980); Erica Harth, *Classical Ideology* (Ithaca: Cornell University Press, 1984), especially her chapter on court historiographers; and Louis Marin, *Le Portrait du Roi* (Paris: Minuit, 1981).

4 For the idea of the integrity of the King's body, cf. E. Kantorowicz, *The King's Two Bodies*, and also J. M. Apostolidès, *Le Roi machine* (Paris: Minuit, 1981). For the concept of the past as Other, cf. M. de Certeau, *L'Ecriture de l'histoire* (Paris: Gallimard, 1975).

5 De Certeau, *L'Ecriture de l'histoire*, p. 13 "(D'une part) le pouvoir doit se légitimer, affecter à la force qui le rend effectif une autorité qui le rende croyable."

6 C. Lévi-Strauss, "Structure du mythe": "Un mythe se rapporte toujours à des événements passés: 'avant la création du monde,' ou pendant les premiers âges, en tout cas, 'il y a longtemps.' Mais la valeur intrinsèque attribuée au mythe provient de ce que les événements censés se dérouler à un moment du temps forment aussi une structure permanente. Celle-ci se rapporte au passé, au présent, au futur."

7 *Ibid.*, p. 229.

8 Cf. A. Green, *Un Œil en trop*, p. 69: "La famille est (donc) l'espace tragique par excellence. Sans doute parce que les nœuds d'amour, donc de haine, sont en elle les tous premiers en date et en importance ..."

9 De Certeau, *L'Ecriture de l'histoire*, p. 30.

10 "ce discours [history] 'autorise' la force qui exerce le pouvoir; il la pourvoit d'une généalogie familiale, politique ou morale; il accrédite l'utilité présente du prince lorsqu'il la transforme en 'valeurs' qui organisent la représentation du passé." *Ibid.*, p. 14.

11 I have chosen to quote the *Poetics* in French (Aristote, *La Poétique*, texte, traduction, notes par R. Dupont-Roc et Jean Lallot, Paris: Seuil, 1980) because of the greater rhetorical emphasis and reinterpretation the editors have given the text.

12 All quotes from Corneille come from *Théâtre complet*, ed. P. Lièvre (Paris: Gallimard, Bibliothèque de la Pléiade, 1950).

13 J. Chapelain, *Les Sentiments de l'Académie*, quoted in *Histoire de l'Académie Française* by M. Pelisson (Paris, 1700), p. 39.

14 For the use of this term cf. J. Derrida, "La double séance," in *La Dissémination* (Paris: Seuil, 1972) and my "L'Hymen de Corneille: Classicism and the Ruses of Symmetry," *Biblio 17, Papers on French Seventeenth-Century Literature*, 21, 1984.

15 J. M. Apostolidès in *Le Prince sacrifié* also uses the analogy of feudality to a primal horde. Cf. "L'univers historique."

16 Cf. Ubersfeld, *Lire le théâtre*, p. 265: "Tout texte théâtral est la réponse à une demande du public, et c'est sur ce point que se fait le plus aisément l'articulation du discours théâtral avec l'histoire et l'idéologie."

17 Cf. P. Bénichou, *Morales du grand siècle*, p. 20: "Le groupe social au nom duquel s'accomplit chez lui l'acte héroique n'est jamais plus vaste que la famille, l'Etat n'étant lui-même autre chose que la famille ..."

18 Cf. Althusser, "Idéologie et Appareils Idéologiques d'Etat," in *Positions*, pp. 101−105.

19 *Ibid.*, p. 105.

20 Cf. S. Freud, *The Interpretation of Dreams, St. Ed.*, 5, p. 349, "dreams take into account in a general way the connection which undeniably exists between all the portions of the dream-thoughts by combining the whole material into a single situation or event. They reproduce logical connections by simultaneity in time."

21 Both S. Doubrovsky (*Corneille et la dialectique du héros*) and P. Bénichou (*Morales du grand siècle*) analyse in different but complementary terms, the importance of the "noble" or "aristocratic" essence as it is represented in and informs Corneille's theater. My own discussion is indebted to theirs. For my discussion of male linking in a generational chain I follow G. Rosolato's essays "La différence des sexes," "Du Père" and "Trois générations d'hommes dans le mythe religieux et la généalogie," in his *Essais sur le symbolique* (Paris: Gallimard, 1969).

22 Cf. Doubrovsky, *Corneille*, and B. Dort, *Pierre Corneille dramaturge*.

23 For the importance of this "natural" sexual symmetry, cf. L. Irigaray, *Speculum de l'Autre Femme* (Paris: Minuit, 1975), S. Kofman, *Freud et l'énigme de la femme: la femme dans les textes de Freud* (Paris: Galilée, 1981), and my own "*Horace*, Classicism and Female Trouble," *Romanic Review*, 74/3, May 1983.

24 Apostolidès, *Le Prince sacrifié*, argues for seeing the theater as the privileged locus for the "sacralization" of the monarchy in the seventeenth century, comparing the theatrical sacrifice to the mass.

25 For the idea of theatrical pleasure as masochistic, cf. J.F. Lyotard, "Œdipe Juif" and P. Lacoue-Labarthe, "Theatrum Analyticum," in *Glyph* II (Baltimore: The Johns Hopkins University Press, 1977), both of whom gloss Freud's "Psychopathic Characters on the Stage" (St. Ed. 8).

3 Passion play: Jeanne des Anges, devils, hysteria and the incorporation of the Classical subject

The two texts most frequently quoted in this chapter are: *Sœur Jeanne des Anges: Autobiographie d'une hystérique possédée, annoté et publié par les docteurs Gabriel Legué et Gilles de la Tourette*, ed. Jerome Millon (Montbonnot-St. Martin, 1985), referred to in the text as *Auto*; and *La Possession de Loudun presentée par M. de Certeau* (Gallimard/Julliard: Paris, 1980), referred to as *La Possession*.

1 The importance of "seeing" for establishing the difference between the sexes in the realm of the symbolic, a need that is always posited as coming

from the male look, a look that is therefore the unexplored, invisible vanishing point of ideology, is discussed at length by S. Heath in his influential article, "Difference," *Screen*, 19/3 (1978), pp. 51–113. Cf. also the discussion of the dynamics of vision in chaps. 6 and 7 *infra*.

2 M. A. Descamps, *L'invention du corps* (Paris, PUF, 1986), p. 19. For an interesting analysis of this same dissection of the female body in Renaissance literature cf. N. Vickers, "Diana Described: Scattered Woman and Scattered Rhyme," in *Writing and Sexual Difference*, ed. E. Abel (Chicago: The University of Chicago Press, 1982).

3 Catherine Clément underlines this point in her essay on sorcery and hysteria in *La Jeune Née* (Paris: 10/18, 1978), p. 17: "Les sociétés ne parviennent pas à offrir à tous la même insertion dans l'ordre symbolique; ceux qui sont, si l'on peut dire, entre les systèmes symboliques, dans les interstices, hors-jeu, ceux-là sont affligés d'une dangereuse mobilité symbolique." She further points out that the position of the witch, the possessed woman, and the "hysteric" must be understood as representing equally a position of resistance and repression.

4 F. Barker, *The Tremulous Private Body*.

5 Richelieu, *Testament Politique*, pp. 257, 244, 112.

6 For an overview of the vast literature on witches, witchcraft and witch-trials in France and Europe in the sixteenth and seventeenth century just a few titles will have to suffice: J. Delumeau, *La Peur en Occident* (Paris: Fayard, 1978), especially chaps. X, XI, XII; J. C. Baroja, *Les Sorcières et leur monde* (Paris: Gallimard, 1972); R. Mandrou, *Magistrats et sorciers en France au XVIIe* (Paris: Seuil, 1980), which contains an extensive bibliography of both sixteenth and seventeenth-century texts and modern scholarship. The most "famous" of the ancient texts consulted include Spenger and Institoris, *Malleus Maleficarum* (Nuremberg, 1494 and 1496), which had many editions (e.g. Lyons 1595, 1620: there is a French translation, *Le Marteau des sorciers*, Paris: Payot, 1970); J. Bodin, *La Démonomanie des sorciers* (Niort, 1616), and, curiously for our interests, F. Hédélin, abbé d'Aubignac, *Des Satyres, brutes, monstres et démons, . . .* (Paris, 1627). Cf. also C. Clément's reading of witches and hysteria in *La Jeune Née*, and L. Irigaray, "La mystérique" in *Speculum*, pp. 238–253. For the history of "possessions," Michelet's *La Sorcière* is still a fascinating read.

7 The expression and judgment are Mandrou's, *Sorciers et magistrats*, p. 219.

8 For the development of the idea of the *corpus mysticum*, in medieval and Renaissance thought cf. the classic work of E. Kantorowicz, *The King's Two Bodies*, especially pp. 216–220.

9 "If sexuality is always a symbolic production, then there is a place for a politics of the unconscious, for, that is, a grasp of the unconscious not as closed but as historically open, taken up in the historical process of its realisation, existing in transformation." Heath, "Difference," p. 74.

10 Barker, *The Tremulous Private Body*, p. 31.

11 The role of exorcism as anti-protestant propaganda is brought out by D. P. Walker, *Unclean Spirits: Possession and Exorcism in France and England in the Late 16th. and Early 17th. Centuries* (Philadelphia: University of Pennsylvania Press, 1981), p. 4.

12 Cf. H. Brémond, *Histoire littéraire du sentiment religieux en France* (Paris, 1921), 2, p. 184.

13 Freud first elaborated the clinical importance of the "primal scene" in his analysis of the "Wolfman" case. Cf. "From the history of an infantile neurosis," *St. Ed.*, 18.

14 "Comme le récit se fragmente en noms (propres) et en rôles, il efface la référence à des êtres pour leur substituer une série d'histoires différentes et combinées: celle du pouls, celle de la digestion, celle de la bouche, de la langue ou des jambes. Ce n'est pas pour rien que le 'je' conscient de la possédée est éliminé ...". De Certeau, *La Possession*, p. 69. Cf. also de Certeau's analysis "Le langage altéré. La parole de la possédée," in *L'Ecriture de l'histoire*, pp. 249—274. The Loudun case was popularized for English-speaking readers by Aldous Huxley in his *The Devils of Loudun* (New York: Harper, 1952). This book served as the basis for Ken Russell's 1971 film *The Devils*.

15 "Ce théâtre consiste à démasquer les forces qui agissent derrière les apparences humaines, à créer des masques pour démasquer. La représentation efface hommes et femmes..." De Certeau, *La Possession*, p. 133.

16 G. Naudé, in R. Pintard, ed., *Le Libertinage érudit dans la première moitié du XVIIᵉ siècle* (Paris: Boivin, 1973), p. 222, quoted by de Certeau, *La Possession*, p. 200.

17 This is brought out by D. P. Walker, *Unclean Spirits*, p. 13.

18 Paris, BN coll. Thoisy, vol. 92, f. 385, etc. quoted in de Certeau, *La Possession*, p. 260.

19 "Sous le second aspect, la parole cesse peu à peu d'être une institution publique pour devenir une relation privée." De Certeau, *La Possession*, p. 90.

20 Quoted in Brémond, *Histoire du sentiment religieux*, p. 200.

21 It should also be noted that for catholic propaganda, especially in the ongoing public relations battle with protestantism, it was those scenes of the elevation of the host and the communion that were the most charged with religico-political significance. Cf. Walker, *Unclean Spirits*, p. 4.

22 S. Freud, "A Neurosis of Demoniacal Possession in the 17th Century," in *St. Ed.* 19, p. 86.

23. Cf., for female masochism, L. Irigaray, *Speculum*, pp. 78—87, and for a discussion of female "passivity," S. Kofman, *Freud et l'énigme de la femme* (Paris: Galilée, 1980), pp. 177—188.

24 Barker, *The Tremulous Private Body*, p. 10.

4 *Rodogune*: sons and lovers

1 All references to *Rodogune* are to *Théâtre choisi de Corneille*, ed. M. Rat (Paris: Garnier Frères, 1962).

2 Doubrovsky, S., *Corneille et la dialectique du héros* (Paris: Gallimard, 1963), p. 292: "*Rodogune* constitue ... une coupure radicale. Encore quelque temps à égalité avec les hommes ... les femmes prendront la succession des hommes pour le maintien de l'éthique héroïque ..." Cf. also the interesting discussion of *Rodogune*, "Ritual in Crisis: *Rodogune*," in H. Stone, *Royal DisClosure: Problematics of Representation in French Classical Tragedy* (Birmingham, Alabama: Summa Publications, 1987).

3 F. Nietzsche, *The Birth of Tragedy* (trans. by F. Golffing, NY Doubleday, 1956), p. 43.

4 *Ibid.*, p. 43.

5 The expression is Geoffroy's, quoted in M. Fumaroli, "Tragique païen et tragique chrétien dans *Rodogune*, in *Revue des Sciences Humaines* (Oct./Dec. 1973).

6 Cf. M. Greenberg, "L'hymen de Corneille," *Biblio 17, Actes de Tucson* (1984), pp. 129–151.

7 M. Fumaroli points out that the princes have been raised in Egypt, traditional land of wisdom and harmony: "les princes ont été préservés de toute compromission, même en pensée, avec les crimes de leurs parents. Dans l'obscurité et la retraite d'une Egypte idéale, terre traditionnelle de la sagesse, ils ont été nourris par Timagène dans le culte des plus hauts exemples et des plus belles vertus, et en particulier de celle que les moralistes antiques mettaient hors pair, l'amitié," "Tragique paien et tragique chrétien," p. 167.

8 Cf. B. Grunberger, who in his *Le Narcissisme* (Paris: Payot, 1972) talks about O. Rank's contribution to the theory of narcissism. "Rank apporte un matériel important pour montrer combien l'homme tient à la possession de son ombre (= double) dont la perte signifie pour lui une véritable castration" (p. 97). On the other hand, we know that the role of the double, discussed by Freud in his "Essay on the Uncanny," is often the projection of hostile, aggressive tendencies, of death. Cf. G. Rosolato's discussion of the double in Freud in *Essais sur le symbolique* (Paris: Gallimard, 1967), p. 190.

9 Cf., for example, R. Jasinski, "Le sens de Rodogune," in *Mélanges d'histoire littéraire offerts à D. Mornet* (Paris: Nizet, 1951), p. 65; "C'est ainsi que Rodogune se croit tenue à demander la tête de Cléopâtre et la demande en effet, mais avec le fervent espoir de ne pas l'obtenir, sachant au surplus que le devoir des deux frères est de la lui refuser."

10 "Je dirai plus: quand cette proposition serait tout à fait condamnable en sa bouche, elle mériterait quelque grâce et pour l'éclat que la nouveauté de l'invention a fait au théâtre, et pour l'embarras surprenant où elle jette les princes et pour l'effet qu'elle produit dans le reste de la pièce qu'elle conduit à l'action historique" (*Examen*, p. 355).

11 For the inherent ambiguity of visual imagery, cf. the introduction of J. Starobinski to his *L'Œil vivant* (Paris: Gallimard, 1961), pp. 14–15.

12 Cf. Doubrovsky's discussion of the importance of the word "nature" and its inversions in the political context of *Rodogune. Corneille*, pp. 290–295.

13 Cf. M. Greenberg, *Corneille, Classicism, and the Ruses of Symmetry*, chap. 2, for a discussion of the importance of Medea in the elaboration of Corneille's mythical universe.

14 L. Irigaray, in *Speculum* (Paris: Minuit, 1975), talks of how this metaphorization of the female as mother is directly related to a process that reproduces masculine ideals and which, at the same time, suppresses any inherently feminine pleasure. Cf. pp. 139–164.

15 Cf. M. Fumaroli, "Tragique paien," p. 161: "Toutes deux sont initiées aux arcanes de la dynastie séleucide ... elles connaissent les tenants et les aboutissements de la crise qui en 'ce jour pompeux' doit être enfin résolue par le sacre du roi."

16 Doubrovsky discusses this dilemma in his analysis of the play, *Corneille*, pp. 297–299.

17 Most specifically in "Female Sexuality" (*St. Ed.* 21, pp. 225–247), "On Narcissism" (*St. Ed.* 14, pp. 73–102), "The Psychogenesis of a Case of Homosexuality in a Woman" (*St. Ed.* 18, pp. 145–175) and "Femininity," in *New Introductory Lectures* (*St. Ed.* 22, pp. 112–136).

18 Cf. "Female Sexuality."

19 Cf. Freud's essay on "Fetishism" (*St. Ed.* 21, pp. 152–159), where he states: "In very subtle cases the fetish itself has become the vehicle both of denying and asseverating the fact of castration." Irigaray, *Speculum*, pp. 87–92, also discusses the importance of Freud's article on fetishism.

20 Doubrovsky, *Corneille*, p. 297: "Toutefois, il ne s'agit pas de n'importe quelle faiblesse, mais d'une faiblesse de femme, qui manifeste précisément la condition féminine qu'elle cherche à fuïr. Car la "haine" de Cléopâtre pour Rodogune, qui se donne complaisamment pour amour du trône, est en fait jalousie de femme."

21 "Suivant la loi, le roi ne meurt jamais, c'est à dire que, par la seule force de la loi, toute l'autorité royale est transmise incontinent, après la mort du monarque, à celui qui a le droit de lui succéder" (art. xxx, chap. II du "Projet des premiers articles de la Constitution, lu par M. Mounier, 28 juillet 1789," quoted in *La Tribune Française*, vol. I (Paris: Aux Presses de la Tribune Française, 1840), p. 67.

5 Molière's *Tartuffe* and the scandal of insight

1 F. Gantheret, "Du coin de l'œil," in *Nouvelle Revue de Psychanalyse* (1987), p. 124.

2 C. Buci-Glucksmann, *La Folie du voir* (Paris: Galilée, 1986), p. 74.

3 Quoted in M. Rat, *Molière, Œuvres complètes* (Paris: Gallimard, 1959, p. 888. (It is from this edition that all quotes from Molière will be taken.)

For the complete discussion of Molière's career, and the debate(s) around the *Tartuffe*, the following works should be consulted: R. Bray, *Molière, homme de théâtre* (Paris: Mercure de France, 1954); A. Adam, *Histoire de la littérature française au XVIIe siècle*, 3 (Paris: del Duca, 1962); J. Guicharnaud, *Molière, une aventure théâtrale* (Paris: Gallimard, 1963); W. D. Howarth, *Molière: a Playwright and His Audience* (Cambridge: CUP, 1982).

4 J. Habermas, *L'Espace public* (French translation by de Launay (Paris: Payot, 1985), pp. 13–17.

5 Cf. for instance E. Thuau, *Raison d'Etat et pensée politique à l'époque de Richelieu* (Paris: Colin, 1966) and W. Church, *Richelieu and Reason of State* (Princeton: Princeton University Press, 1973).

6 Cf. C. Mauron, *Psychocritique du genre comique* (Paris: Corti, 1985), pp. 31–33.

7 L. Gossman, *Men and Masks, A Study of Molière* (Baltimore: The Johns Hopkins Press, 1963), p. 106.

8 Cf. Siguret, *L'Œil surpris*.

9 J. Rose, *Sexuality in the Field of Vision* (London: Verso, 1986), p. 227.

10 Cf. Lacan, *Les Quatre Concepts* (Paris: Seuil, 1973), p. 95.

11 Cf., for an analysis of "femininity" as "lack," S. Heath's discussion of Lacan in "Difference," Lacan's *Encore* (Paris: Seuil, 1975), especially pp. 76–82; and J. Rose, *Sexuality*.

12 "Je me voyais me voir" dit quelque part la Jeune Parque ... Assurément cet énoncé a sons sens plein et complexe à la fois quand il s'agit du thème que développe 'la Jeune Parque,' celui de la féminité ..." (*Les Quatre Concepts*, p. 76).

13 *Ibid.*, pp. 97–98.

14 N. Gross, *From Gesture to Idea: Esthetics and Ethics in Molière's Comedy* (NY: Columbia Un. Press, 1982), pp. 14–15.

15 J. Lacan, *Ecrits* (Paris: Seuil, 1966), p. 90.

16 Cf. "The Uncanny," in *On Creativity and the Unconscious*, p. 141.

17 Cf. G. Rosolato, "Narcisses," p. 8: "Et ce sera sans oublier que ... dans sa problématique propre, la mort est un repère banal, toujours présent. Narcisse se mirait encore jusque sur les eaux du Styx."

18 A. Green, *Narcissisme de vie, narcissisme de mort*, p. 34: "Parti du regard, Freud noue le narcissisme au domaine du visible ... Il passe de l'image de soi comme objet d'amour à la fleur de la résurrection en omettant de citer le moment narcissique par excellence, celui de la fusion de l'objet et de son image dans l'élément liquide, fascinant, mortifère et régressif jusqu'à la pré-naissance."

19 J. Baudrillard, *De La Séduction* (Paris: Denoel, 1979), p. 87.

20 "On Narcissism, an Introduction," *St. Ed.* 14, p. 88–89; cf., too, S. Kofman's reading of narcissism, in *L'Enigme de la femme* (Paris: Galilée, 1980), pp. 60–77.

21 A. Green, *Narcissisme*, p. 35; "le narcissisme est lui-même apparence et [que] derrière lui se cache toujours l'ombre de l'objet invisible."

22 *Ibid.*, p. 55.

23 For the linking of the "imaginary" to the maternal cf. Rose, *Sexuality*, p. 218.

24 Cf. *Les Mots et les choses, passim.*

25 G. Defaux, *Molière, ou les métamorphoses du comique* (Lexington: French Forum, 1983), pp. 98–99.

26 This is what Bourdaloue's quote – "La fausse piété et la vraie ... ont des dehors presque tous semblables" (in Rat, *Molière...*, p. xvi) – perceives.

27 Cf. Green, *Narcissisme*, p. 68: "Si la parole est médiation entre corps et langage, corps-à-corps psychique, la parole est psyché. Miroir, ou plutôt jeu de miroirs prismatiques, décomposant la lumière des corps ou recomposant le spectre des rayons lumineux." For an extended commentary, in a feminist perspective, on this same psycho-sexual dynamic, cf. K. Silverman, *The Acoustic Mirror: The Female Voice in Psychoanalysis and Cinema* (Bloomington: Indiana University Press, 1988).

28 Cf. Rosolato, *Essais sur le symbolique* (Paris: Gallimard, 1969), especially the chapter "Trois générations ..."; and my chap. 5, "Racine's Children," *infra*, pp. 141–173.

29 *Jokes and their Relation to the Unconscious, St. Ed.* 8, p. 100.

30 Cf. L. Irigaray, *Speculum de l'autre femme* (Paris: Minuit, 1975), p. 140.

31 Cf. J. Laplanche and J.-B. Pontalis, *Fantasme originaire, fantasmes des origines, origines du fantasme* (Paris: Hachette, 1985), p. 51.

32 Freud, "A Case of Infantile Neurosis," *St. Ed.* 17, pp. 35–36.

33 "Some Psychological Consequences of the Anatomical Distinction of the Sexes ...", *St. Ed.* 19, p. 249. Cf. also note of Green, *Narcissisme*, p. 240.

34 For another similar reading of the prince's panoptic power cf. J. Creech, "Marivaux and the Classical Episteme: or Suis-je chez moi, Marie?" *L'Esprit Créateur* (Fall, 1985), pp. 30–41.

6 Racine's children

1 All references to Racine are to *Racine, Théâtre complet*, ed. M. Rat (Paris: Garnier Frères, 1960).

2 Charles Mauron, *L'Inconscient dans l'œuvre et la vie de Racine* (Paris: J. Corti, 1969), p. 37.

3 J. Schérer, *Racine et/ou la cérémonie* (Paris: PUF, 1982), p. 89.

4 Cf. Mauron, *L'Inconscient*, pp. 135 and 198, and R. Barthes, *Sur Racine* (Paris: Seuil, 1963), pp. 37 and 48.

5 L. Bersani, *A Future for Astyanax* (Boston: Little, Brown and Co., 1976), p. 50.

6 Cf. Barthes, *Sur Racine*, p. 114, "Toutes ces personnes ... sont agitées, opposées, ou plus encore liées au sein d'une réalité qui est en fait le personnage central de la pièce: la famille."

7 M. Foucault, *Les Mots et les choses*, Introduction, *passim*.

8 Cf. Barthes, *Sur Racine*, p. 25: "La division du monde racinien en forts et en faibles, en tyrans et en captifs, est en quelque sorte extensive au partage des sexes: c'est leur situation dans le rapport de force qui verse les uns dans la virilité et les autres dans la féminité, sans égard à leur sexe biologique."

9 Cf. J. Starobinski, *L'Œil vivant* (Paris: Gallimard, 1961), p. 87: "Chaque fois la culpabilité des personnages se constitue sous le regard suprême de ce témoin ou mieux, de ce Juge transcendant. Tous les regards échangés par les héros humains sont épiés par un œil inexorable, qui reprouve et qui condamne."

10 Cf. Phillip Lewis, "Sacrifice and Suicide: Some Afterthoughts on the Career of J. Racine," *Biblio 17, Actes de Baton Rouge* (1986), pp. 58–59.

11 G. Rosolato, "Trois générations," p. 92.

12 Cf. Mauron, *L'Inconscient*, pp. 132 and 169. For other, more sociological or literary-historical attempts to situate the tragedies of Racine within the cultural and religious context of the seventeenth century the reader should consult: Bénichou, *Morales du grand siècle*; Goldmann, *Le Dieu caché*; J. Orcibal, *La Genèse d'Esther et d'Athalie* (Paris: Vrin, 1950); R. Picard, *La Carrière de Jean Racine* (Paris: Gallimard, 1956) and E. Zimmerman, *La Liberté et le destin dans le théâtre de Jean Racine* (Saratoga: Anma Libri, 1982).

13 This is, of course, Freud's main argument in *Totem and Taboo*, that he will expand upon in his other metapsychological works: *Moses and Monotheism, Civilization and Its Discontents*, etc. Cf. Introduction.

14 G. Rosolato, *Le Sacrifice, repères psychanalytiques* (Paris: PUF, 1987), pp. 83–123.

15 Cf. Green, *Un Œil en trop*, p. 210.

16 "Quant au meurtre du père je poserai que dans le mythe monothéiste il n'apparaît jamais directement. Toute l'opération a, en effet, pour but d'en éviter l'accomplissement. Il faut donc admettre que ce meurtre constitue un noyau secret, fondamental, par rapport auquel s'organisent les substitutions du sacrifice, moyennant quoi se réalise l'alliance." Rosolato, *Le Sacrifice*, p. 74.

17 Rosolato, *La Relation d'inconnu* (Paris: Gallimard, 1978), p. 87: "Cependant les psychanalystes, depuis Freud ... ont mis en évidence dans ce schéma une autre ligne de force latente, d'autant plus camouflée que le système patriarcal est plus puissant. Sous couvert du meurtre du fils s'insinuent les souhaits de mort à l'égard du père. La victime rituelle, de remplacement, seconde en quelque sorte, symbolise le père ..."

18 S. Leclaire, *On tue un enfant* (Paris: Seuil, 1975), p. 20.

19 Cf. Mauron, *L'Inconscient*, p. 73. For an interpretation of Racine's "modernity," cf. M. F. Bruneau, *Racine, le jansénisme et la modernité* (Paris: Corti, 1986).

20 "Lentement s'impose la logique 'archaïque' de l'inconscient: de même que la mère en position de puissance y apparaît pourvue de pénis, de même le père en position de protecteur peut y apparaître gros d'un enfant." Leclaire, *On tue* ..., p. 18.

21 Cf. Rosolato, *Le Sacrifice*, pp. 63–64.

22 "J'avoue que je ne m'étais pas formé l'idée d'un bon homme en la personne de Néron: je l'ai toujours regardé comme un monstre. Mais c'est ici un monstre naissant. Il n'a pas encore mis le feu à Rome; il n'a pas encore tué sa mère, sa femme, ses gouverneurs." *Première préface*, ed. Rat, p. 233.

23 *Ibid.*, p. 233.

24 *La Violence et la sacré* (Paris: Grasset, 1972), p. 223.

25 *Ibid.*, p. 349.

26 Cf. S. Moscovici, *Society against Nature* (Atlantic Highlands, NJ: Humanities Press, 1976); for a further discussion of the ethnological and philosophical importance of the incest taboo, pp. 125–136.

27 Cf. Freud's essay on the Uncanny, and this comment by Rosolato, *Le Sacrifice*, p. 30: "ce double devient dangereux par la rivalité redoutable qu'il suscite. Le dédoublement efface les différences, supprime l'Autre, donc perd le repoussoir pour l'unicité. La mort et la destruction se centrent alors sur la relation au double."

28 *Ibid.*, p. 29: "L'identification narcissique est porteuse d'aggressivité ... la charge destructrice de la relation spéculaire illustrée par la valeur représentative de la mort qu'a le double."

29 A point made repeatedly in *Totem and Taboo, Moses and Monotheism*. Cf. Introduction.

30 Cf. Freud, "A Neurosis of Demoniacal Possession in the Seventeenth Century," pp. 277–278.

31 Cf. E. Enriquez, *De La Horde à l'etat*, p. 246: "l'ambivalence des sentiments et d'agressivité caractérisent de manière structurale, les rapports père-fils" and p. 247 "Le père est toujours un être interdicteur et un objet d'identification, le fils est toujours le créateur et le destructeur de son père."

32 *Ibid.*, p. 243: "Si sans père, il ne peut y avoir d'enfants (au sens social du terme), sans enfants, c'est à dire, sans individus capables de reconnaître la loi du père et de s'identifier aux idéaux qu'elle véhicule, il ne peut y avoir de père non plus."

33 *Ibid.*, p. 92: "la vie naissante, l'enfant, est aussi dans une semblable réduction une menace qui pousse vers la tombe la génération précédente, d'où les fantasmes de mort dressés vers lui, générateurs de culpabilité inconsciente."

34 *Sur Racine*, p. 55.

35 Cf. Rosolato, *Essais:*, pp. 168–169 for the two contradictory positions vis à vis the father, either "inféodation" or "révolte."

36 For a fuller discussion of this particular play cf. G. Defaux, "Violence et passion dans l'*Iphigénie*," *Biblio 17* (1984); and J.M. Apostolidès, *Le Prince sacrifié* (Paris: Minuit, 1985), pp. 108–127.

37 Girard, *La Violence*, p. 375.

38 In the "*Essay on the Uncanny.*"

39 Girard, *La Violence*, p. 375: "Il ne faut pourtant pas conclure ... que la victime émissaire doit être perçue comme simplement étrangère à la communauté. Elle ne fait qu'un avec le 'double monstrueux.' Elle a absorbé toutes les différences et notamment, la différence entre le dedans et le dehors; elle passe pour circuler librement de l'intérieur à l'extérieur. Elle constitue donc, entre la communauté et le sacré, à la fois un trait d'union et de séparation."

40 Rosolato, *La Relation d'inconnu*, p. 88: "On a noté la similitude qui rapproche le Roi (on pourrait dire le monarque, ou le dictateur) de la victime émissaire: son pouvoir et son ascendant s'exercent aussi par le danger même qu'il appelle, qui reste suspendu sur lui et qu'il conjure. Sa position d'exception le lie à la victime comme à un pôle d'opposition, vers lequel il peut toutefois basculer, dans la défaite, l'attentat, ou le coup d'Etat."

41 Rosolato, *Le Sacrifice*, p. 75: "Que l'on songe aux caractères de la victime émissaire: son innocence ou son humanité, sa faiblesse surtout sont le négatif du Père Idéalisé, tout-puissant, féroce et haï par envie collective, et coupable de toutes ses violences arbitraires. La victime révèle ainsi par renversement le sens de la substitution et son effet d'occultation."

42 L. Bersani, *A Future for Astyanax*, p. 42.

43 *Le Dieu caché*, p. 47.

44 Mauron, *L'Inconscient*, p. 258: "Depuis Alexandre, depuis Titus, nous savons avec quelle délectation Racine n'a cessé de vouloir s'identifier au roi. Cette assimilation a longtemps pour lui le symbole du salut. Toute participation a la majesté royale l'enivre."

45 *Ibid.*, p. 153–154 and Bersani, *A Future for Astyanax*, p. 25.

46 Rosolato, *Le Sacrifice*, p. 9: "le meurtre du père [est] à la base du mythe sacrificiel. ... l'opération sacrificielle sur le fils est le déplacement d'une action qui vise en premier le père et qui a pour fonction essentielle de détourner les désirs mortifères à l'égard de son substitut idéalisé et de l'autorité suprême."

7 "Visions are seldom all they seem": *La Princesse de Clèves* and the end of Classical illusions

1 For the etymology of "theory/theater," cf., among others, N. Miller, *Subject to Change* (NY: Columbia Un. Press, 1988), p. 179, and G. Balandier, *Pouvoirs sur scène* (Paris: Balland, 1980), p. 12.

2 *Les Quatre Concepts fondamentaux de la psychanalyse* (Paris: Seuil, 1973), p. 98.

3 Quoted in Heath, "Difference," p. 53.

4 Cf., for example, M. A. Doane, *The Desire to Desire* (Bloomington: University of Indiana Press, 1987), p. 104: "paranoia demands a split between the known and the unknown, the seen and the unseen"; and J. Rose, "Paranoia and the Film System," *Screen* (Winter, 1976), p. 87: "Freud describes paranoia as the untoward projection of a rejected idea – the content of a desire – which reappears as perceived reality, against which repression manifests itself anew as opposition," and pp. 100–101: "paranoia is a pre-oedipal structure of aggressivity which threatens the stabilization of symbolic positions in so far as they constitute the social overdetermination of the subject's self-cohesion in the imaginary."

5 Cf. J. Raitt, *Madame de Lafayette and La Princesse de Clèves* (London: Harrap, 1971), p. 80: "The sources of Mme de Clèves' situation and behaviour are to be found more in the early seventeenth-century theatre than in the early seventeenth-century novel ... It was in the thematic freedom of the theatre that the Platonic attitude to love was first attached to the primitive and classical idea of the fatality of physical passion." Cf. also p. 172: "The novel divides naturally into five parts, corresponding perhaps to the exposition, peripeteia, crisis, catastrophe and dénouement of a classical play."

6 Valincour, in Laugaa, *Lectures de Mme de Lafayette* (Paris: Armand Colin, 1971), p. 87, and pp. 89–90.

7 "Sur *La Princesse de Clèves*" in *Répertoire* (Paris: Minuit, 1960), pp. 74–78.

8 A scene that has attracted the attention of several feminist critics. Cf. J. de Jean, "Female Voyeurism: Sappho and Lafayette," *Rivista di Letterature Moderne e Comparate*, 40 (1987), pp. 201–215; N. Miller, *Subject*, pp. 184ff., and N. Schor, "The Portrait of a Gentleman: Representing Men in (French) Women's Writing," in *Representations*, 20 (Fall, 1987), pp. 113–134.

9 S. Lotringer, "La structuration romanesque," *Critique* (1970), p. 498.

10 For a "history" of this change, beside the works mentioned in the introduction cf. *Histoire de la vie privée*, ed. Ph. Ariès and G. Duby (Paris: Seuil, 1985, 1987), vols. 2 and 3. At the same time, what this representation of a supposedly "conservative" projection of the "public–private" split would seem to confirm is our statement (in the Introduction) that these great "epistemic" changes are never monolithic, but rather are fragmentary, oscillatory, and indeterminate in any one particular example.

11 Cf. L. Marin, *Le Portrait du roi* (Paris: Minuit, 1981), p. 289: "Ainsi le secret du monarque absolu, le secret éthique, retrait du politique sur son portrait, le secret du roi tout-puissant, c'est qu'il ne l'est pas; pensée cachée, jamais dite, pensée qui n'est peut-être jamais pensée – et là

serait la force de la figure, de la fiction, du figuratif, de penser cette
pensée – celle de l'impossible oubli qu'il n'est pas ce qu'il est."

12 Cf. Lacan, "Du regard," in *Les Quatre Concepts*, p. 92: "Imiter, c'est
sans doute reproduire une image. Mais foncièrement, c'est, pour le
sujet, s'insérer dans une fonction dont l'exercice le saisit."

13 "Je ne vois que d'un point, mais dans mon existence je suis regardé de
partout." *Ibid.*, p. 69.

14 Cf. N. Bryson's comments on Vermeer, in *Vision and Painting*,
pp. 111–117.

15 Lacan, *Les Quatre Concepts*, p. 98.

16 Cf. N. Elias, *The Court Society*, trans. E. Jephcott (NY: Pantheon
Books, 1983), chaps. IV, V, VI, pp. 66–117.

17 Cf. Introduction, for reference to the internalization of the interdictions
of sexuality in J. Mitchell and S. Moscovici.

18 J. Rose, *Sexuality in the Field of Vision* (London: Verso, 1986), p. 226.

19 Heath, "Difference," p. 55.

20 Cf. M. A. Hirsh, "A Mother's Discourse: Incorporation and Repetition
in *La Princesse de Clèves*," *Yale French Studies* 62 (1981); P. Kamuf,
"A Mother's Will," in *Fictions of Feminine Desire* (Lincoln: University
of Nebraska Press, 1982) and N. Miller, *Subject*.

21 E. Lemoine-Luccioni, *Partage des Femmes* (Paris: Seuil, 1976), p. 55.

22 J. Mitchell, *Psychoanalysis and Feminism* (New York: Random House,
1974), p. 404: "The girl only acquires her secondary feminine identity
within the law of patriarchy in her positive Oedipus complex when she
is seduced/raped by, and/or seduces the father. As the boy becomes heir
to the law with his acceptance of symbolic castration from the father,
the girl learns her feminine destiny with this symbolic seduction."

23 Cf. Heath, "Difference," p. 59: "male or female, the subject is implicated
from and in the phallus, phallic jouissance, but differently: there is a
male and female way of failing relation."

24 A point made over and over again since *Totem and Taboo*. Cf. Introduction, and G. Rosolato, "Trois Génerations," in *Essais sur le symbolique* (Paris: Gallimard, 1969).

25 Cf. in particular P. Kamuf, *Fictions*.

26 "Difference," p. 53.

27 Cf. J. Rose, *Sexuality*, p. 232. Cf. also L. Mulvey's statement that the
male gaze functions in two ways, either sadistically to punish or endanger
the woman, or fetishistically to overvalue her beauty in an attempt
to master the threat of castration. "Visual pleasure and the narrative
cinema," in *Women and the Cinema*, ed. K. Kay and G. Peary (NY:
Dutton, 1977), pp. 412–429.

28 R. Barthes, *S/Z* (Paris: Seuil, 1970).

29 Cf. P. Kamuf, *Fictions*, pp. 86–88.

30 Freud, *Three Essays on the Theory of Sexuality* (NY: Norton, 1963),
p. 23.

31 Cf. J. Rose, *Sexuality* ..., p. 277: "The sexuality lies less in the content of what is seen than in the subjectivity of the viewer ... The relationship between viewer and scene is always one of fracture, partial identification, pleasure and distrust."

32 *The Desire*, p. 177.

33 Lacan, *Les quatre Concepts*, p. 76: " 'Je me voyais me voir', dit quelque part la Jeune Parque. Assurément cet énoncé a son sens plein et complexe à la fois, quand il s'agit du thème que développe *la Jeune Parque*, celui de la féminité ..."

34 Cf. Lacan particularly *Le Séminaire, livre xx, Encore* (Paris: Seuil, 1975), and Lemoine-Luccioni, *Partage des Femmes*.

35 S. Heath, "Difference," pp. 65—66. Cf. also Lacan, *Les Quatre Concepts*, p. 99: "Sans aucun doute, c'est par l'intermédiaire des masques que le masculin, le féminin, se rencontrent de la façon la plus aiguë, la plus brûlante." The primary reference for this discussion is J. Rivière's article, "Womanliness as Masquerade," reprinted in *Formations of Fantasy*, ed. V. Burgin, J. Donald and C. Kaplan (London: Methuen, 1979).

36 In *De la séduction* (Paris: Denoël, 1979), p. 23.

37 Cf. M. A. Doane, *The Desire*, p. 168: "The desire to be looked at is thus transformed into a fear of being looked at, or a fear of the apparatus which systematizes or governs that process of looking."

38 "A Case of Paranoia," *St. Ed.* 14, p. 265.

39 Cf., for an interesting analysis of female voyeurism, J. de Jean, "Female Voyeurism," and N. Schor, "The Portrait of a Gentleman."

40 Lacan, "Du Regard," in *Les Quatre Concepts*, p. 95.

41 Cf., for the entire discussion of the "invraisemblance" of the confession, G. Genette, "Vraisemblance et Motivation," in *Figures*, II (Paris: Seuil, 1966), pp. 71—99; J. de Jean, "Lafayette's Ellipses: The Privileges of Anonymity," in *PMLA* (1984), pp. 884—902; N. K. Miller, "Emphasis Added: Plots and Plausibilities in Women's Fiction," *PMLA* (1981), pp. 36—48 (reprinted in *Subject to Change*); and J. Lyons, "Narrative Interpretation and Paradox: *La Princesse de Clèves*," *Romanic Review* (nov. 1981), pp. 383—401.

42 Cf. Heath, "Difference," p. 77.

43 Quoted in Laugaa, *Lectures*, pp. 329—330.

44 For an extended discussion of hysteria, cf. chap. 2. Cf. also Heath, "Difference," p. 56 for a definition of hysteria as "being unsure as to being woman or man, the hysterical position — having or not having the phallus."

45 Mitchell, *Psychoanalysis*, p. 404.

INDEX

Index

Koch, P., 219 (n. 12)
Kofman, S., 222 (n. 23), 224 (n. 23), 227 (n. 20)

Laborde, clinic, 78
Lacan, J., 11, 19, 37, 123, 124, 125, 157, 175, 183, 217 (n. 68), 227 (nn. 10, 11, 18), 235 (nn. 12, 15), 234 (nn. 33, 34, 40)
Lacoue-Labarthe, P., 222 (n. 25)
Laing, R. D., 78
Lamoignon, G. de, 114
Laplanche, J., 228 (n. 31)
La Popelinière, 49
La Rochefoucauld, F., xi
Laslett, P., 12, 215 (n. 40)
Laugaa, M., 220 (n. 16)
Lauretis, T. de, 217 (n. 63)
Law of the Father, as castration, 83
Le Bon, G., 2
Le Cid, 53–58
Leclaire, S., 153, 229 (n. 18), 230 (nn. 20, 21)
Lemoine-Luccioni, E., 186, 220 (n. 23), 233 (n. 21)
Levi-Strauss, C., 16, 45, 50, 220 (n. 24), 221 (n. 6)
Lewis, Philip, 146, 229 (n. 10)
Lotringer, S., 184, 232 (n. 9)
Louis XIII, 13, 18, 67
Louis XIV, 1, 2–3, 4, 5, 6, 13, 18, 212 (n. 4), 214 (n. 36)
Lublinskaya, A. D., 215 (n. 37)
Lyons, J., 218 (n. 6), 234 (n. 41)
Lyotard, J. F., 217 (n. 64), 222 (n. 25)

Machiavelli, N., 49
Malherbe, F., 15
Mandrou, R., 13, 215 (n. 46), 223 (nn. 6, 7)
Marin, L., 3, 212 (n. 3), 213 (nn. 10, 17), 216 (n. 53), 221 (n. 3), 232 (n. 11)
marriage, importance for monarchy, 17
masochism, female, in Absolutism, 136
"masquerade," as femininity, 123; as female sexuality, 198–99
Mauron, C., 172, 227 (n. 6), 228 (nn. 2, 4), 229 (n. 12), 231 (n. 44), 232 (n. 19)
Medea, 103
Medici, Marie de, 5
Michelet, J., 233 (n. 6)
Miller, N., 231 (n. 1), 232 (n. 8), 233 (n. 20), 234 (n. 41)

mimetic order, of 16th C, 23
mirror-stage, 128
Mitchell, J., 11, 16, 18, 207, 214 (n. 34), 216 (n. 52), 233 (n. 22), 234 (n. 45)
Molière, 113–140 passim
monarch, as referent for time, desire, 63
monarchy, object of desire, 49
monotheism, and Oedipal scenario, 149
monster, child as, 169
Moscovici, S., 16, 237 (n. 26)
mother, as hysteric in Corneille, 63
Mousnier, R., 215 (nn. 32, 38), 219 (n. 12)
Mulvey, L., 233 (n. 27)
Murray, T., 14, 215 (n. 48), 216 (n. 10)
myth, the Astrée myth for Classicism, 46; as "fetish," 147; of family, 148

Nancy, J. L., 46, 220 (n. 24)
narcissism, 20, 126–128; and death, 6; masochism, 7; relation to death, 1, 26; as pre-Oedipal unity of mother and child, 128
Narcissus, as "sun" God, 4
Naudé, G., 224 (n. 16)
Nelson, R. J., 220 (n. 1)
Neoplatonic concept of love, in Astrée, 33
Neoplatonism, 39–40
Nietzsche, F., 88, 225 (n. 3)

Oedipal constellation, 95
Oedipal scenario, 17, 169; as capitalist structure, 183
Oedipus, 162; in Racine, 146; as structure of Racinian tragedy, 172
Oedipus complex, as a "vision", 175

Pascal, B., xi, 150
patriarchy, and castration, 172
patricide and regicide, 118
Péréfixe, archbishop of Paris, 119
phallic mother, 17, 101, 103, 114
Picard, R., 229 (n. 12)
Plato, 39
politics, definition, 31; as suppression of sexuality, 168
Pontalis, J. B., 228 (n. 31)
possession, as desymbolization, 74
Poussin, N., 147
pre-Oedipal, as textual economy of L'Astrée, 45
primal scene, 136; exorcism as, 74; as origins of subject, 137

237

Index

Cambridge Studies in French

General editor: MALCOLM BOWIE

240